THEORETICAL CONCEPTS AND FORMULAS IN FOOD PROCESS ENGINEERING

Dr. Md. Irfan Ahmad Ansari

Dr. Pramod Rai

2019

JAIN BROTHERS (New Delhi)

16/873, East Park Road, Near Dr. N.C. Joshi Hospital,
Karol Bagh, New Delhi-110005, Ph. : (011) 23618426, 45097398
E-mail : jain_bros@hotmail.com
www. thejainbrothers.com

Published y :

Shri Sunil Kumar Jain
for
Jain Brothers (New Delhi)
16/873, East Park Road,
New Delhi – 110 005

Branch Office at :

1. **M/s Sunil Book Service**
   FATIMA NAGAR, KAZIPET-506004
   Ph. (0870) 2459617
2. **M/s Jain Brothers**
   Vidya Vihar, Pilani (Raj.)
   Ph. : (01596) 242144

First Edition : 2010
Second Edition : Nov. 2018

***Price* : ₹ 190.00**

ISBN : 978-81-8360-146-7

Laser Typesetting by :

CINOGRAPHICS
E–41, New Multan Nagar,
New Delhi – 110 056

Dedicated
To
Our Parents

Preface

Food processing industries are growing at very rapid pace to develop quality and safe processed products to cater the need of burgeoning Indian population but there is acute shortage of trained technical man power in the field of food process engineering. To meet this shortage, a number of universities, institutes, colleges are now offering the courses related to food processing. Admission to post graduate programme and Ph. D programme are done through competitive examinations in which many questions are numerical based. Knowledge of basic theoretical concepts related to food process engineering is essential to solve the numerical problems in food process engineering. At present, a book on theoretical concepts and formulas related to food process engineering in not available in market which can fulfill the requirement. We feel that there is an urgent need of such book covering all aspects of food process engineering. Keeping the need and latest syllabus in view, an attempt has been made to compile the relevant theoretical concepts and formulas of food process engineering applications at one place. The information in this book is compiled from numerous sources such as books, journals, scientific literatures, etc. Each topic is presented in the book in such a way that we have presumed that the readers have basic knowledge of the topic. The book, divided into fourteen chapters is logically organized and covers general mathematical formulae, basic physical quantities, engineering properties of foods, momentum transfer, heat transfer, mass transfer, and the most common unit operations that find applications in food process engineering such as cleaning, size reduction and mixing, thermal processing of foods, refrigeration and freezing, psychometrics, drying, evaporation, etc. For the reader's convenience, Greek alphabets, units and dimensions, and conversion factors are also presented in appendices. The book is intended for a wide range of students, teachers, scientists and practicing engineers engaged in the fields of Agricultural Engineering, Post Harvest Engineering, Dairy Engineering, Food Engineering, Biological Systems Engineering, Food Process Engineering, Food Technology, Dairy Technology, Food Science, etc. We hope that this book will meet the long felt need of teachers and students of the subject and will be a valuable addition to the food process engineering literature. We also hope this book will serve as a good problem solving tool for those students preparing for different competitive examinations such as ARS, ICAR-NET, GATE, JRF, SRF, IFS, etc apart from their semester examinations and teaching aid for teachers in the field of food process engineering. Any errors or repetitions that may have escaped our attention are regretted. The constructive criticisms, useful suggestions and detection of errors from readers for further improvement in the present compilation will be gratefully acknowledged.

October, 2010

Md. Irfan Ahmad Ansari
E-mail : irfan262@yahoo.com

Pramod Rai
E-mail : pramod_kgp@yahoo.co.uk

Acknowledgements

We would like to express our deep sense of gratitude to publishers and authors of the books and journals for the materials which we have used in preparing the book. We are very much thankful to Dr. A.K Sarkar, Dean, Faculty of Agriculture and Prof. Anil Kumar, Head, Department of Agricultural Engineering, for providing all possible support and encouragement during preparation of the book. We also would like to thank to Dr. Z. A. Haider, Associate Dean, College of Biotechnology and Dr. A. K. Datta, Department of Agricultural and Food Engineering, Indian Institute of technology, Kharagpur for moral support and encouragement during writing the book. We wish to express our sincere thanks to fellow colleagues of our Department Er. B. Oraon, Er. Mintu Job and Er. Uttam Kumar for moral support and encouragement.

We would like to thank to our all family members and relatives for continuous encouragement, affection and support throughout our career. Finally we would like to thank the staff members of the publisher Jain Brothers for their help in editing the manuscript and timely publishing the book. Last but not the least, we would like to thank Almighty for giving us life and the opportunity to gain knowledge to pursue higher education and research work.

October, 2010

Md. Irfan Ahmad Ansari
E-mail : irfan262@yahoo.com

Pramod Rai
E-mail : pramod_kgp@yahoo.co.uk

Contents

Chapter 1

General Mathematical Formulae

A basic knowledge of mathematics is essential to understand the principles that govern the unit operations found in the food processing industry. This chapter presents the general mathematical formulae commonly used in food process engineering.

1.1 ALGEBRA

Identities :

$$(a+b)^2 = a^2 + 2ab + b^2$$

$$(a-b)^2 = a^2 - 2ab + b^2$$

$$a^2 - b^2 = a^2 - b^2 = (a+b)(a-b)$$

$$(a+b)^3 = a^3 + 3a^2b + 3ab^2 + b^3 = a^3 + b^3 + 3ab(a+b)$$

$$(a-b)^3 = a^3 - 3a^2b + 3ab^2 - b^3 = a^3 - b^3 - 3ab(a-b)$$

$$a^3 + b^3 = (a+b)(a^2 - ab + b^2)$$

$$(a+b+c)^2 = a^2 + b^2 + c^2 + 2ab + 2bc + 2ca$$

Linear Equation :

A linear equation is represented by:

$$y = mx + c$$

A plot of y versus x gives a straight line with slope m and intercepts c.

This formula is also known as the slope-intercept form.

The equation of point-slope form is:

$$y - y_1 = m(x - x_1)$$

where m = slope, and y_1 and x_1 represent coordinates of a point (x_1, y_1) through which the line must pass.

The equation of slope for two given points is given by:

$$m = \frac{(y_2 - y_1)}{(x_2 - x_1)}$$

$$d = \sqrt{(y_2 - y_1)^2 + (x_2 - x_1)^2}$$

where d = distance between two points.

Interpolation of Tabular Data :

Tabular data are widely used for many applications and the linear procedure is widely used to interpolate between tabulated values. To have value of Prandtle numbers (Pr) at any temperature between the tabulated values (Table 1), interpolation of data is required.

TABLE 1

Values of Prandtl Number at Different Temperatures

T (°C)	Pr
0	13.7
5	114
10	9.5

Mathematically, the relationship between ratios can be expressed as:

$$y = y_1 - \left(\frac{y_1 - y_2}{x_1 - x_2}\right) \times (x_1 - x)$$

Taking x values as temperature and y values as Prandtl numbers, Prandtl number at 2.5 °C can be calculated as:

$$Pr = 13.7 - \left(\frac{13.7 - 11.4}{0 - 5}\right) \times (0 - 2.5) = 13.7 - 2.3 \times 0.5 = 12.55$$

The equations for slope (m) and intercept (c) of a line obtained by regression analysis of N pairs of experimental data are given by:

$$m = \frac{\sum xy - {\left(\sum x \sum y\right)}/{N}}{\sum x^2 - \left[{\left(\sum x\right)^2}/{N}\right]}$$

$$c = \frac{\sum y \sum x^2 - \sum x \sum xy}{N\left(\sum x^2 - \left[{\left(\sum x\right)^2}/{N}\right]\right)}$$

The process of regression involves minimizing the square of the difference between value of y calculated by the regression equation and y_i, (the experimental value of y). In linear regression, $\sum (mx + c - y)^2$ is called the explained variation, and $\sum (y_i - y)^2$ is called the *random error* or *unexplained variation.*

The ratio of the explained and unexplained variation is called the *correlation coefficient.*

The formula for the linear correlation coefficient (r) between the independent variable (x_i) and dependent variables (y_i) is given by:

$$r = \frac{N\sum xy - \sum x \sum y}{\left[\left[N\sum x^2 - \left(\sum x\right)^2\right]\left[N\sum y^2 - \left(\sum y\right)^2\right]\right]^{0.5}}$$

Mean of x is: $\bar{x} = \frac{\sum x}{N}$

Mean of y is: $\bar{y} = \frac{\sum y}{N}$

Nonlinear Equations :

The polynomial equation $y = a + bx + cx^2 + dx^3$ is often used to represent experimental data. In this equation, linear, quadratic and cubic terms are present. The objective of polynomial regression is to determine the coefficients of the polynomial such that the sum of the squares of the difference between experimental and predicted value of the response variable is minimum.

Linearization of Nonlinear Equations :

S.No.	*Function*	*General Form*	*Linearized Form*	*Remarks*
1.	Hyperbolic function	$y = \frac{1}{b+x}$	$\frac{1}{y} = b + x$	Plot of $1/y$ against x will be linear
2.	Exponential	$y = ab^x$	$\log y = \log a + x \log b$	Plot of $\log y$ against x will be linear
3.	Geometric function	$y = ax^b$	$\log y = \log a + b \log x$	Plot of $\log y$ against $\log x$ will be linear

Logarithmic and Semi-Logarithmic Graphs :

A full logarithmic or log-log graph has both abscissa and ordinate in the logarithmic scale. A semi-logarithmic graph has the ordinate in the logarithmic scale and the abscissa in the arithmetic scale. Full logarithmic graphs are used for geometric functions and semi-logarithmic graphs are used for exponential functions. The logarithmic and arithmetic scales are shown in Fig. 1. One cycle semi-logarithmic and full logarithmic graph are shown in Fig. 2.

The slope on semi-logarithmic graph is calculated by:

$$\text{slope} = \frac{\log y_2 - \log y_1}{x_2 - x_1}$$

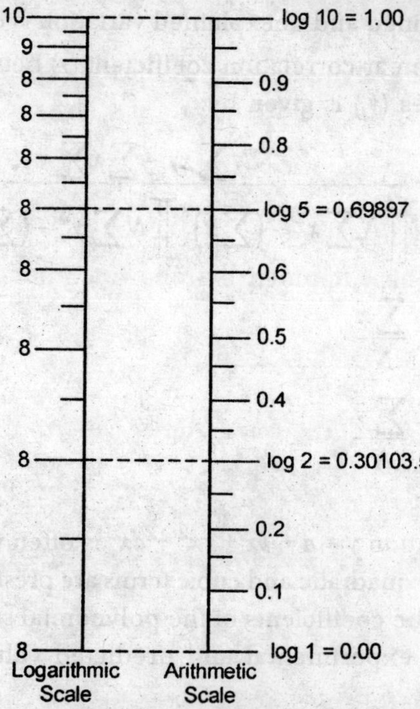

FIG. 1.1—Logarithmic and arithmetic scales

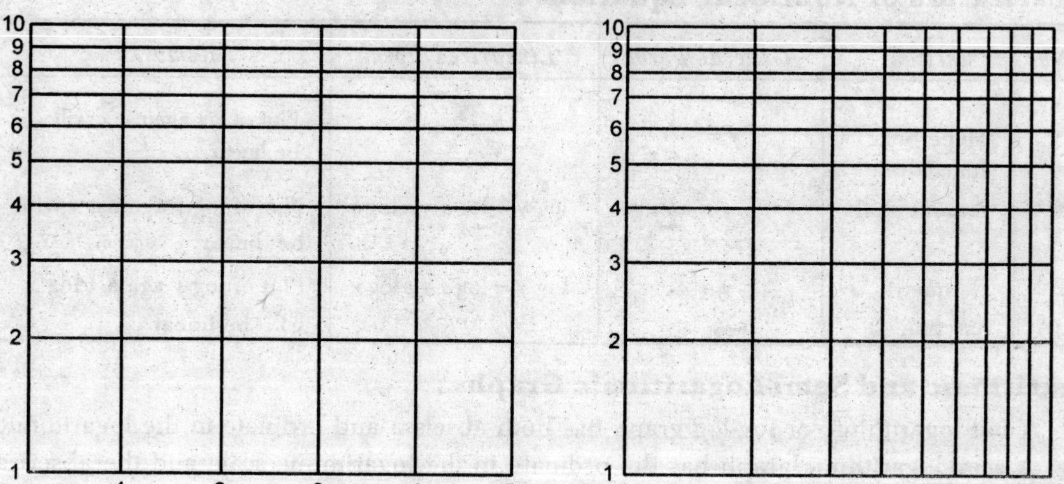

FIG. 1.2—One cycle semi-logarithmic and full logarithmic graph

The slope on log-log graph is calculated by:

$$\text{slope} = \frac{\log y_2 - \log y_1}{\log x_2 - \log x_1}$$

where (x_1, y_1) and (x_2, y_2) are coordinates of points.

Quadratic Equation :

Equations with 2 as the highest power of the variable are called quadratic equations, and the root is obtained using the quadratic formula. The general form of quadratic equation is:

$$ax^2 + bx + c = 0$$

where a, b, and c are constant values.

The value of x may be computed by following equation:

$$x = \frac{-b \pm \sqrt{b^2 - 4ac}}{2a}$$

If α and β are the roots of the quadratic equation, then α and β are given by:

$$\alpha = \frac{-b + \sqrt{b^2 - 4ac}}{2a}$$

and $$\beta = \frac{-b - \sqrt{b^2 - 4ac}}{2a}$$

The sum and product of roots are given by:

$$\text{sum of roots} = \alpha + \beta = \frac{-b}{a}$$

$$\text{product of roots} = \alpha\beta = \frac{c}{a}$$

Radical Combinations :

$\sqrt[n]{ab} = \sqrt[n]{a} \times \sqrt[n]{b}$	$\sqrt[n]{a} = a^{1/n}$	$\sqrt[n]{\frac{a}{b}} = \frac{\sqrt[n]{a}}{\sqrt[n]{b}}$
$\sqrt[n]{a^m} = a^{m/n}$	$\sqrt[n]{\sqrt[m]{a}} = \sqrt[mn]{a}$	$\sqrt{a^n} = (a^n)^{1/2} = a^{2/n}$

Exponents :

$a^{-n} = \frac{1}{a^n}$	$a^m \times a^n = a^{m+n}$	$(a^m)^n = a^{mn}$
$\frac{a^m}{a^n} = a^{m-n}$	$(ab)^n = a^n b^n$	$a^\circ = 1$

Note : $a \neq a$ is base and n is exponent.

Logarithms :

The logarithm of x to the base b is defined by:

$\log_b (x) = c,$ where $bc = x$

$\ln x$ (Base = e) (natural log)

$\log x$ (Base = 10)

$\log (xy) = \log x + \log y$

$\log (x/y) = \log x - \log y$

$\log xy = y \log x$

$\log (1/x) = -\log x$

$\log 1 = 0$

$\log a^a = 1$

$\log b\ b^n = n$

$\log xc = c \log x$

$xc = \text{antilog}\ (c \log x)$

$\ln (x) = .303 \log (x)$

$\log 10 = 1$

$\log 100 = 2$

1.2 TRIGONOMETRY

Pythagoras' Law :

$$c^2 = a^2 + b^2$$

Basic Ratios :

$\sin\theta = \frac{b}{c}$	$\cos\theta = \frac{a}{c}$	$\tan\theta = \frac{b}{a}$
$\cot\theta = \frac{a}{b}$	$\sec\theta = \frac{c}{a}$	$\cos ec\theta = \frac{c}{b}$

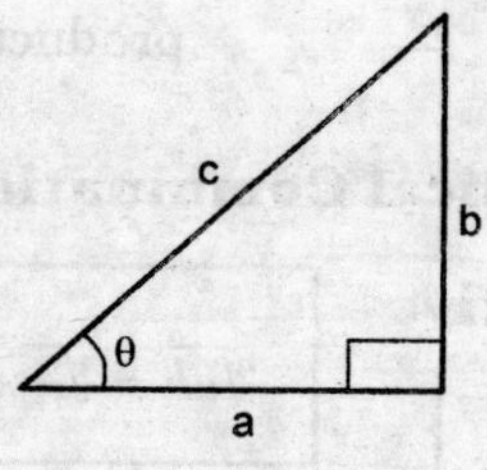

$\tan\theta = \frac{\sin\theta}{\cos\theta}$	$\cot\theta = \frac{\cos\theta}{\sin\theta}$	$\sec\theta = \frac{1}{\cos\theta}$
$\cos ec\theta = \frac{1}{\sin\theta}$	$\tan\theta = \frac{1}{\cot\theta}$	$\cot\theta = \frac{1}{\tan\theta}$

Pythagorean Identities :

$$\sin^2\theta + \cos^2\theta = 1$$

$$1 + \tan^2\theta = \sec^2\theta$$

$$1 + \cot^2\theta = \cos ec^2\theta$$

Sign of Functions :

Quadrant	*sin* / *cosec*	*cos* / *sec*	*tan* / *cot*
I	+	+	+
II	+	−	−
III	−	−	+
IV	−	+	−

Angle/Function	*sin*	*cos*	*tan*
$-\theta$	$-\sin\theta$	$\cos\theta$	$-\tan\theta$
$90° - \theta$	$\cos\theta$	$\sin\theta$	$\cot\theta$
$90° + \theta$	$\cos\theta$	$-\sin\theta$	$-\cot\theta$
$180° - \theta$	$\sin\theta$	$-\cos\theta$	$-\tan\theta$
$180° + \theta$	$-\sin\theta$	$-\cos\theta$	$\tan\theta$
$270° + \theta$	$-\cos\theta$	$-\sin\theta$	$\cot\theta$
$270° + \theta$	$-\cos\theta$	$\sin\theta$	$-\cot\theta$
$360° + \theta$	$-\sin\theta$	$\cos\theta$	$-\tan\theta$

Co-function Identities :

$\sin\left(\frac{\pi}{2}-\theta\right)=\cos\theta$	$\tan\left(\frac{\pi}{2}-\theta\right)=\cot\theta$	$\sec\left(\frac{\pi}{2}-\theta\right)=\cos ec\theta$
$\cos\left(\frac{\pi}{2}-\theta\right)=\sin\theta$	$\cot\left(\frac{\pi}{2}-\theta\right)=\tan\theta$	$s\cos ec\left(\frac{\pi}{2}-\theta\right)=\sec\theta$

Negative Angle Identities :

$\sin(-\theta)=-\sin\theta$	$\tan(-\theta)=-\tan\theta$	$\sec(-\theta)=\sec\theta$
$\cos(-\theta)=\cos\theta$	$\cot(-\theta)=-\cot\theta$	$\cos ec(-\theta)=-\cos ec\theta$

Values of Trigonometric Functions :

Function/ Angle	*0°*	*30°*	*45°*	*60°*	*90°*	*120°*	*145°*	*150°*
sin	0	$\frac{1}{2}$	$\frac{1}{\sqrt{2}}$	$\frac{\sqrt{3}}{2}$	1	$\frac{\sqrt{3}}{2}$	$\frac{1}{\sqrt{2}}$	$\frac{1}{2}$
cos	1	$\frac{\sqrt{3}}{2}$	$\frac{1}{\sqrt{2}}$	$\frac{1}{2}$	0	$-\frac{1}{2}$	-1	$-\frac{1}{\sqrt{3}}$

Radians Versus Degrees :

- ❖ π radian = 180°
- ❖ 1 rad = 57.3°
- ❖ 1 = 60′
- ❖ A circle in degree contains 360 degrees
- ❖ A circle in radians contains 2π radians
- ❖ 2π radian = 1 revolution = 360°.

1.3 GEOMETRY

Items	*Circumference/ Perimeter*	*Area*	*Lateral/ Curved Surface Area*	*Total Surface Area*	*Volume*	*Shape*
Scalene Triangle	$a + b + c$	$\sqrt{s(s-a)(s-b)(s-c)}$ where $s = \frac{a+b+c}{2}$ S is semiperimeter				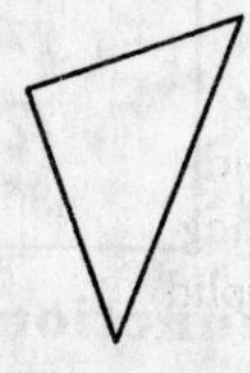
Equilateral Triangle	$3a$ where a is the length of each side	$\frac{1}{2}ah = \frac{\sqrt{3}}{4}a^2$ where $h = \frac{\sqrt{3}}{2}a$				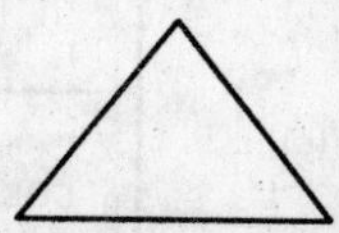
Right Angled Triangle	$a + b + c$	$\frac{1}{2}bh$ b = base h = perpendicular height				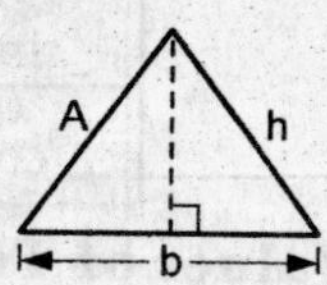
Rectangle	$2(l + b)$	lb where l = length and b = breadth of the rectangle				

Contd......

Items	*Circumference/ Perimeter*	*Area*	*Lateral/ Curved Surface Area*	*Total Surface Area*	*Volume*	*Shape*
Square	$4a$	a^2 where a = side of the square				
Cube			$4a^2$ where a = side of cube	$6a^2$	$6a^3$	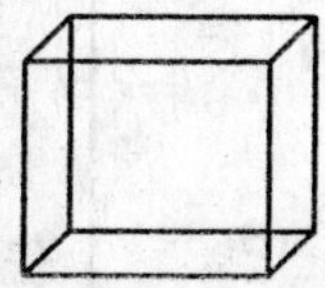
Cuboid (Rectangular Solid)			$2h(l+b)$ where l = length, b = breadth, h = height	$2(lb+bh+hl)$	lbh	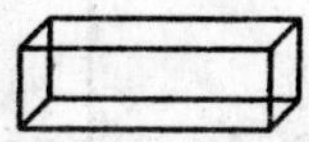
Trapezium	Sum of all sides	$A = \left(\frac{a+b}{2}\right)h$ where a and b = length of parallel sides h = height (distance between the parallel sides)				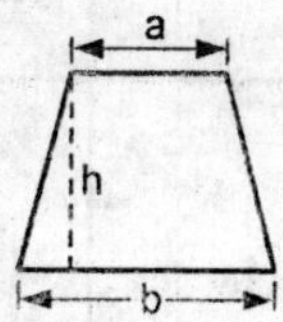
Parallelogram		$A = bh$ where b = base and h = height				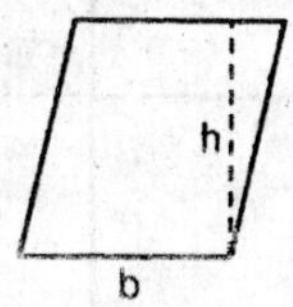
Hexagon	$6a$	$6 \times \frac{\sqrt{3}}{4} a^2$ where a is the length of side				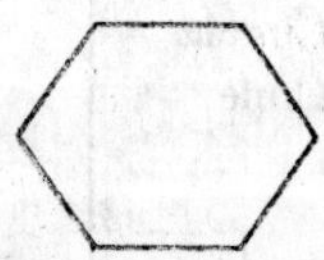

Contd......

Items	*Circumference/ Perimeter*	*Area*	*Lateral/ Curved Surface Area*	*Total Surface Area*	*Volume*	*Shape*
Octagon	$8a$	$4.83a^2$ where a is the length of one side				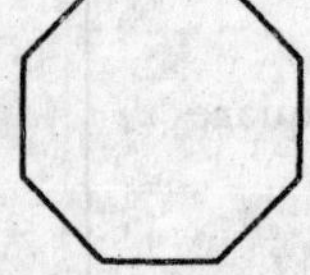
Circle	$2\pi r = \pi d$	$\pi r^2 = \dfrac{\pi d^2}{4}$ where, r = radius d = diameter				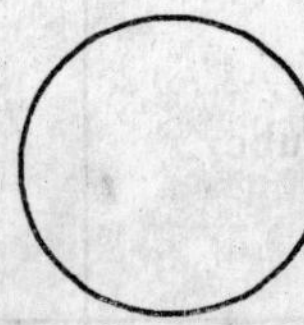
Circle Sector	$2r + l$ where l = arc length	$\dfrac{\pi r^2 \theta}{360}$ where θ = angle of the sector, r = radius of sector				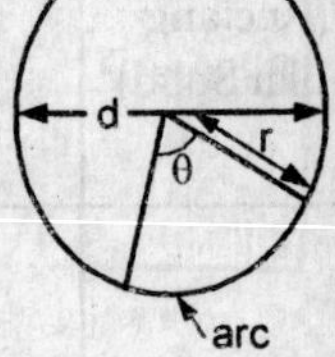
Right Circular Cylinder			$2\pi rh$ $= \pi dh$	$2\pi r^2$ $+ 2\pi rh$ $= 2\pi r$ $(r + h)$	$\pi r^2 h$ $= \dfrac{\pi}{4} d^2 h$	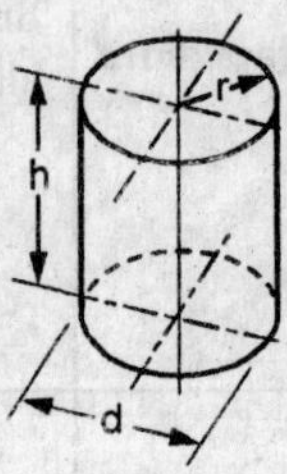
Right Circular Cone			πrl where l = slant height of cone r = radius h = height	πr^2 $+ \pi rl$ $= \pi r$ $(l + r)$	$\dfrac{1}{3}\pi r^2 h$	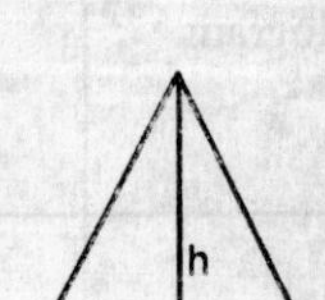

Contd.....

Items	Circumference/ Perimeter	Area	Lateral/ Curved Surface Area	Total Surface Area	Volume	Shape
Sphere			$4\pi r^2 = \pi d^2$ where r = radius d = diameter	$4\pi r^2 = \pi d^2$	$\frac{4}{3}\pi r^3 = \frac{\pi d^3}{6}$	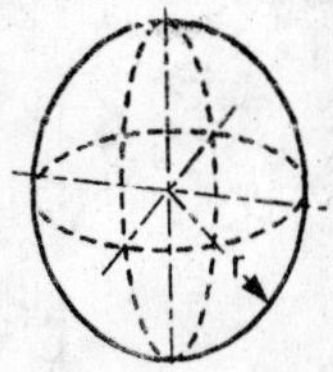
Hemisphere:			$2\pi r^2$	$2\pi r^2 + \pi r^2 = 3\pi r^2$	$\frac{2}{3}\pi r^3$	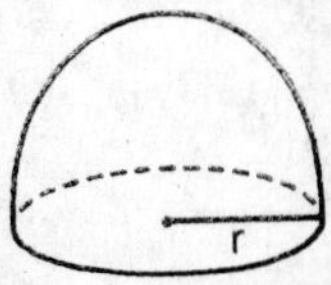
Ellipse	$\pi\frac{(D+d)}{2}$	$\frac{\pi}{4}Dd$ where d, D = smaller and larger diameter				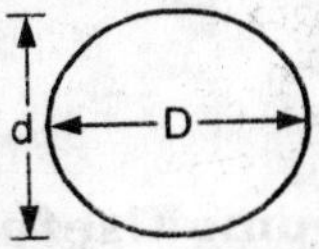

Surface Area to Volume Ratio of can :

The total surface area (TSA) and curved surface area (CSA) of a can of radius r and length h is given by:

$$TSA = 2\pi r^2 + 2\pi rh = 2\pi r(r+h)$$
$$CSA = 2\pi rh = \pi dh$$

The volume of a can in terms of radius r and height h is given by:

$$V = \pi r^2 h$$

Hence, the ratio of total surface area to volume ratio of a can may be expressed as:

$$\frac{TSA}{V} = \frac{2(r+h)}{rh}$$

Note : Among various geometric shapes, sphere has the largest surface area to volume ratio and hence faster heating at geometrical centre of retort pouch is preferred over cylindrical cans.

1.4 CALCULUS

Some Useful Derivatives :

$y = f(x)$	dy/dx
a (constant)	0
x	1
$u + v$	$du/dx + dv/dx$
uv	$u(dv/dx) + v(du/dx)$
x^n	nx^{n-1}
e^x	e^x
e^{kx}	ke^{kx}
$\log(x)$	$1/x$
$\log(ax + b)$	$a/(ax + b)$
$\sin x$	$\cos x$
$\cos x$	$-\sin x$
$\sin(ax + b)$	$a\cos(ax + b)$
$\cos(ax + b)$	$-a\sin(ax + b)$

Some Useful Integrals :

$\int x^n dx = \frac{x^{n+1}}{n+1} \quad (n \neq -1)$	$\int \frac{dx}{x} = \log x$
$\int \frac{dx}{ax+b} = \frac{\log(ax+b)}{a}$	$\int six\ dx = -\cos x$
$\int \cos dx = \sin x$	$\int e^n dx = e^x$
$\int e^{kx} dx = \frac{e^{kx}}{k}$	$\int \ln x\ dx = x(\ln x - 1)$
$\int a^x dx = \frac{a^x}{\log a}$	

Chapter 2

Basic Physical Quantities

Knowledge of basic physical quantities is essential to gain an understanding of principles that govern the unit operations found in the food process engineering. This chapter deals with the commonly used basic physical quantities.

2.1 LINEAR AND ANGULAR VELOCITY

Linear Velocity :

Linear velocity (v) is defined as the rate of change of linear displacement (s) with respect to time (t) for motion in a straight line and given as :

$$\text{linear velocity} = \frac{\text{change of displacement}}{\text{change of time}}$$

i.e.
$$v = \frac{s}{t}$$

The SI unit of linear velocity is meter per second (m/s).

Angular Velocity :

Angular velocity is a measure of the speed at which an object spins and is given by the equation:

$$\omega = \frac{v}{r}$$

where r is the radius and v is velocity. The SI unit of angular velocity is radian per second.

An object rotating at a constant speed of N revolutions per second subtends an angle of $2\pi n$ radians in one second has an angular velocity:

$$\omega = 2\pi n, \text{ rad/s}$$

Frequency :

This is defined as cycles per second. The unit of frequency is hertz.

$$1 \text{ Hz} = 1 \text{ cycle/s}$$

The following formula converts angular velocity into frequency:

$$f = \frac{\omega}{2\pi}$$

The frequency and time period (T) are related as:

$$T = \frac{1}{f}$$

Relationship between angular velocity and linear velocity :

The linear velocity or tip speed v of an object rotating with an angular velocity? situated at a distance r from the centre is given by:

$$v = \omega r = 2\pi N r$$

where v is linear velocity in m/s, ω is angular velocity in radians/s and N is rotational speed in revolution per second (rps).

The relationship between angle in radians (θ), arc length (s) and radius of a circle (r) is:

$$s = r\theta$$

2.2 LINEAR AND ANGULAR ACCELERATION

Linear Acceleration :

It is defined as the rate of change of velocity with time and is given by:

$$\text{linear acceleration} = \frac{\text{change of linear velocity}}{\text{time taken}}$$

i.e.

$$a = \frac{\Delta v}{t}$$

where a is acceleration and v is velocity. The SI unit of accelerations m/s^2.

Angular Acceleration :

It is defined as the rate of change of angular velocity with respect to time and is given by:

$$\text{angular acceleration} = \alpha = \frac{\text{change of angular velocity}}{\text{time taken}}$$

The SI unit of angular accelerations rad/s^2.

Relationship between angular acceleration and linear acceleration :

$$a = r\alpha$$

where a = linear acceleration, r = radius, a = angular acceleration.

Mass and Weight :

The mass (m) of a body is the measure of the amount of material present in that body. The weight of an object is the force of gravity acting vertically downwards due to the force of gravity acting on the object. Mass and weight are related as:

$$W = mg$$

where, W is weigh in Newton, m is mass in kg and g is acceleration due to gravity which is equal to 9.81 m/s^2.

Force :

The force acting on a body is defined by Newton's second law of motion. It is the product of mass and acceleration. The SI unit of force is Newton (N). A force of one Newton produces an acceleration of 1 m/s^2 when applied to a mass of 1 kg.

$$1 \text{ N} = 1 \text{ kg m/s}^2$$

Linear Momentum :

The momentum of a body is defined as the product of mass (m) and velocity (v) and is given by:

$$M = mv$$

The SI unit ofmomentum is kg m/s.

Impulse :

It is defined as the product of force (F) and time (t) and is given by :

$$\text{impulse} = \text{force} \times \text{time} = F \,.\, t$$

The SI unit of impulse is $N \,.\, s$.

Work :

The amount of work done is defined as the product of force (F) and the displacement (d) of an object and is given by:

$$w = F \,.\, D$$

where W = work.

The SI unit of work is Joule (J), which is defined as the amount of work done when a force of 1 Newton acts for a distance of 1 m in the direction of the force. Thus,

$$1 \text{ J} = 1 \text{ Nm}$$

It can also be described as the product of the applied pressure and the displaced volume.

The energy per unit mass is called specific energy. The SI unit of specific energy is J/kg.

Energy :

It is the ability to do work. The SI unit of all types of energy is J. It may also be expressed as kJ and kilowatt hours (kWh). In FPS unit, the unit of thermal energy is British Thermal Units (Btu) which is the amount of heat required to raise 1 lb of water by 1°F.

$$1 \text{ Btu} = 1055 \text{ J}$$

$$1 \text{ kWh} = 3600 \text{ kJ}$$

$$1 \text{ kWh} = 3412 \text{ Btu}$$

Kinetic Energy (*KE*) :

It is the energy possessed by a body by virtue of its motion and is given by:

$$KE = \frac{1}{2} mv^2$$

where KE is kinetic energy, m is mass of an object and v is velocity.

The SI unit of kinetic energy is also Joule (J). Kinetic energy is of importance in the movement of all objects in the food processing industry.

Potential Energy (*PE*) :

It is the energy possessed by virtue of its position or state or configuration of an object and is given by:

$$PE = mgh$$

where PE is potential energy, m is mass of an object, g is acceleration due to gravity and h is height above some specified datum.

The SI unit of potential energy is also Joule (J).

Power :

It is defined as the rate of doing work and is given by the following equation:

$$P = \frac{\text{work done}}{\text{time taken}} = \frac{W}{t}$$

Or,
$$P = \frac{\text{energy used}}{\text{time taken}} = \frac{E}{t} = \frac{F \times d}{t} = F \times v$$

Or, P = force × velocity where d is distance and v is velocity.

The SI unit of power is J/s or Watt (W).

Efficiency is defined as the ratio of the useful output energy to the input energy and is given as :

$$\text{efficiency} = \frac{\text{output energy}}{\text{input energy}} = \frac{\text{output power}}{\text{input power}}$$

Efficiency has no units and is normally expressed in percentage.

Centripetal (Centrifugal) Acceleration :

An object moving in a circle at constant speed v experiences a centripetal/centrifugal acceleration that is proportional to the square of its speed and inversely proportional to the radius of the circle which it circumscribes. Centripetal (centrifugal) acceleration (a_c) is given by :

$$a_c = \frac{v^2}{r} = \omega^2 r$$

where ω is angular velocity in rad/s.

Centripetal (Centrifugal) Force :

It is given by :

$$F_c = \frac{mv^2}{r} = m\omega^2 r$$

where r is the radius in m, m is mass in kg and ω is angular velocity in rad/s. The SI unit of centrifugal/centripetal force is Newton (N).

The acceleration due to centrifugal force (a) can be calculated by the formula:

$$a = \omega^2 R$$

where R = radial distance from centre of rotation, m

ω = angular velocity, rad/s

The angular velocity can be calculated as:

$$\omega = 2\pi N$$

where N = revolutions per second (rps)

The centrifugal force is used in high speed separator or clarifier's for removal of particular matter or separation of immiscible liquids of different densities (cream from milk). The efficiency of a separator can be defined in terms of number of gravitational force or g forces where number of g force is equal to centrifugal force divided by gravitational force and is given by:

$$g \text{ force} = \frac{\text{centrifugal force}}{\text{gravitational force}} = \frac{mr\omega^2}{mg} = \frac{v^2}{gr} = \frac{4\pi^2 N^2 r}{g}$$

Torque :

The turning moment of a couple is called a *torque*. It is equal to the force (F) multiplied by the perpendicular distance (d) between the line of action of the force and the center of rotation at which it is exerted and is given by :

$$T = F \times d$$

where T is torque. The SI unit of torque is Nm.

Power Transmission :

A shaft rotating with a constant angular velocity ω acted on by a twisting moment T transmits a power P is given by the equation:

$$P = T\omega = 2\pi NT$$

Mass Density :

The mass density is defined as the ratio of mass and volume and is given by:

$$\rho = \frac{m}{V}$$

where, m = mass, kg

V = volume, m^3

The density of a substance is the reciprocal of its specific volume. The SI unit of mass density is kg/m^3.

Specific Volume :

The specific volume of a substance is the total volume of that substance divided by the total mass of that substance and it is the reciprocal of the density.

Generally the term 'specific' is used to denote a property of a unit mass of a substance. Mathematically:

$$v_s = \frac{V}{m} = \frac{1}{\rho}$$

where v_s = specific volume, m^3/kg

ρ = density, kg/m^3

m = mass, kg

V = volume, m^3

The SI unit of specific volume is m^3/kg.

Specific Gravity :

It is a ratio of the density of a substance (ρ_s) and the density of pure water (ρ_w) at standard temperature and pressure (*STP*). It is a measure of the relative density of a substance as compared to the density of water. If the specific gravity of a substance is known at a particular temperature, its density at that temperature can be found using:

$$\rho_s = (sg)_T \cdot \rho_w$$

where ρ_s = density of substance at T °C,

$(SG)_T$ = specific gravity at T °C, and

ρ_w = density of water at temperature T °C.

Temperature :

Temperature is the degree of hotness or coldness of an object. Temperature (T) is a thermodynamic quantity related to the velocity of motion of molecules. The SI unit of temperature is Kelvin (K) and MKS unit is °C.

Temperature Scales :

The three temperature scales most commonly employed in food process engineering applications are degree Celsius (°C) scale, degree Fahrenheit (°F) scale and Kelvin (K) scale. The absolute zero, freezing and boiling point in different scales are given below :

Temperature	°C	°F	°K
Absolute zero	– 273	– 460	0
Boiling point of water	100	212	373
Freezing point of water	0	32	273

Temperatures Conversion Formulas :

One temperature scale to another temperature scale can be converted by using following equations:

Fahrenheit scale to Celsius scale	$T_C = \frac{(T_F - 32)}{1.8}$
Celsius scale to Fahrenheit scale	$T_F = 1.8 \times T_C + 32$
Celsius scale to Kelvin scale	$T_K = T_C + 273$
Kelvin scale to Celsius scale	$T_C = T_K - 273$

The relation between the temperatures on above scales may also be given by:

$$\frac{T_C}{100} = \frac{T_F - 32}{180} = \frac{T_K - 273}{100}$$

Or $$\frac{T_C}{5} = \frac{T_F - 32}{9} = \frac{T_K - 273}{5}$$

Note : *TC, TF* and *TK* are temperatures in Celsius, Fahrenheit and Kelvin scale.

Pressure :

It is defined as the force per unit area and is given by:

$$P = \frac{F}{A}$$

where, F = force, N

A = area, m^2

Force may be expressed in term of pressure and area as by the following relation:

force = pressure × area

The SI unit of pressure is Pascal (Pa) and one Pascal is equal to one N/m^2. One bar is equal to approximately one atmosphere.

1 bar = 10^5 Pa = 0.1 MPa ≅ 1 atmosphere

Pressure Scales :

When pressure is measured relative to a perfect vacuum, then it is called ***absolute pressure*** and when pressure is measured relative to atmospheric pressure, then it is called gauge pressure. If the pressure is below that of the atmosphere, it is designated as a vacuum. A perfect vacuum would correspond to absolute zero pressure. Gauge pressures are positive if they are above atmospheric pressure and negative if they are below atmospheric pressure. The atmospheric pressure is also called the ***barometric pressure***. Fig. 1 shows the relationships between absolute, gauge, vacuum, and atmospheric pressures.

The relationships between absolute pressure, gauge pressure and vacuum may be expressed by the following equations:

Absolute pressure = atmospheric pressure +gauge pressure

Absolute pressure = atmospheric pressure −vacuum pressure

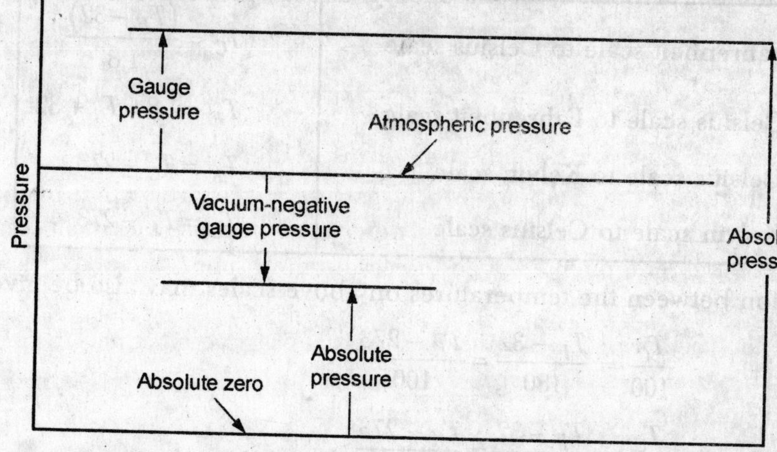

FIG. 2.1. Pressure Relationships

The lowest theoretically possible absolute pressure is zero.

The equation for gauge pressure is given by:

$$P_{gauge} = \text{density} \times \text{height} \times \text{acceleration due to gravity}$$

Or, $$P_{gauge} = \rho g h$$

Hence, Absolute pressure can be expressed as:

$$\text{absolute pressure} = \text{gauge pressure} + \text{atmospheric pressure}$$
$$= \rho g h + P_{atmospheric}$$

where h = head, m

g = acceleration due to gravity, m/s^2

ρ = density of fluid, kg/m^3

Pressure Head :

The equation for head of fluid is given by:

$$h = \frac{P}{\rho g}$$

The SI unit of pressure head is m.

2.3 MIXTURES OF GASES

Dalton's Law of Partial Pressure :

Dalton's law for mixtures of ideal gases states that the total pressure of a gas mixture is equal to the sum of the individual partial pressures and is given by:

$$P = p_A + p_B + p_C + \ldots\ldots\ldots$$

where P is total pressure and $p_A, p_B, p_C, \ldots$ are the partial pressures of the components A, B, C, ... in the mixture.

Since the number of moles of a component is directly proportional to its partial pressure, hence the mole fraction of a component may be written as:

$$n_A = \frac{p_A}{P} = \frac{p_A}{p_A + p_B + p_C + ...}$$

Gas mixtures are always represented in terms of mole fractions.

The mole fraction of a component in a mixture is the proportion of the number of molecules of the component present to the total number of the molecules of all the components. Partial pressures of the components are additive, and their sum is equal to the total pressure of the mixture.

In ambient air, total pressure consists of the partial pressure of air plus the partial pressure of water vapor. The total partial pressure of air is the sum of the partial pressures of oxygen, nitrogen, carbon dioxide, hydrogen, and other gases.

Amalgat's law :

Amalgat's law of partial volumes states that the total volume (*Vt*) of a mixture is the sum of the volumes of the components of the mixture.

Where V_1, V_2, V_3, ... are volume of components present in the mixture.

Gas Laws :

The relationships that exist between pressure, volume and temperature in a gas are given in a set of laws called the gas laws.

Boyle's Law :

Boyle's law states that when gas temperature is constant, the volume (V) of a given mass of gas is inversely proportional to the pressure (P).

i.e. $V \propto \frac{1}{P}$ or, $V = \frac{K}{P}$ or, $PV = K$ where K = constant

When a fixed mass of gas at constant temperature changes from pressure P_1 and volume V_1 to pressure P_2 and volume V_2 then :

$$P_1 V_1 = P_2 V_2$$

Charles' Law :

Charles' law states when gas pressure is constant, the volume (V) of a given mass of gas varies directly as the absolute temperature (T).

i.e. $V \propto T$ or, $V = KT$ or $\frac{V}{T} = K$

where K = constant, T = absolute temperature, K

If a given mass of gas at a constant pressure occupies a volume V_1 at a temperature T_1 and a volume V_2 at temperature T_2, then

$$\frac{V_1}{T_1} = \frac{V_2}{T_2}$$

Gay-Lussac's Law :

When gas volume is constant, the pressure (P) of a given mass of gas varies directly to the absolute temperature (T).

i.e. $$P \propto T \quad \text{or} \quad P = KT \quad \text{or} \quad \frac{P}{T} = K$$

where K = constant

When a fixed mass of gas at constant volume changes from pressure P_1 and temperature T_1, to pressure P_2 and temperature T_2 then:

$$\frac{P_1}{T_1} = \frac{P_2}{T_2}$$

P-V-T Relationships for Ideal Gases :

$$\frac{PV}{T} = \text{constant}$$

Or, $$\frac{P_1V_1}{T_1} = \frac{P_2V_2}{T_2}$$

With gases, concentrations are primarily measured in weight concentrations per unit volume or as partial pressures. These can be related through the gas laws which is represented in the following form:

$$PV = nRT = \frac{mRT}{M}$$

where, V = volume, m^3

T = absolute temperature, K

n = molar mass of gas in mol

M = molecular weight

R = gas constant, J/kg K

P = pressure, Pa

The molar concentration of a gas is given by:

$$C = \frac{n}{V} = \frac{\text{Total number of mole}}{\text{Volume of gas}}$$

Or, $$C = \frac{P}{RT}$$

Partial pressure exerted in a mixture of ideal gases is given by the product of the mole fraction of that component and total pressure.

i.e. $$p_A = y_A P$$

P-V-T Relationships for Ideal Gases in Thermodynamic Processes :

Thermodynamic Processes	*Governing Equation*	*Remark*
Isothermal Processes	$P_1V_1 = P_2V_2$	temperature remains constant
Isobaric processes	$\frac{V_1}{T_1} = \frac{V_2}{T_2}$	pressure remains constant
Isocratic processes	$\frac{P_1}{T_1} = \frac{P_2}{T_2}$	volume remains constant

The pressure P and volume V of a gas undergoing adiabatic transformation are related by the equation:

$$PV^{\gamma} = \text{constant } t$$

where $\gamma = \frac{C_p}{C_v}$, C_p and C_v are heat capacity of gas at constant pressure and volume.

Also, $$TV^{\gamma-1} = \text{constant } t$$

Expression for Temperature Rise in Adiabatic Compression :

Since $$PV^{\gamma} = \text{constant } t$$

Hence we may write:

$$P_1V_1^{\gamma} = P_2V_2^{\gamma}$$

Also $$\frac{P_1V_1}{T_1} = \frac{P_2V_2}{T_2}$$

From these two equations, we may write:

$$T_1V_1^{\gamma-1} = T_2V_2^{\gamma-1}$$

$$\frac{T_2}{T_1} = \left(\frac{V_1}{V_2}\right)^{\gamma-1}$$

Since $$\frac{V_1}{V_2} = \left(\frac{P_2}{P_1}\right)^{1/\gamma}$$

Hence $$\frac{T_2}{T_1} = \left(\frac{P_2}{P_1}\right)^{\frac{\gamma-1}{\gamma}}$$

Thermal Expansion of Solids :

When solids are heated, there is expansion in length, area and volume. These expansions are known as *linear expansion, superficial expansion* and *volumetric expansion.*

Coefficient of linear expansion : It is defines as the increase in length per unit length of a material for 1 °C rise of temperature and is given by:

$$\alpha = \frac{\Delta l}{l \Delta T}$$

where Δl is the change in length, l is original length and ΔT is the rise in temperature.

Coefficient of superficial expansion : It is defines as the increase in area per unit area of a material for 1 °C rise of temperature and is given by:

$$\beta = \frac{\Delta A}{A \Delta T}$$

where ΔA is the change in original area A and ΔT is the rise in temperature.

Coefficient of volumetric expansion : It is defines as the increase in volume per unit volume of a body for 1 °C rise of temperature and is given by:

$$\gamma = \frac{\Delta V}{V \Delta T}$$

where ΔV is the change in original volume V and ΔT is the rise in temperature.

2.4 RELATIONSHIP BETWEEN α, β AND γ

Coefficient of volumetric expansion = coefficient of linear expansion × 3

i.e. $\gamma = 3\alpha$

Coefficient of superficial expansion = coefficient of linear expansion × 2

i.e. $\beta = 2\alpha$

Concentrations :

Concentrations can be expressed in the following ways:

(i) Weight/weight percentage (w/w %)
(ii) Weight/volume percentage (w/v %)
(iii) Volume/ volume percentage (v/v %)
(iv) Molar concentration (M)
(v) Mole fraction

$$\text{Weight/weight percentage (w/w \%)} = \frac{\text{weight of solute}}{\text{total weight of solution}} \times 100$$

Example : A food containing 15% solids (w/w) will contain 15 kg of solid matter in every 100 kg of foods (solid or liquid).

$$\text{Weight/volume percentage (\% w/v)} = \frac{\text{weight of solute (gram)}}{\text{total volume of solution (ml)}} \times 100$$

$$\text{Volume/volume percentage (\% v/v)} = \frac{\text{volume of solute (ml)}}{\text{total volume of solution (ml)}} \times 100$$

Molarity of Solution : The molar concentration is the number of molecular weights of the solute expressed as moles in 1 m^3 of the solution.

Mole Fraction : The mole fraction is the ratio of the number of moles of the solute to the total number of moles of all species present in the solution. Mixture may be a solid, a liquid solution, or a gas.

$$\text{mole fraction} = n_i = \frac{\text{mole component } i}{\text{total moles}}$$

A mixture which contains w_A kg of component A of molecular weight M_A and w_B kg of component B of molecular weight M_B, the mole fraction of both components may be expressed as:

$$n_A = \frac{\text{number of moles of } A}{\text{number of moles of } A + \text{number of moles of } B} = \frac{n_A}{n_A + n_B} = \frac{\frac{w_A}{M_A}}{\frac{w_A}{M_A} + \frac{w_B}{M_B}}$$

and, $$n_B = \frac{\text{number of moles of } B}{\text{number of moles of } A + \text{number of moles of } B} = \frac{n_B}{n_A + n_B} = \frac{\frac{w_B}{M_B}}{\frac{w_A}{M_A} + \frac{w_B}{M_B}}$$

Since $n_A + n_B = 1$ hence $n_B = 1 - n_A$ or $n_A = 1 - n_B$

The definition of the mole fraction can be extended to any number of components in a multi component mixture.

Mole fraction of water n_w in a given product may also be expressed as:

$$n_w = \frac{\frac{m_w}{M_w}}{\frac{m_w}{M_w} + \sum \frac{m_i}{M_i}}$$

where m_w = mass fraction of water

M_w = molecular weight of water

m_i = mass fraction of the ith component of soluble solids

M_i = molecular weight of ith component of soluble solid.

Composition Fractions :

Most material streams in process units are mixtures of compounds. The composition of the stream is expressed in various ways. The composition fractions can be based on mass or on moles.

Mass fraction : Mass fraction of a component is given by:

$$\text{mass fraction} = x_i = \frac{\text{mass component } i}{\text{total mass}}$$

The mass fraction of A component in a mixture consisting of masses mA and mB of components A and B is given by:

$$x_A = \frac{m_A}{m_A + m_B}$$

A mass percentage is the mass fraction multiplied by 100.

Material Balances :

Material (mass) balances are based on the principle that matter is neither created nor destroyed. Thus, in any process, a mass balance can be made as follows:

Inflow = Outflow + Accumulation

If accumulation is 0,

Inflow = Outflow, then the process is at steady state.

If the accumulation is not 0, then the process is at unsteady state.

Mass balances are essential in processes involving material flow. For example, liquid handling systems, evaporation and dehydration systems can be analyzed using mass balances.

Heat Balances :

Heat balance calculations are treated in the same manner as material balances. The amount of heat entering a system must equal the amount of heat leaving a system, or:

Heat in = heat out + accumulation

At a steady state, the accumulation term is zero. Heat balance problems are facilitated by using diagrams that show process streams bringing heat and taking heat out of a system.

Flux :

Transfer of any physical quantity passing through a unit area in unit time is called *flux* of that quantity. Some examples of flux are heat flux, momentum flux and mass flux. The unit of heat flux is J/sm^2 or W/m^2. The unit of momentum flux is (kgm/s)/m^{2}s or kg/ms^2 same as the unit of shear stress (N/m^2 = kg/ms^2). The unit of mass flux is kg/sm^2.

The heat flux is the rate of heat transfer per unit area and equation for heat flux is given as :

$$\text{heat flux} = \frac{q}{A}$$

where q is rate of heat transfer, W and A is heat transfer area.

Rate Equation :

The rate of transport (i.e. quantity transported per unit time) is proportional to the driving force and inversely proportional to the resistance of the medium to the transport. For any kind of molecular transport processes (heat or thermal energy, momentum, and mass), the general rate equation can be written as follows :

$$\text{rate of transfer process} = \frac{\text{driving force}}{\text{resistance}}$$

Example : For heat transfer –

$$\text{Rate of heat transfer} = \frac{\text{temperature difference}}{\text{heat flow resistance of medium}}$$

Electricity :

Ohm's Law : This law states that the current flowing in a conductor at uniform temperature is proportional to the potential difference V at its end. Mathematically, it is expressed as:

$$V \propto I$$

or,

$$V = IR$$

where R = resistance of the conductor, ohms

I = current, amperes (A)

V = potential difference, volt (V)

The electric current is defined as the rate of flow of charge (q). The equation for current is given by :

$$I = \frac{q}{t}$$

The potential difference V between two points is the work per unit charge required to move the charge between the points.

For two parallel plates with potential difference V, separated by distance d, the strength of the E field between the plates is :

$$E = \frac{V}{d}$$

Specific resistance or resistivity : The equation of specific resistance is:

$$\rho = \frac{RA}{l}$$

where ρ = Specific resistance (ohm-m),

l = length of conductor (m) and

A = cross sectional area of conductor (m^2)

Resistors in Series and Parallel :

For series connections, the current in all resistors is the same and the equivalent resistance for n resistors in series is given by:

$$R_S = R_1 + R_2 + \ldots + R_n$$

For parallel connections of resistors, the voltage drop across each resistor is the same and the equivalent resistance (Rp) for n resistors in parallel is given by:

$$RP = \frac{1}{\left(\frac{1}{R_1} + \frac{1}{R_2} + \ldots + \frac{1}{R_n}\right)}$$

For two resistors R_1 and R_2 in parallel, the equivalent resistance is given by:

$$R_p = \frac{R_1 R_2}{R_1 + R_2}$$

Power absorbed by a resistive element is given by:

$$P = VI = I^2 R = \frac{V^2}{R}$$

where P is power (watt), I is current (amp), R is resistance (Ohm) and V is volt.

Electrical Energy :

The total amount of electrical energy E when a current I flow over a potential difference V for a time t is given by:

$$E = VIt = I^2 Rt$$

where E is in Joule, I in amperes, V in volt, R in ohms and t in second.

The amount of electrical energy used by the consumer is measured in terms of kilowatt hours or number of units. The number of units used is equal to the product of the power rating in kilowatts and the time in hours:

$$\text{Number of units used (kWh)} = \text{power rating (kW)} \times \text{time (h)}$$

Chapter 3

Engineering Properties of Foods

Engineering properties of food and biological materials are required in the design of food process equipments to ensure food quality and safety. This chapter covers the various engineering properties of food such as thermal, physical, mechanical and electrical properties.

Thermal Properties :

The thermal properties of foods are of considerable importance in food process engineering. The important thermal properties of particular importance are specific heat, thermal conductivity, and thermal diffusivity, enthalpy and latent heat of phase transition.

Specific heat : Specific heat is the amount of heat required to increase the temperature of 1 kg of material by 1 °C at a given temperature and can be thought of as the ability of a substance to absorb heat. It is denoted by *Cp*. The SI unit for *Cp* is J/kg K or J/kg °C.

The specific heat (*Cp*) may be expressed by the following relationship :

$$C_p = \frac{Q}{m\Delta T}$$

where, C_p = specific heat at constant pressure, J/kg K
Q = heat transferred, J
m = mass, kg
ΔT = temperature difference, K

The specific heat of a food having different mass fraction and specific heat is calculated by:

$$C_p = \sum_{i=1}^{n} x_i C_{pi}$$

where, x_i = mass fraction of component i
C_{pi} = specific heat of component i (J/kg K)

Thermal Conductivity :

It represents the quantity of heat Q that flows per unit time through a food material of unit thickness and unit area having unit temperature difference between faces. It is denoted by k. The SI unit of thermal conductivity is W/m K. The rate of heat flow through a food material by conduction can be predicted by Fourier's law of heat conduction which is given by:

$$Q = \frac{kA(T_1 - T_2)}{x}$$

where A is the surface area of the food, x is its thickness, T_1 is the temperature at the outer surface where heat is absorbed and T_2 is the temperature at the inner surface.

Thermal conductivity of food is an important property used in calculation involving rate of heat transfer. Most high moisture food has thermal conductivity value close to that of water.

Thermal Conductivity of Gas :

Thermal conductivity of gas increases approximately as the square root of the absolute temperature.

i.e. $$k \propto \sqrt{T} \propto v_s$$

where, T = absolute temperature, K

v_s = mean speed of molecules, m/s

At very low pressure (vacuum), k approaches zero.

Thermal Conductivity of Liquid :

Thermal conductivity of liquids varies moderately with temperature and expressed as:

$$k = a + bT$$

where a and b are constant.

Thermal conductivity of liquids is essentially independent of pressure.

Thermal Diffusivity :

It defines the rate at which heat diffuses by conduction through a food material. It is denoted by a and its SI unit is m^2/s. It is related to thermal conductivity (κ) and specific heat C_p through density (ρ) as follows :

$$\alpha = \frac{\kappa}{\rho C_p}$$

Physically, thermal diffusivity can be interpreted as the ratio of the material's ability to transfer heat to its capacity to store heat.

Heat Content (Sensible Heat) of a Material :

The heat which causes an increase or decrease in the temperature of a body without changing its state is known as *sensible heat*. The heat content or sensible heat of a material is given by the following equation:

Sensible heat = mass specific heat temperature difference

i.e. $$Q = mC_p\Delta T = mC_p(T_2 - T_1)$$

where Q = heat content or sensible heat, J

m = mass, kg

C_p = specific heat, J/kg K

ΔT = temperature difference = $T_2 - T_1$, K

T_1 = initial temperature, K

T_2 = final temperature, K

Rate of Change of Heat Content :

The equation for rate of change of heat content of a material is given by:

$$q = \dot{m} C_p \Delta T = A\rho v C_p \Delta T = \frac{\pi}{4} d^2 \rho v C_p \Delta T$$

where q = rate of change of heat content, J/s or W

$\dot{m}$ = mass flow rate, kg/s

C_p = specific heat, J/kg K

ΔT = temperature difference, K

d = diameter of pipe, m

v = velocity of flow, m/s

ρ = dnsity of fluid, kg/m^3

Latent Heat :

The amount of heat absorbed or given out by a unit mass of the substance to change its state without change of temperature is called *latent heat*. The different types of latent heat are latent heat of fusion, latent heat of vaporization and latent heat of sublimation. All types of phase changes are presented in Fig. 3.1.

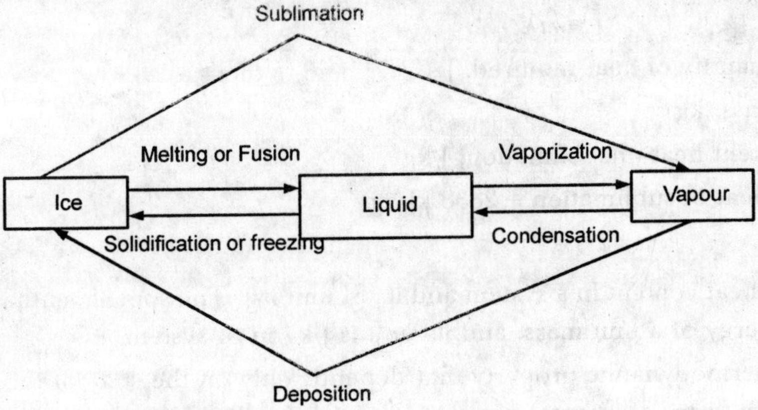

FIG. 3.1. Depiction of phase change

Latent Heat of Fusion :

The amount of heat required to covert a unit mass of the substance from solid state to the liquid state without change of temperature is called *latent heat of fusion*. The equation for latent heat of fusion or solidification is given by:

$$Q_f = m\lambda_f$$

where Q_f = quantity of heat required or liberated, J

m = mass of material solidified or melted, kg

λ_f = latent heat of solidification or fusion, J/kg

Latent heat of fusion of ice = 335 kJ/kg

Latent heat of freezing of water = 335 kJ/kg.

Latent Heat of Vaporization :

The amount of heat required to convert a unit mass of saturated liquid to saturated vapour at constant temperature and pressure is called *latent heat of vaporization.* The latent heat removed or supplied for condensation or vaporization can be calculated from the relationship:

$$Q_v = m\lambda_v$$

where, Q_v = quantity of heat required or liberated, J

m = mass of a given material evaporated or condensed, kg

λ_v = latent heat of vaporization or condensation, J/kg

Latent heat of steam at 100°C = 2257 kJ/kg

Latent Heat of Sublimation :

The amount of heat required to covert a unit mass of the substance from solid state to directly vapour state without change of temperature is called *latent heat of sublimation* and reverse of this process is called deposition. The latent heat of sublimation can be calculated from the relationship:

$$Q_s = m\lambda_s$$

where, Q_s = quantity of heat required, J

m = mass, kg

λ_s = latent heat of sublimation, J/kg

Latent heat of sublimation = 2838 kJ/kg

Enthalpy :

It is the heat content in a system and its SI unit is J. The specific enthalpy is a measure of the total energy of a unit mass, and its unit is J/kg in SI system.

It is a thermodynamic property that depends only on the state of the system and can be expressed in terms of internal energy (U), pressure (P), and volume (V) by the following relation :

$$H = U + PV$$

Gibbs free energy (G) is the difference of enthalpy and product of temperature (T) and entropy (S) and is given by :

$$G = H - TS$$

Entropy :

It is referred to as a measure of the inability to do work for a given heat transferred. Changes in entropy take place when evaporation or condensation occurs. The entropy changes are given by the formula :

$$S_{fg} = S_f - S_g$$

where S_f = specific entropy of saturated liquid, J/kg K

S_g = specific entropy of saturated vapour, J/kg K

S_{fg} = specific entropy change of vaporization, J/kg K

Since phase changes occur at constant pressure, the following relationship can be applied:

$$S_{fg} = \frac{h_{fg}}{T}$$

Enthalpy of steam = 2500 + 1.88 T

Latent heat of vaporization at temperature T is given by:

$$\lambda_1 = 2501 + 1.88\ \mathrm{T} - 4.18\ \mathrm{T}$$

Latent heat of vaporization may also be expressed in term of enthalpy as:

$$h_{fg} = h_g - h_f$$

where h_g is specific enthalpy of steam and h_f is specific enthalpy of liquid water.

The difference between specific enthalpy of the saturated liquid and saturated vapour is equal to latent heat of vaporization.

Steam Quality :

Steam quality also known as *dryness fraction* (x) is defined as the mass of steam present per unit mass of steam-water mixture. The steam quality or dryness fraction(x) is given by:

$$x = \frac{\text{mass of dry steam}}{\text{total mass of wet steam}} = \frac{\text{mass of dry steam}}{\text{mass of dry steam + mass of water}}$$

It is expressed as a decimal fraction between 0 (saturated liquid) and 1 (saturated steam).

The specific enthalpy of wet steam is given by :

$$h = h_f + xh_{fg}$$

The specific volume (v) of wet steam is given by :

$$v = v_f + xv_{fg}$$

The quality of the mixture at any point in the liquid-vapor region can be found using the following relationship:

$$x = \frac{\upsilon - \upsilon_f}{\upsilon_{fg}}$$

$$x = \frac{h - h_f}{h_{fg}}$$

where υ = specific volume of the mixture (m^3/kg)
x = quality of the mixture in decimal fraction
υ_g = specific volume of the vapor (m^3/kg)
υ_f = specific volume of the liquid (m^3/kg)
υ_{fg} = specific volume change of vaporization (m^3/kg) or $v_{fg} = vg - v_f$
h = specific enthalpy of the mixture (J/kg)
h_g = specific enthalpy of the saturated vapor (J/kg)
h_f = specific enthalpy of the saturated liquid (J/kg)
h_{fg} = specific enthalpy change of vaporization (J/kg) or $h_{fg} = h_g - h_f$

In a process where there is a change of phase between saturated liquid and saturated vapour, the rate at which heat is supplied or removed is given by:

$$q = \dot{m} h_{fg}$$

where $\dot{m}$ = mass flow rate, kg/s
h_{fg} = latent heat of vaporization = $h_g - h_f$, J/kg
h_f = enthalpy of saturated liquid, J/kg
h_g = enthalpy of water vapour, J/kg
q = heat transferred rate, J/s or W

The enthalpy at temperature T_2 can be calculated by following expression if enthalpies at temperature T_1 and T_3 are known :

$$h_2 = h_1 + \frac{T_3 - T_1}{h_3 - h_1}(h_2 - h_1)$$

This equation can be used under a given set of conditions where linear interpolation of data is required to obtain the properties from steam table.

Physical Properties :

Shape : Shape is important in heat and mass transfer calculations, screening solids to separate foreign materials, grading of fruits and vegetables, and evaluating the quality of food materials. The shape of a food material is usually expressed in terms of its sphericity and aspect ratio.

Sphericity : It indicates deviation of shape of an object from a sphere. Sphericity is the defined as the ratio of volume of solid to the volume of a sphere that has a diameter equal to the major diameter of the object so that it can circumscribe the solid sample. For a spherical particle of diameter D_p, sphericity is equal to 1.

$$\text{sphericity} = \left(\frac{\text{volume of solid sample}}{\text{volume of circumscribed sphere}}\right)^{1/3}$$

Sphericity may also be written as :

$$\phi = \frac{(abc)^{1/3}}{a}$$

where the major, intermediate, and minor diameters (Fig. 3.2) are $2a$, $2b$, and $2c$, respectively.

The equivalent diameter of a particle can be determined by the following equation:

$$\text{equivalentadiameter} = (abc)^{1/3}$$

The equivalent diameter is diameter of a sphere having the same ratio of surface to volume as the actual particle. It is also known as *geometric mean diameter.*

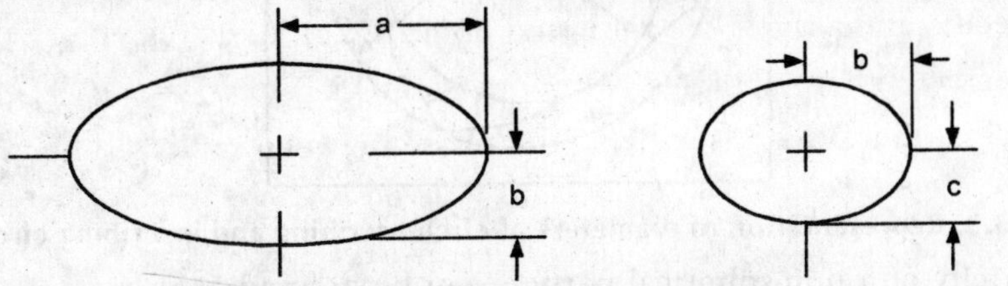

FIG. 3.2. Representation of dimension

Sphericity is also defined as the ratio of surface area of a sphere having the same volume as the object to the actual surface area of the object. Mathematically:

$$\phi = \frac{\pi D_e^{\ 2}}{S_p} = \frac{6V_p}{D_e S_p}$$

where D_e = equivalent diameter or nominal diameter of the particle (m)

S_p = surface area of one particle (m^2)

V_p = volume of one particle (m^3)

The equivalent diameter is sometimes defined as the diameter of a sphere having the same volume as the particle. The equivalent diameter is usually taken as the nominal size based on screen analysis or microscopic examination in granular materials.

The number of particles (N) in a sample having mass (m), density of the particles (ρ_p) and volume of one particle (V_p) is given by:

$$N = \frac{m}{\rho_p V_p}$$

where N = number of particles

m = mass of the sample (kg)

ρ_p = density of the particles (kg/m^3)

V_p = volume of one particle (m^3)

Total surface area of the particles is given by:

$$A = S_p N = \frac{6m}{\phi \rho_p D_e}$$

Another definition of sphericity is the ratio of the diameter of the largest inscribed circle (d_i) to the diameter of the smallest circumscribed circle (d_c) (Fig. 3.3) and which is given by:

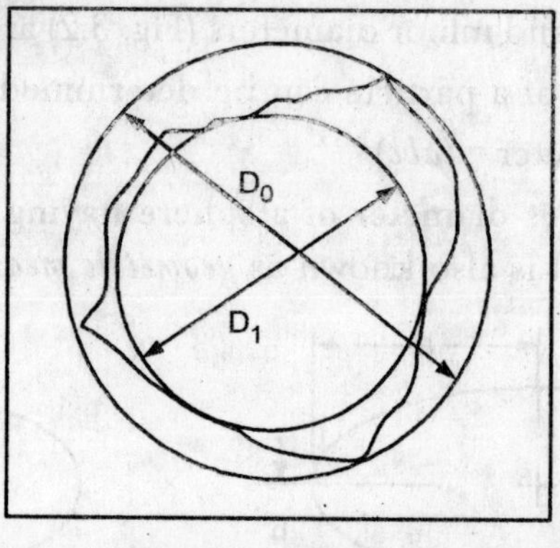

FIG. 3.3. Representation of diameters of circumscribing and inscribing circles

The sphericity of a non-spherical particle can be defined as:

$$\phi = \frac{\text{surface area of a sphere having the same volume as the particle}}{\text{surface area of paricle}} = \frac{SA_s}{SA_p}$$

For non-spherical particles, an equivalent diameter (*de*)can be defined as the diameter of a sphere with same volume *V* as the original particle.

Volume of particle (V_p) = volume of sphere (V_s)

$$V_s = \frac{\pi}{6} d_e^{\,3}$$

Since $$V_s = V_p$$

Hence, $$V_s = \frac{\pi}{6} d_e^{\,3} = V_p$$

Or, $$d_e = \left(\frac{6\,V_p}{\pi}\right)^{1/3}$$

Sphericity of Particle of Rectangular Block Shape :

The surface area of a rectangular block is:

$$SA_p = 2\,(lb + lh + bh)$$

where l is length, h is height and b is breadth.

The volume of the rectangular block is:

$$V_p = lbh$$

The equivalent diameter *de* is:

$$d_e = \left(\frac{6V_p}{\pi}\right)^{1/3} = \left(\frac{6lbh}{\pi}\right)^{1/3}$$

$$SA_s = \pi d_e^2$$

Hence,
$$\phi = \frac{SA_s}{SA_p} = \frac{\pi d_e^2}{2(lb + lh + bh)} = \frac{\pi\left(\frac{6lbh}{\pi}\right)^{\frac{2}{3}}}{2(lb + lh + bh)}$$

Sphericity of a Cubical Particle :

Let a = side of cubical particle

$$V_p = a^3$$

$$SA_p = 6a^2$$

The equivalent diameter de is:

$$d_e = \left(\frac{6V_p}{\pi}\right)^{1/3} = \left(\frac{6a^3}{\pi}\right)^{1/3}$$

$$SA_s = \pi d_e^2$$

Hence,
$$\phi = \frac{SA_s}{SA_p} = \frac{\pi d_e^2}{6a^2} = \frac{\pi\left(\frac{6a^3}{\pi}\right)^{2/3}}{6a^2} = \frac{\pi\left(\frac{6}{\pi}\right)^{2/3}}{6} = 0.8059 \approx 0.806$$

Sphericity of a Cylindrical Particle Having Equal Diameter and Length:

Let d = diameter of cylindrical particle and l = length of cylindrical particle

$$V_p = \frac{\pi d^2 l}{4} = \frac{\pi d^3}{4} \qquad \text{(Since } d = l\text{)}$$

$$SA_p = \frac{3}{2}\pi d^2$$

The equivalent diameter de is :

$$d_e = \left(\frac{6V_p}{\pi}\right)^{1/3} = \left(\frac{6}{4\pi}\frac{\pi d^3}{}\right)^{1/3} = \left(\frac{3d^3}{2}\right)^{1/3}$$

$$SA_s = \pi d_e^2$$

Hence,
$$\phi = \frac{SA_s}{SA_p} = \frac{\pi d_e^2}{\frac{3}{2}\pi d^2} = \frac{\pi\left(\frac{3d^3}{2}\right)^{2/3}}{\frac{3}{2}\pi d^2} = \frac{\pi\left(\frac{3}{2}\right)^{2/3}}{\frac{3}{2}} = 0.87358 \approx 0.874$$

Aspect Ratio :

The aspect ratio (R_a) is used to express the shape of a material and is calculated using the length (a) and the width (b) of the sample as:

$$R_a = \frac{a}{b}$$

Roundness :

It is a measure of the sharpness of the corners of a solid (Fig. 3.5). Mathematically, it is expressed as :

$$R = \frac{A_p}{A_c}$$

where A_p = largest projected area of object in natural position

A_c = area of smallest circumscribing circle

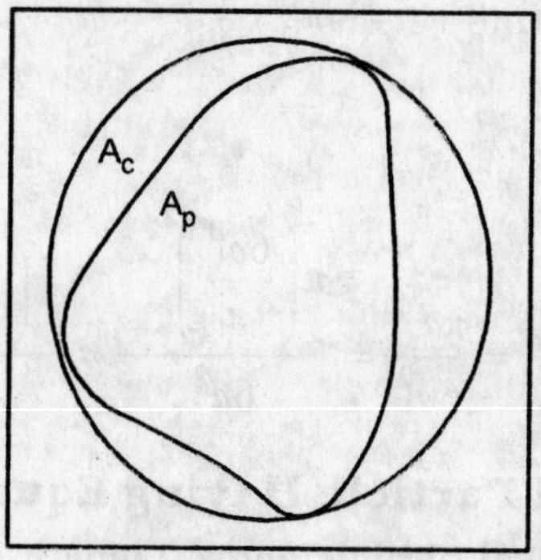

FIG. 3.5. Representation of roundness of a particle

Bulk Density :

It is the mass of a group of individual particles divided by the space occupied by the entire mass, including the air space. Density of food materials is useful in mathematical conversion of mass to volume. Bulk density is the density of a material when packed or stacked in bulk.

True Density :

True density also known as *solid density* or *particle density* (ρ_T) is the ration of weight of particles and volume of particles. The particle density of a pure substance or a composite material calculated from the densities of its components considering conservation of mass and volume. If the densities and volume or mass fractions of constituents are known, density can be determined from:

$$\rho_T = \sum_{i=}^{n} X_i^v \rho_i = \frac{1}{\sum_{i=1}^{n} X_i^w / \rho_i}$$

where ρ_i = density of ith component (kg/m^3)

X_i^v = volume fraction of ith component

X_i^w = mass fraction of ith component

n = number of components

Porosity :

Porosity is the percentage of air between the particles compared to a unit volume of particles. Porosity is an important physical property that is required in modeling and design of various heat and mass transfer processes such as drying, frying, baking, heating, cooling, and extrusion. It is an important parameter in predicting diffusional properties of cellular foods.

The porosity of the packed material is that fraction of total volume which is occupied by the air i.e.

$$\text{porosity } (\varepsilon) = \frac{\text{air or void volume}}{\text{total volume}}$$

Relationship Between Porosity, Bulk Density and Solid Density :

The relationship is given by :

$$\text{porosity} = \frac{\text{solid density-bulk density}}{\text{solid density}} 1 - \frac{\text{bulk density}}{\text{solid density}} = 1 - \frac{\rho_b}{\rho_p}$$

Overrun :

The inclusion of air into liquids (ice cream and whipped cream) reduces the density of the product. The amount of air that is incorporated is referred to as the over-run. The term overrun is defined as the percentage increase in volume attributed to air and expressed as:

$$\text{overrum} = \frac{\text{increase in volume}}{\text{original volume}} = \frac{V_f - V_l}{V_l} \times 100$$

where V_f is the volume of the foam and V_l is the volume of the original liquid.

For ice-cream, % overrun is given as :

$$\%\text{Overrun} = (\text{Volume of ice cream} - \text{Volume of mix used}) \times \frac{100}{\text{Volume of mix used}}$$

Typical over-run values are 60–100% for ice cream and 100–120% for whipped cream.

Foam :

Foams can be defined as a colloidal dispersion in which gas is the dispersed phase and liquid is the continuous phase.When a bubble in foam is considered, there are two forces acting on the bubble: dynamic forces and surface tension forces. The dynamic forces can be regarded as shear stress. The ratio of these forces, which is the Weber number is used to determine the maximum stable bubble size possible and is given by :

$$We = \frac{\tau D_{max}}{\sigma}$$

where τ is shear stress, s is surface tension, and D_{max} is the maximum diameter of the bubble.

Frictional Properties :

The frictional properties such as angle of repose and coefficient of friction are important in designing of storage bins, material conveying systems, etc.

Angle of Repose :

It is the angle θ between the base and slope of the cone formed on a free vertical fall of the granular material or powder to a horizontal plane. The angle of repose depends on size, shape, orientation and moisture content of the material.

Coefficient of Friction :

The coefficient of friction (μ) is a measure of the amount of friction existing between two surfaces. A low value of coefficient of friction indicates that the force required for sliding to occur is less than the force required when the coefficient of friction is high. The value of the coefficient of friction is given by:

$$\mu = \frac{\text{frictional force}}{\text{normal force}} = \frac{F}{N}$$

Or, $$F = \mu N$$

Relationship Between Coefficient of Friction and Angle of Repose :

$$\mu = \tan\theta$$

where μ = the coefficient of friction, and θ = the angle of repose.

Mechanical Properties :

Stress : Stress is the ratio of the applied force (*F*) to cross-sectional area (*A*) of the material. The SI unit of stress is N/m^2 or Pa.

$$\text{stress} = \frac{\text{applied force}}{\text{cross sectional area}} = \frac{F}{A}$$

Strain : Strain is usually expressed as a dimensionless ratio, such as the elongation as a percentage of the original length. Strain, like stress, can be categorized into two groups: normal strain and shear strain. Normal strain (ε) is the change in length per unit length in the direction of the applied normal stress and is expressed as:

$$\text{strain} = \frac{\text{change in length}}{\text{original length}} = \frac{\Delta l}{L_o}$$

Strain is dimension-less and is often expressed as a percentage, i.e.

$$\text{percentage strain} = \frac{\Delta l}{L_o} \times 100$$

The ratio of stress to strain is known as modulus while the ratio of strain to stress is known as *compliance*. Different types of moduli are defined for a Hookean solid.

Modulus of Elasticity :

Young's modulus or Modulus of elasticity (E) is defined as the ratio of normal stress (σ) to normal tensile or compressive strain (ε).

$$E = \frac{\text{stress}}{\text{strain}} = \frac{F / A_0}{\Delta L / L_0}$$

where, E = Young's modulus of elasticity, Pa

F = force applied, N

A_0 = original cross-sectional area, m^2

ΔL = elongation, m

L_0 = original length, m

$$\%\ \text{elongation} = \left(\frac{\Delta L}{L_0}\right) \times 100$$

Material showing elastic behavior is known as a *Hookean solid.*

Modulus of Rigidity :

Shear modulus or modulus of rigidity (G) is used to describe the relationship between the shear stress and shear strain.

$$G = \frac{\text{shear stress}}{\text{shear strain}} = \frac{\tau}{\gamma}$$

$$\text{Share stress} = \tau = \frac{\text{tangential force}}{\text{area under shear}}$$

$$\text{Shearstrain} = \frac{x}{L}$$

Shear stress (τ) is defined as the force applied parallel to the plane per unit area.

If the force is applied from all directions which results in a volume change, modulus is called *bulk modulus* (K).

$$K = \frac{\text{pressure change}}{\text{volume change/original volume}}$$

Poisson's Ratio :

Poisson's ratio (μ) is defined as the ratio of transverse strain to the corresponding axial strain. It provides a measure of the change in length vs. change in width of the sample during loading.

$$\mu = \frac{\text{change in width per unit width}}{\text{change in length per unit length}} = \frac{\Delta D / D}{\Delta L / L}$$

The deformation distance of spring (x) varies linearly with the force acting on the system (F) is given by:

$$F = k\,x$$

where k is the spring constant. The spring is considered as an ideal solid element obeying Hooke's law.

Deborah Number :

In viscoelastic fluids, stress is a function of the strain similar to a solid and it is also a function of strain rate like a liquid. The degree that a fluid can return to its original position depends on its elastic and viscous characteristics. Deborah number is important for viscoelastic materials. For any fluid, Deborah number (De) is defined as:

$$De = \frac{\lambda_{rel}}{\theta}$$

where λ_{rel} is the characteristic relaxation time of the material and θ is the characteristic time of the deformation process.

The Deborah number represents the ratio of duration of fluid memory to the duration of the deformation process and is used as a measure of degree of viscoelasticity.

If $De < 1$, the fluid appears to be more viscous than elastic and if $De > 1$, then the fluid appears to be more elastic than viscous.

Electrical Properties :

Electrical conductivity : Electrical conductivity is a measure of how electric current flows through a food of unit cross-sectional area A, unit length L, and resistance R. It is the inverse value of electrical resistivity (measure of resistance to electric flow).

$$\sigma = \frac{L}{AR}$$

The SI unit of electrical conductivity is S/m.

Colligative Properties :

Freezing point depression : The freezing point depression of any food product can be estimated using the following equation:

$$\ln n_s = \frac{\lambda_f}{R}\left(\frac{1}{T_0} - \frac{1}{T_f}\right)$$

where T_0 = freezing point of pure solvent, K

T_f = freezing point of solution, K

R = gas constant, J/mol K

λ_f = latent heat of fusion, J/mol

n_s = mole fraction of solute

Boiling Point Elevation :

The boiling point elevation can be estimated using the following equation:

$$\ln n_s = \frac{\lambda_v}{R}\left(\frac{1}{T} - \frac{1}{T_o}\right)$$

where T_0 = boiling point of pure solvent, K

T_f = boiling point of solution, K

R = gas constant, J/mol K

λ_f = latent heat of vaporization, J/mol

n_s = mole fraction of solute

Chapter 4

Momentum Transfer

Momentum transfer deals with flow of fluid over surface, in pipes and ducts. This chapter discusses basic of fluid flow, fluid handling equipments, compressible fluid flow, flow measurement and fluid flow in porous media.

Fluid :

A fluid is a substance which deforms continuously or flows when subjected to shearing forces. The force that moves the liquid is known as the shearing force or shear stress and the velocity gradient is known as the *shear rate*. Momentum transfer occurs in fluid flow due to velocity gradient.

Newton's Law of Viscosity :

Newtonian fluids are those that exhibit a linear relationship between the shear stress and the rate of shear.

Newton's law of viscosity is given by:

$$\tau = \mu \frac{dv}{dy}$$

where μ is viscosity of fluid and may be written as:

$$\mu = \frac{\text{Shearing stress}}{\text{Rate of shearing strain}} = \frac{\tau}{\frac{dv}{dy}} = \frac{\tau}{\gamma}$$

where γ is shear rate, rate of shearing strain or velocity gradient.

The above equation may be written as:

$$\tau = \mu\gamma$$

The shear stress (τ) is shearing force per unit area and is given by:

$$\tau = \frac{F}{A}$$

where F = shearing force and A = area

Gases, water, milk and dilute solutions of low molecular weight solutes are practically Newtonian fluids.

Viscosity :

Viscosity is defined as the resistance of a fluid to shearing action. Viscosity is the ratio of the shearing stress (F/A) to the velocity gradient in a fluid. It is also called *dynamic viscosity*, *absolute viscosity*, or *simple viscosity*.

Momentum Diffusivity or Kinematic Viscosity :

Kinematic viscosity is a measure of the resistive flow of a fluid under the influence of gravity. It conveys information about the rate at which momentum may diffuse through the fluid because of molecular motion. The kinematic viscosity (ν) is the ratio of the viscosity to the density (ρ) and is given by:

$$\nu = \frac{\mu}{\rho}$$

Effect of Temperature on Viscosity :

The viscosity of liquids is strongly temperature-dependent and almost pressure independent. Viscosity of liquids in general, decreases with increasing temperature. The most frequently used empirical equation used to relate changes in viscosity with changes in temperature is:

$$\ln \mu = A + \frac{B}{T}$$

where μ is viscosity, T is absolute temperature and A and B are constants. The constants B and A are slope and intercept respectively of the plot of ln (μ) against $1/T$.

The viscosity of a gas increases with increase in temperature approximately in accordance with an equation given below :

$$\mu = \mu_0 \left(\frac{T}{273}\right)^n$$

where μ is viscosity at absolute temperature T, μ_0 is the viscosity at an absolute reference temperature 0 °C (273 K) and n is an empirical exponent that best fits the experimental data. For gases, the kinematic viscosity increases more rapidly with temperature than does the absolute viscosity.

The temperature effect on viscosity can be described by an Arhenius type relationship:

$$\mu = A \exp\left(\frac{E_a}{RT}\right).$$

where E_a = activation energy (J/kg mol),

R = gas constant (8314.34 J/kg mol K)

T = absolute temperature (K)

A = constant (Pa · s)

The equation may also be expressed in terms of a reference viscosity (μ_r) given at a reference temperature (T_r):

$$\ln\left(\frac{\mu}{\mu_r}\right) = \frac{E_a}{R}\left(\frac{1}{T} - \frac{1}{T_r}\right)$$

Types of Fluid Flow and Reynolds Number :

The types of fluid flow depends on the mass flow rate, the density, viscosity of the fluid and the geometry of the flow channel. These variables are combined in a dimensionless group known as the Reynolds number (Re). The Reynolds number is a dimensionless quantity that can be used as an index of laminar or turbulent flow. Reynolds number is a product of a characteristic length, a characteristic velocity and a density of fluid divided by its viscosity which is given by:

$$Re = \frac{\rho \overline{v} D}{\mu} = \frac{\overline{v} D}{\nu} = \frac{GD}{\mu} = \frac{\rho Q D}{A\mu}$$

where G = Mass velocity or mass flux (kg/m^{2}s)

D = pipe diameter in case of flow in a circular pipe, m

$\overline{v}$ = average velocity of the fluid, m/s

ρ = density of the fluid, kg/m^3

μ = viscosity of the fluid, Pa . s.

ν = kinematic viscosity, m^2/s

A = cross sectional area of flow, m^2

For a straight circular pipe, following types of flow occurs based on Reynolds number:

Laminar flow	:	$Re < 2000$
Transitional flow	:	$2000 < Re < 4000$
Turbulent flow	:	$Re > 4000$

A laminar regime is common in food processes where the velocities are relatively low and the viscosities relatively high.

The mass flow rate for a fluid flowing in a pipe may be related as:

$$\dot{m} = \rho \overline{v} A$$

Volumetric flow rate for a fluid flowing in a pipe is:

$$Q = A\overline{v}$$

Hence,

$$\dot{m} = Q\rho$$

The mass flow rate may also be expressed as:

$$\text{mass flow rate} = \dot{m} = \frac{\text{mass of fluid collected in a container}}{\text{time taken to collect the fluid}}$$

The average (mean) velocity is often referred to as superficial velocity which is expressed in term of mass flow rate as given below:

$$\overline{v} = \frac{\dot{m}}{\rho A} = \frac{4\dot{m}}{\pi D^2 \rho}$$

A = cross sectional area of flow

$$A = \frac{\pi}{4}D^2$$

where $\bar{v}$ = average velocity

ρ = density of fluid

D = diameter of tube

The average velocity may be calculated by dividing the volumetric flow rate by the cross-sectional area of the tube by using following equation:

$$\text{average velocity} = \bar{v} = \frac{\text{volumetric flow rate}}{\text{cross sectional area of flow}} = \frac{Q}{A}$$

For a pipe or tube of circular cross section and diameter d, the average velocity is given as:

$$\frac{Q}{A} = \frac{Q}{\frac{\pi}{4}D^2} = \frac{4Q}{\pi D^2}$$

Mass velocity is calculated by dividing mass flow rate by cross sectional area of channel and is given by:

$$G = \frac{\dot{m}}{A} = \rho v$$

Reynolds number in term of mass flow rate may be expressed as :

$$Re = \frac{4\dot{m}}{\pi D\mu}$$

where refers to mass flow rate (kg/s).

Reynolds number in term of volumetric flow rate may be expressed as:

$$Re = \frac{4Q\rho}{\pi D\mu}$$

Important Dimensionless Numbers Involved in Fluid Flow:

$$\text{Euler number} = Eu = \frac{\text{Pressure Force}}{\text{Inertial Force}} = \frac{\Delta p}{\rho v^2}$$

$$\text{Froude number} = Fr = \frac{\text{Inertial Force}}{\text{Gravity Force}} = \frac{v}{\sqrt{gD}}$$

$$\text{Mach number} = Ma = \frac{\text{Local Velocity}}{\text{Sonic Velocity}} = \frac{v}{c}$$

$$\text{Weber number} = We = \frac{\text{Inertial Force}}{\text{Surface Tension Force}} = \frac{\rho v^2 L}{\sigma}$$

where Δp = pressure difference across the pipe
L = length of the pipe
v = velocity of flowing fluid
ρ = density of the fluid
μ = fluid viscosity
c = speed of sound in the fluid
o = surface tension of the fluid
D = diameter of pipe
g = acceleration due to gravity

Equivalent Diameter :

When fluid flow occurs through a duct with a non-circular cross-section, or a partially filled duct, diameter (D) is replaced by the hydraulic mean diameter or equivalent diameter defined by:

Hydraulic mean diameter

$$D_H = \frac{4 \times \text{cross sectional area}}{\text{wetted perimeter}} = \frac{4A}{P_w} = 4 \times R_H$$

where R_H is hydraulic radius.

For a circular pipe or tube of diameter D, hydraulic mean diameter is given by:

$$D_H = \frac{4 \times \frac{\pi D^2}{4}}{\pi D} = D$$

For a duct of rectangular cross sectional area 'a' by 'b', hydraulic mean diameter is given by:

$$D_H = \frac{4ab}{2(a+b)} = \frac{2ab}{(a+b)}$$

when $a = b$ (square duct), then

$$D_H = \frac{2a^2}{2a} = a$$

For an open rectangular channel with depth of liquid h and width w, hydraulic mean diameter is given by:

$$D_H = \frac{4wh}{w+2h}$$

For flow through a narrow gap or slit (Fig. 4.1) as in plate heat exchanger hydraulic mean diameter is given by:

$$D_H = \frac{4 \times w \times b}{2(w+b)} = \frac{4bw}{2w} \approx 2b \qquad \text{(as } w >> b \text{ so } b \text{ can be neglected)}$$

where w = breadth of passage
b = distance between plates (width of passage)

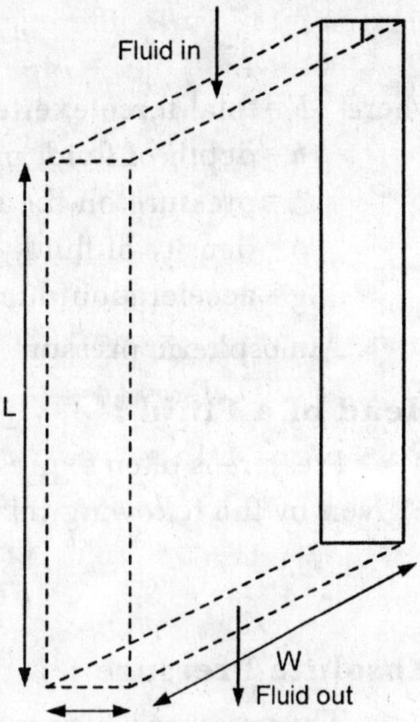

FIG. 4.1. Fluid flow in plane narrow slit

For fluid flowing through annular space with outside diameter D_0 and inside diameter D_i,

$$D_H = 4 \times \frac{\frac{\pi}{4}\left(D_0^2 - D_i^2\right)}{\pi\,(D_0 + D_i)} = D_0 - D_i$$

The equivalent diameter of annulus is simply the difference between outer and inner diameters.

The Reynolds number in term of equivalent diameter may be expressed as:

$$Re = \frac{\rho v D_H}{\mu} = \frac{4 R_H v \rho}{\mu}$$

Continuity Equation :

The principle of conservation of mass in fluid dynamics is referred to as the continuity principle.

The continuity relation for one dimensional flow in a tube is given as:

$$\dot{m} = \rho \bar{v} A$$

where $\dot{m}$ refers to mass flow rate, v is mean velocity and A is cross sectional area.

For fluid having constant density we may write:

$$A_1 v_1 = A_2 v_2 = Q$$

where Q is volumetric flow rate (m^3/s).

This equation is frequently used in solving flow problems.

Volumetric Flow Rate :

The volume flow rate (Q) is the volume of fluid flowing per unit time. Mathematically:

$$\text{volumetric flow rate} = Q = \frac{\text{volume of fluid}}{\text{time}} = \frac{\text{mass of fluid}}{\text{density} \times \text{time}} = \frac{\text{mass flow rate}}{\text{density}}$$

So, the volumetric flow rate (m^3/s) may be obtained by dividing mass flow rate by the density:

$$Q = \frac{\dot{m}}{\rho}$$

The volumetric flow rate can also be calculated from the equation:

$$Q = A\bar{v} = \frac{\pi}{4} D^2 \bar{v}$$

Pressure in a Fluid :

The static pressure at the base of the fluid column (P) is expressed as follows (Fig. 4.2):

$$P = \frac{F}{A} = P_0 + \rho g h$$

where F = total force exerted on the area A

h = depth of fluid, m

P_o = pressure on the surface of liquid

ρ = density of fluid

g = acceleration due to gravity

Atmospheric pressure at sea level is 101.325 kPa.

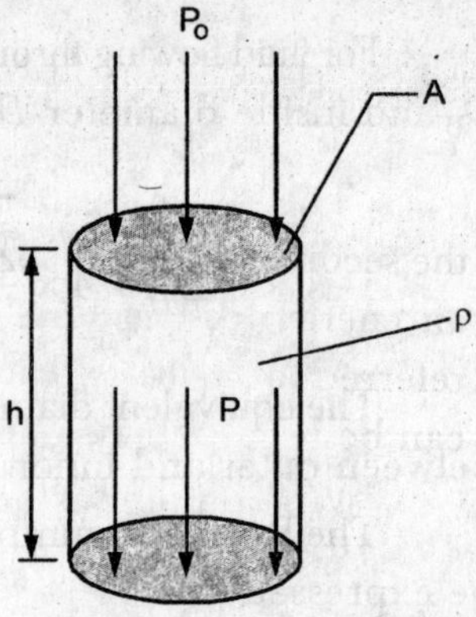

FIG. 4.2. Pressure at a vertical column of fluid

Head of a Fluid :

Pressure is often expressed as fluid head (h) and pressure is given by the following relation:

$$h = \frac{P}{\rho g}$$

Absolute Pressure :

The pressure which is measured from the datum of a perfect vacuum is called *absolute pressure.*

Absolute pressure = Gauge pressure + Atmospheric pressure

Gauge Pressure :

The pressure which is measured from the datum of the atmospheric pressure is called *gauge pressure.*

Aauge pressure = Absolute pressure – Atmospheric pressure

Pressures above atmospheric always yield a positive gauge pressure and a vacuum or negative pressure is the pressure below that of the atmosphere.

The relationship among absolute, gauge, and vacuum pressure is shown in Fig. 4.3.

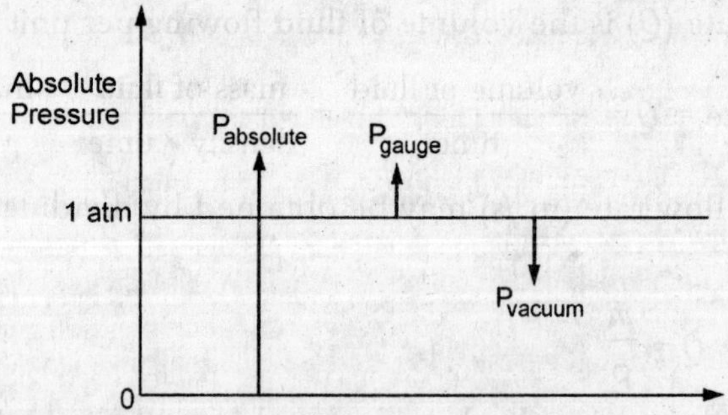

FIG. 4.3. Relationship among absolute, gauge, and vacuum pressure

Bernoulli's Equation :

Bernoulli's equation is one of the most important equations in fluid transport. The conservation of energy relationship for a flowing fluid is known as Bernoulli's equation which is given as:

$$\frac{v_2^2}{2g} + z_2 + \frac{p_2}{\rho_2 g}$$

The subscript 1 indicates the first position in the pipework and the subscript 2 indicates the second position in the pipework. Each term of this equation has unit of meter and represents an energy loss in term of a head of the fluid. The term on each side of the equation are referred to as the velocity head, potential head and pressure head respectively. The equation can be used between any two positions in a flow system.

When a pipe is horizontal, then $z_1 = z_2$, then the above equation becomes:

$$\frac{v_1^2}{2g} + z_1 + \frac{p_1}{\rho_1 g} = \frac{v_2^2}{2g} + z_2 + \frac{p_2}{\rho_2 g}$$

Including friction loss in pipe, the equation becomes:

$$\frac{v_1^2}{2g} + z_1 + \frac{p_1}{\rho_1 g} = \frac{v_2^2}{2g} + z_2 + \frac{p_2}{\rho_2 g} + \Delta H_f$$

where z_1, z_2 = elevation at inlet and outlet, m

v_1, v_2 = velocity at inlet and outlet, m/s

g = gravitational acceleration, 9.8 m/s^2

p_1, p_2 = pressure at inlet and outlet, N/m^2

ΔH_f = pressure drop due to friction, divided by ρg = friction head

This equation is widely used for the calculation of the pump work necessary to transport a fluid from one point of the process to another.

Total head of a liquid (H) is given by:

$$H = \text{potential head} + \text{pressure head} + \text{velocity head} = z + \frac{P}{\rho g} + \frac{v^2}{2g}$$

Total head of a liquid (H_1) at inlet is given by:

$$H_1 = z_1 + \frac{P_1}{\rho g} + \frac{v_1^2}{2g}$$

Total head of a liquid (H_2) at exit is given by:

$$H_2 = z_2 + \frac{P_2}{\rho g} + \frac{v_2^2}{2g}$$

Power Requirements for Pumping :

The pump power requirements for a liquid flow system may be determined by using the energy conservation equation. The power supplied to the pump drive from an external source is denoted by P_B is:

$$P_B = \dot{m}W_p = \dot{m}\frac{\Delta H}{\eta} \quad \text{J/s or W}$$

where W_p = pump work, J/kg

$\Delta H = H_b - H_a$

H_b = total discharge head, m

H_a = total suction head, m

The power delivered to the fluid is calculated from the mass flow rate and head developed by pump. It is denoted by P_f and defined by:

$$P_f = \dot{m}\Delta H$$

$$\therefore \quad P_B = \frac{P_f}{\eta}$$

where, η = overall mechanical efficiency of pump

The energy supplied by a pump is given by:

$$E_p = \Delta PE + \Delta KE + \frac{\Delta p}{\rho} + E_f$$

where ΔPE = change in potential energy, J/kg

ΔKE = change in kinetic energy, J/kg

E_f = total loss in energy due to friction, J/kg

Power rating of pump is determined by:

$$\text{Power} = mE_p$$

where $\dot{m}$ = mass flow rate, kg/s

E_p = energy supplied by pump, J/kg

Reciprocating (Piston) Pump :

It consists of a stationary cylindrical chamber containing a reciprocating piston or plunger. For an incompressible fluid, the volumetric capacity is given by:

$$Q = \frac{\pi}{4}D^2 \cdot L \cdot N \cdot \eta_v$$

where Q = volumetric flow rate, m^3/s

N = pump speed, strokes per second, s^{-1}

D = diameter of the cylinder (bore), m

L = length of the piston movement (stroke), m

η_v = volumetric efficiency

Pump Affinity Laws :

The performance of a centrifugal pump is affected by a change in speed or impeller diameter. For a given pump, the flow rate (Q), the discharge head (H) and the power requirement

(*P*) all increase with increasing speed of revolution (*N*). An approximate rule-of-thumb, known as the *rule of one-two-three states* that (impeller diameter (*D*) held constant):

$$Q \propto N$$
$$H \propto N^2$$
$$P \propto N^3 \qquad \text{(as power is product of discharge and head)}$$

For geometrically similar pumps with speed constant and varying diameter, following relation holds:

$$Q \propto D^3$$
$$H \propto D^2$$
$$P \propto D^5 \qquad \text{(as power is product of discharge and head)}$$

Combining pump laws we may write:

$$Q \propto ND^3$$
$$H \propto N^2 D^2$$
$$P \propto N^3 D^5$$

These relations may be expressed as:

$$\frac{Q_1}{Q_2} = \frac{N_1 D_1^3}{N_2 D_2^3}$$

$$\frac{H_1}{H_2} = \frac{N_1^2 D_1^2}{N_2^2 D_2^2}$$

$$\frac{P_1}{P_2} = \frac{N_1^3 D_1^5}{N_2^3 D_2^5}$$

Laminar Flow in a Cylindrical Pipe or Tube:

The velocity distribution of a Newtonian fluid for laminar flow in a pipe is represented by the following equation:

$$v = v_{max}\left[1 - \left(\frac{r}{R}\right)^2\right]$$

where R = radius of pipe or tube

r = radial distance from centre line of pipe

v_{max} = maximum velocity at the centre where $r = 0$

v = velocity at radial distance 'r' from the centre of pipe

The maximum velocity occurs at $r = 0$ and is given by:

$$v_{max} = \frac{\Delta p R^2}{4\mu L}$$

where R is radius of pipe, Δp is pressure drop, μ is viscosity of fluid and L is length of pipe.

The average velocity of a fluid is flowing in laminar flow in a pipe of radius R and length L under the influence of a pressure drop across the pipe is:

$$\bar{v} = \frac{\Delta p R^2}{8\mu L} = \frac{\Delta p D^2}{32\mu L} = \frac{v_{max}}{2}$$

Hence, the ratio of the average velocity to the maximum velocity for Newtonian fluid flow in a circular tube is 1/2.

The volumetric flow rate Q (volume per unit time) is the cross sectional area of tube multiplied by average velocity is:

$$Q = A\bar{v} = \pi R^2 \bar{v} = \frac{\pi \Delta p R^4}{8\mu L} = \frac{\pi \Delta p D^4}{128\mu L}$$

This equation is called the Hagen-Poiseuille equation for laminar flow in a tub/pipe. From this expression, it is clear that the pressure drop is directly proportional to the volumetric flow rate of fluid. This equation can be used to determine the viscosity of a Newtonian fluid from pressure drop data when the fluid is allowed to flow through a tube or a capillary.

For same flow rate, we may write:

$$\Delta p \propto \frac{L}{R^4}$$

$$\Rightarrow \quad \frac{\Delta p_1}{\Delta p_2} = \frac{L_1 R_2^{\,4}}{L_2 R_2^{\,4}}$$

For piston flow in a pipe, $\bar{v} = v_{max}$

For turbulent flow in a pipe, $v_{max} = 1.18\bar{v}$

Maximum velocity for parallel planes in laminar flow, $v_{max} = 1.5\bar{v}$

Where $\bar{v}$ is average velocity.

Pressure Drop and Friction Loss in Laminar Flow :

Flow through a tubular conduit is accompanied by a drop in pressure. The drop in pressure is equivalent to the stress that must be applied on the fluid to induce flow.

The equation for pressure drop due to friction in a pipe under laminar flow is given by:

$$\Delta p_f = P_1 - P_2 = \frac{4fL\rho\bar{v}^2}{2D}$$

where Δp_f = pressure drop

P_1, P_2 = pressure at point 1 and 2 respectively

$\bar{v}$ = average velocity

L = length of pipe

D = inside diameter of pipe

L = length of a pipe

The pressure drop equation may be expressed as:

$$\Delta p = \rho g h$$

This equation is used to calculate the pressure drop that occurs when liquids flow in pipes.

The friction energy loss (F_f) and pressure drop in a pipe are related as:

$$F_f = \frac{\text{pressure drop}}{\text{density of fluid}} = \frac{\Delta p}{\rho} = \frac{4flv^2}{2D}, \quad \text{J/kg (N.m/kg)}$$

where, f = Fanning friction factor

Friction Factors :

Friction factors are dimensionless numbers needed to determine energy losses in pipeline. Two friction factors are the Fanning friction factor and the Darcy friction factor.

Fanning friction factor (f) is defined as drag force per unit wetted surface area (shear stress, τ_w) divided by the kinetic energy (product of density times velocity head) and is given by:

$$\text{friction factor} = \frac{\text{shear stress}}{\text{velocity head} \times \text{density}}$$

$$f = \frac{\tau_w}{\frac{1}{2}\rho\bar{v}^2} = \frac{\frac{\pi R^2 \times \Delta p}{2\pi RL}}{\frac{1}{2}\rho\bar{v}^2} = \frac{\Delta pR}{\rho L\bar{v}^2} = \frac{\Delta pD}{2\rho L\bar{v}^2}$$

$$\Delta p = \frac{\rho f L\bar{v}^2}{R} = \frac{4\rho f L\bar{v}^2}{2D}$$

The characteristic area used for fluid flowing through a pipe is the wetted area which is equal to $2\pi RL$ where R is the pipe radius and L is the pipe length.

Fanning's friction factor is also called Skin friction coefficient.

Fanning friction factor (f) for laminar flow in a pipe is calculated as:

$$f = \frac{16}{\text{Re}} = \frac{16}{\rho vD/\mu}$$

The Darcy friction factor (f') is defined as:

$$f' = 2\frac{\Delta pD}{\rho L\bar{v}^2} = 2 \times 2\left(\frac{\Delta pD}{2\rho L\bar{v}^2}\right) = 4 \times f \qquad \left(\text{as } f = \frac{\Delta pD}{2\rho L\bar{v}^2}\right)$$

Hence, Darcy friction factor (f') = 4 × Fanning friction factor (f)

The Darcy friction factor is also known as Blasius friction factor or (Moody) friction factor.

Darcy friction factor for a fully developed laminar flow is:

$$f' = \frac{64}{Re}$$

Entry Length :

The entry length of a tube is an example of the buildup of a boundary layer. The length of tube/pipe which is required for velocity profile to be fully developed is called *entry length* (transition length). The approximate entry length Le (m) of a pipe having a diameter D (m) for a fully developed velocity profile to be formed in laminar flow is:

$$Le = 0.0575 D \, Re$$

where Re is Reynolds number.

The entry length for a turbulently flowing fluid can be predicted from the equation:

$$Le = 4.4 D \, (Re)^{1/6}$$

Shear Stress :

The shear stress profile for laminar flow in a tube is linear (Fig. 4.4), varying from 0 at center ($r = 0$) of the tube to a maximum at the wall ($r = R$). The maximum shear stress is given by:

$$\tau_w = \frac{\Delta p D}{4L} = \frac{\Delta p R}{2L} = \frac{4\mu}{R}\frac{\Delta p R^2}{8\mu L} = \frac{4\mu\bar{v}}{R} = \frac{8\mu\bar{v}}{D} = \mu\left(\frac{8\bar{v}}{D}\right)$$

where D = diameter of pipe and = shear stress at the wall

Hence, shear rate at the wall of pipe for laminar flow is.

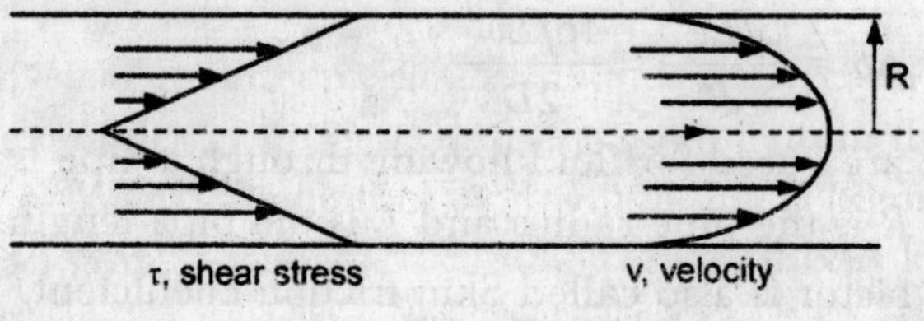

FIG. 4.4 Shear stress and velocity profile in laminar flow in a tube

Pressure loss in a pipe in terms of the pipe diameter and the shear stress at the wall on the pipe is:

$$\Delta P = \frac{4\tau_w L}{D}$$

where ΔP is the pressure drop causing flow, L is length of cylindrical tube and D is diameter of tube.

Drag Force :

The total drag force (retarding force) on the fluid resulting from the shear force transmitted from fluid to the tube wall is the product of wetted area of the wall and shear stress at the wall

The drag force due to shear stress by the wall in a pipe is given as:

$$\text{drag force} = \text{shear stress} \times \text{area over which it acts}$$
$$= \tau_w \times \text{area of pipe wall} = \tau_w \pi DL = 2\pi RL\tau_w$$

Or,
$$F_d = 2\pi RL \times \tau_w = 2\pi RL \times \frac{\Delta p R}{2L} = \Delta p \pi R^2$$

$\because$
$$\bar{v} = \frac{\Delta p R^2}{8\mu L}$$

$\therefore$
$$F_d = 8\pi\mu L\bar{v}$$

where F_d = drag force and Δp = pressure drop

Hence, the drag force is directly proportional to the average velocity for laminar flow in a pipe.

Drag Coefficient :

The drag coefficient C_D is defined as the ratio of total drag force per unit area to kinetic energy per unit volume. Mathematically,

$$C_D = \frac{F_D / A_p}{\frac{1}{2}\rho v^2}$$

where F_D is the total drag force on a totally immersed body, A_p is an area, v is free stream velocity and ρ is density of fluid.

The projected area is the area obtained by projecting the body on a plane perpendicular to direction of flow.

For spherical object of radius 'r' and diameter d_p, the projected area is:

$$A_p = \pi r^2 = \frac{\pi}{4} d_p^2$$

For a cylindrical object of height 'h' and diameter 'd_p' whose axis is perpendicular to flow, the projected area is:

$$A_p = hd_p$$

For a cylinder of height 'h' and diameter d_p whose axis is parallel to direction of flow, the projected area is:

$$A_p = \frac{\pi}{4} d_p^2$$

Drag force acting on a sphere as a function of fluid viscosity, velocity and particle size is (Stoke's equation):

$$F_D = 3\pi\mu d p_v$$

Since, also we have:

$$F_D = \frac{1}{2} C_D \rho v^2 A_p = \frac{1}{2} C_D \rho v^2 \frac{\pi d_p^2}{4} = \frac{1}{8}\pi C_D \rho v^2 d_p^2$$

Solving these two equations, we may write:

$$C_D = \frac{24\mu}{\rho v d_p} = \frac{24}{\frac{\rho v d_p}{\mu}}$$

The Reynolds number for a given solid immersed in a flowing fluid is given by:

$$\text{Re} = \frac{\rho v d_p}{\mu}$$

Hence,
$$C_D = \frac{24}{\text{Re}}$$

The magnitude of the drag acting on a sphere, as a function of fluid viscosity, velocity and particle size can be derives as:

$$F_D = \frac{C_d \rho v^2 A_p}{2} = \frac{24}{\text{Re}} \times \frac{\rho v^2}{2} \times \frac{\pi d_p{}^2}{4} = \frac{24}{\frac{\rho v d_p}{\mu}} \times \frac{\rho v^2}{2} \times \frac{\pi d_p{}^2}{4} = 3\pi\mu v d_p$$

Turbulent Flow in a Cylindrical Pipe or Tube:

The velocity distribution for turbulent flow in a pipe is represented by the following equation:

$$v = v_{\max}\left(1 - \frac{r}{R}\right)^{\frac{1}{7}}$$

where r is the radial distance from the centre and R is radius of pipe and $v_{\max}$ is the maximum velocity at the centre where $r = 0$.

Relationship between average velocity and maximum velocity under turbulent flow is given by:

$$\bar{v} = \frac{49}{60} v_{\max} = \frac{4}{5} v_{\max} = 0.817 v_{\max} \text{ and } v_{\max} = 1.25\bar{v}$$

For Newtonian fluid in turbulent flow, maximum velocity is given by:

$$v_{\max} = \frac{\bar{v}}{0.0336 \log(\text{Re}) + 0.662}$$

Pressure Drop and Friction Factor in Turbulent Flow:

For turbulent flow, pressure drop in pipe flow is given by:

$$\Delta p = \frac{4 f L \rho \bar{v}^2}{2D}$$

The friction energy loss and pressure drop in turbulent flow in a pipe is given by:

$$F_f = \frac{\Delta p}{\rho} = \frac{4 f l \bar{v}^2}{2D}, \text{ J/kg}$$

Degree of surface roughness or relative roughness of a pipe

$$= \frac{\text{roughness}}{\text{hydraulic mean diameter of pipe}} = \frac{\varepsilon}{D_H}$$

where ε = height of effective roughness, m

D_H = hydraulic diameter of pipe, m

The surface roughness (ε) characterizes the surface condition of a pipe.

Blasius equation can be used for calculating friction factor in turbulent flow in smooth pipes for Reynolds numbers 4000 < Re < 100000:

$$f = \frac{0.079}{\text{Re}^{0.25}} = 0.079\,\text{Re}^{-0.25}$$

The Moody chart presents the friction factor as function of Reynolds number for various magnitudes of relative roughness of the pipes.

For laminar flow, f is not a function of pipe roughness.

Laminar Fluid Flow Between Parallel Plates:

The liquid flow on flat surfaces as a thin film is of interest in many practical situations such as in film evaporators and plate heat exchangers.

The velocity profile for fluid moving down a vertical plate in laminar flow at steady state is:

$$v = \frac{\rho g \delta^2}{2\mu}\left[1 - \left(\frac{x}{\delta}\right)^2\right]$$

where δ is the thickness of the layer, x is the distance from the free surface of the liquid toward the plate and v is the velocity at a distance x from the free surface.

The velocity profile for fluid moving along an inclined flat surface in laminar flow at steady state is:

$$v = \frac{\rho g \delta^2}{2\mu}\cos\alpha\left[1 - \left(\frac{x}{\delta}\right)^2\right]$$

where x = distance taken from the free surface of the liquid

g = gravitational acceleration

δ = thickness of a falling film

α = angle of inclination with vertical

Maximum velocity of falling film along an inclined flat surface is:

$$v_{max} = \frac{\rho g \delta^2}{2\mu}\cos\alpha$$

Average velocity for falling film along an inclined flat surface is:

$$\bar{v} = \frac{\rho g \delta^2}{3\mu} \cos\alpha$$

For the shear stress profile:

$$\tau = \rho g \delta \cos\alpha$$

The volumetric flow rate Q, in a channel of width w is:

$$Q = A\bar{v} = (\delta \times w) \times \frac{\rho g \delta^2 \cos\alpha}{3\mu} = \frac{\delta^3 w \rho g \cos\alpha}{3\mu}$$

where A = cross sectional area.

For vertical wall, $\cos\alpha = 1$

So, $$\delta^3 = \frac{3Q\mu}{\rho g w}$$

This equation can be used for the calculation of the thickness (δ) of a falling film, corresponding to a given flow rate Q.

Maximum velocity of falling film along vertical surface is:

$$v_{max} = \frac{\rho g \delta^2}{2\mu}$$

Average velocity for falling film along vertical surface is:

$$\bar{v} = \frac{\rho g \delta^2}{3\mu}$$

Relationship between average velocity (bulk velocity) and maximum velocity of liquid film flowing under laminar flow is given by:

$$\bar{v} = \frac{2}{3} v_{max}$$

Thus, the ratio of the average velocity to the maximum velocity for Newtonian fluid flow in a narrow slit is 2/3.

Shear stress at the wall for a falling film in term of average velocity is:

$$\tau_w = \rho g \delta = \frac{\rho g \delta^2}{3\mu} \times \frac{3\mu}{\delta} = \mu\left(\frac{3\bar{v}}{\delta}\right)$$

So, shear stress at the wall for a falling film is $\left(\frac{3\bar{v}}{\delta}\right)$.

For slit flow, pressure drop may be predicted by the equation:

$$\Delta p = \frac{3\mu L \bar{v}}{\delta^2}$$

where 2δ = gap between plates

Another equation which can be used to predict the pressure drop in slit flow is:

$$\Delta p = 2f\rho\frac{L}{2\delta}\frac{\bar{v}^2}{2}$$

where 2δ =gap between plates

For slit flow in laminar range, friction factor is given by:

$$f_s = \frac{24}{\text{Re}}$$

Since for pipe flow, friction factor is given by:

$$f_p = \frac{16}{\text{Re}}$$

Solving these equations, we may write:

$$f_s = \frac{3}{2} \times f_p = 1.5 \times f_p$$

Thus, friction factor for slit flow is 50% higher than that for pipe flow.

Mass flow rate per unit width of wall is given by:

$$\Gamma = \frac{\dot{m}}{w} = \rho\bar{v}\delta \text{ kg/s.m}$$

where Γ is called liquid loading.

The mass flow rate ($\dot{m}$) is the product of the density ρ, the cross-sectional area (δw) and the average velocity.

Hydraulic diameter of a falling film/slit flow = 4δ

Where 2δ is total thickness of film.

Reynolds number for slit flow is given by:

$$\text{Re} = \frac{\rho\bar{v}(4\delta)}{\mu} = \frac{4\Gamma}{\mu}$$

For falling film, laminar flow occurs for Re < 1200.

Non-Newtonian Liquid Flow:

Fluids which do not obey the Newton's law of viscosity are called as non-Newtonian fluids or power law fluid. Shear thinning or shear thickening fluids obey the power law model (Ostwald-de Waele equation).The shear stress/shear rate relationship for a power law fluid is given by the following equation:

$$\tau = k\left(\frac{dv}{dr}\right)^n = k(\gamma)^n$$

where k = consistency coefficient/index (Pa · s^n or N-s^n/m^2)

n = flow behavior index (dimensionless)

$dv/dr = \gamma$ = shear rate

The Herschel –Bulkley model is the most commonly used model to describe the flow behaviour of most liquid food products and is given by:

$$\tau = t_0 + k\,(g)^n$$

where τ_0 is yield stress.

For a Newtonian fluid, τ_0, $n = 1$

For a Bingham fluid, τ_0, $n = 1$

For a shear thinning fluid, τ_0, $0 < n < 1$

For a shear thickening fluid, τ_0, $n > 1$

For a Herschel-Buckley fluid, τ_0, $n > 0$

The slope of shear stress versus shear rate graph is not constant for non-Newtonian fluids.

Newtonian model can be considered as a special case of this model in which $n = 1$ and $k = \mu$.

For all the types of non-Newtonian fluids, apparent viscosity depends on the shear rate. For shear thinning and shear thickening fluids (so-called *Power law fluids*), the apparent viscosity is given by:

$$\mu_{opp} = k\gamma^{n-1}$$

The apparent viscosity has the same units as viscosity but the value varies with the rate of shear.

Velocity Profile and Shear Rate for a non-Newtonian Fluid

The equations for the velocity distribution for a non-Newtonian fluid in laminar flow in a circular pipe given by:

$$v = \left(\frac{n}{n+1}\right)\left(\frac{\Delta p}{2kL}\right)^{1/n}\left[R^{\frac{n+1}{n}} - r^{\frac{n+1}{n}}\right] = \left(\frac{n}{n+1}\right)\left(\frac{\Delta p}{2kL}\right)^{1/n} R^{\left(\frac{n+1}{n}\right)}\left[1-\left(\frac{r}{R}\right)^{\frac{n+1}{n}}\right]$$

This equation represents the velocity profile of a power law fluid.

The relationship between average velocity and pressure drop ΔP and maximum velocity and pressure drop ΔP in laminar flow for non-Newtonian fluids is given by:

$$\bar{v} = \left(\frac{n}{3n+1}\right)\left(\frac{\Delta p}{2kL}\right)^{1/n} R^{\frac{n+1}{n}}$$

and $$v_{\max} = \left(\frac{n}{n+1}\right)\left(\frac{\Delta p}{2kL}\right)^{1/n} R^{\frac{n+1}{n}}$$

From these two expressions, we may write:

$$v_{\max} = \frac{3n+1}{n+1}\bar{v}$$

where $v_{\max}$ is maximum velocity and $\bar{v}$ is average velocity.

The volumetric flow rate of power law fluid is:

$$Q = \pi\left(\frac{n}{3n+1}\right)\left(\frac{\Delta p}{2kL}\right)^{1/n} R^{\frac{3n+1}{n}}$$

where R is radius of pipe.

The velocity profile in terms of the maximum velocity may be written as:

$$v = v_{\max}\left[1-\left(\frac{r}{R}\right)^{\frac{n+1}{n}}\right] \qquad \text{(as } r = 0 \text{ and } v = v_{\max}\text{)}$$

For $n < 1$, a relatively flat velocity profile is obtained.

$n = 0$, rod like flow is obtained

$n > 1$, much sharper profile is obtained.

The velocity profile in terms of the average velocity is:

$$v = \bar{v}\left(\frac{3n+1}{n+1}\right)\left[1-\left(\frac{r}{R}\right)^{\frac{n+1}{n}}\right]$$

where k is consistency index ($Pa.\ s^n$), n is flow behaviour index, L is pipe length (m), and R is pipe diameter (m).

The relationship between the pressure drop (Δp) and the volumetric flow rate (Q) when a power law fluid moves through a pipeline under laminar flow conditions is :

$$\frac{\Delta pR}{2L} = k\left[\left(\frac{3n+1}{4n}\right)\left(\frac{4Q}{\pi R^3}\right)\right]^n$$

Or,

$$\frac{\Delta pd}{4L} = k\left[\left(\frac{3n+1}{4n}\right)\left(\frac{32Q}{\pi d^3}\right)\right]^n$$

where L is length and d is diameter of pipe.

This equation can be used to predict pressure drop for power law fluid under laminar flow for a given condition.

The maximum shear rate found in a pipe is:

$$\gamma_{\max} = \left(\frac{3n+1}{4n}\right)\left(\frac{4Q}{\pi R^3}\right)$$

where shear rate correction factor $= \left(\frac{3n+1}{4n}\right)$.

The minimum value of shear rate in a pipe is zero and it occurs at the centre of pipe ($r = 0$) but varies non-linearly with radius as:

$$\gamma = \left[\left(\frac{3n+1}{4n}\right)\left(\frac{4Q}{\pi R^3}\right)\right]\left(\frac{r}{R}\right)^{1/n}$$

This equation is valid for laminar flow.

The generalized coefficient of viscosity is given by:

$$\gamma = k\left(\frac{3n+1}{4n}\right)^n 8^{n-1}$$

or, $\gamma = K'\, 8^{n-1}$

where, $K' = k\left(\frac{3n+1}{4n}\right)^n$

Generalized Reynolds number for non-Newtonian fluid is given by:

$$Re_{\text{gen}} = \frac{D^n \bar{v}^{(2-n)} \rho}{k\left(\frac{3n+1}{4n}\right)^n 8^{(n-1)}} = \frac{8(\bar{v})^{2-n} R^n \rho}{k\left(\frac{3n+1}{n}\right)^n} = \frac{D^n \bar{v}^{(2-n)} \rho}{\gamma}$$

Generalized Reynolds number (Re_{gen}) and friction factor (f) for laminar flow for a power law fluid are related as:

$$f = \frac{16}{Re_{gen}}$$

Frictional Pressure Drop to Flow of Non-Newtonian Fluids

The frictional pressure drop in pipe for power law fluid in laminar flow is given by:

$$\Delta p = \frac{4K'L}{D}\left(\frac{8\bar{v}}{D}\right)^{n'} = 32\gamma\frac{L}{D}\left(\frac{\bar{v}}{D}\right)^n \qquad (\text{as } \gamma = K'\, 8^{n-1})$$

Or,

$$\bar{v} = \frac{D}{8}\left(\frac{\Delta p D}{4K'L}\right)^{1/n}$$

Pressure drop of power law fluid in laminar flow can also be computed by friction factor method. The formula is:

$$\Delta p = \frac{4fL\rho\bar{v}^2}{2D} \qquad \text{where } f = \frac{16}{Re_{gen}}$$

This equation may be written in terms of the radius of the tube and the Reynolds number as follows:

$$\Delta p = \frac{2\left(\frac{16}{Re_{gen}}\right)(\bar{v})^2 \rho L}{D}$$

Frictional loss can be evaluated by:

$$F_f = \frac{\Delta p}{\rho}, \text{J/kg}$$

Similarly pressure drop in turbulent can also be computed based on generalized Reynolds number.

Non-Newtonian Liquid Flow in Slit:

The expression of velocity profile for a non-Newtonian fluid film flowing down a plane inclined at an angle with the vertical plane is:

$$v = \left(\frac{n}{n+1}\right)\left(\frac{\rho g\cos\alpha}{k}\right)^{1/n}(\delta)^{\left(\frac{n+1}{n}\right)}\left[1-\left(\frac{x}{\delta}\right)^{\frac{n+1}{n}}\right]$$

where L is length of the film, δ is film thickness and x is distance measured from the film surface.

The thickness of the film δ can be expressed in terms of an average velocity of flow as:

$$\bar{v} = \left(\frac{n}{2n+1}\right)\left(\frac{\rho g\cos\alpha}{k}\right)^{1/n}(\delta)^{\left(\frac{n+1}{n}\right)}$$

The film thickness is:

$$\delta = \left[\frac{\bar{v}(2n+1)k^{1/n}}{n[\rho g\cos\alpha]^{1/n}}\right]^{\frac{n}{n+1}}$$

The average velocity and maximum velocity are related as:

$$\bar{v} = \frac{n+1}{2n+1}v_{max}$$

The average velocity is given as:

$$\bar{v} = \frac{\delta}{3}\left(\frac{\Delta p\delta}{K''L}\right)^{1/n}$$

where 2δ = gap between plates

$$\gamma = k\left(\frac{2n+1}{3n}\right)^n 3^{n-1}$$

The pressure drop is given by:

$$\Delta p = f\rho\frac{L}{\delta}\frac{\bar{v}^2}{2}$$

where L = length and 2δ = gap between plates

Another equation used to calculate pressure drop is given by:

$$\Delta p = 3\gamma\frac{L}{\delta}\left(\frac{\bar{v}}{\delta}\right)^n$$

where L = length and 2δ = gap between plates

The generalized Reynolds number is:

$$Re_{gen} = \frac{4\bar{v}^{(2-n)}\delta^n \rho}{\gamma}$$

where 2δ = gap between plates

Fluid Flow Measurement :

The measurement of flow rate in a liquid transport system is an essential component of the fluid transport operation. There are various types of flow measurement devices that are used for quantification of mass flow rate or velocity. These methods include venture meter, orifice meter, pitot tube, etc.

Venturimeter : The velocity at throat of venturimeter is:

$$v = \frac{Cv}{\sqrt{1-\beta^4}}\sqrt{\frac{2(p_1 - p_2)}{\rho}}$$

$$\beta = \frac{D_2}{D_1}$$

The volumetric flow rate of venturimeter is:

$$Q = \frac{CvA_2}{\sqrt{1-\beta^4}}\sqrt{\frac{2(p_1 - p_2)}{\rho}}$$

$$A^2 = \frac{\pi D_2^{\,2}}{4}$$

where C_v = venturi coefficient
D_2 = diameter of throat
D_1 = diameter of pipe
p_1–p_2 = pressure drop
ρ = density of flowing fluid

The volumetric flow rate of venturimeter can also be expressed as:

$$Q = C_D A_1 \sqrt{\frac{2gh}{\left[\left(\frac{A_1}{A_t}\right)^2 - 1\right]}}$$

where A_t = cross sectional area of throat
A_1 = cross sectional area of pipe

Orifice Meter : An orifice (a hole in a plate) placed normal to flow in a pipeline is a restriction and causes pressure drop.

The mass flow is give by:

$$\dot{m} = C_D A_1 \rho v_1 = C_D A_1 \rho \sqrt{\frac{2(p_1 - p_2)}{\rho\left[\left(\frac{A_1}{A_o}\right)^2 - 1\right]}}$$

If the pressure difference is replaced by the term $\rho g h$, where h is the head loss then the mass flow rate equation becomes:

$$\dot{m} = C_D A_1 \rho \sqrt{\frac{2gh}{\left[\left(\frac{A_1}{A_o}\right)^2 - 1\right]}}$$

where A_1 = cross sectional area of pipe

A_o = cross sectional area of orifice

C_D = Coefficient of discharge

Volumetric flow rate is given by:

Rotameter : Velocity of flow of fluid is given by:

$$v = C_r \sqrt{\frac{2gV_f(\rho_f - \rho)}{A_f \rho}}$$

where C_r = rotameter coefficient

V_f = volume of float

ρ_f = density of float

ρ = density of fluid

A_f = maximum cross sectional area of float

For same rotameter:

$$\frac{v_1}{v_2} = \sqrt{\frac{\frac{(\rho_f - \rho_1)}{\rho_1}}{\frac{(\rho_f - \rho_2)}{\rho_2}}} = \sqrt{\frac{(\rho_f - \rho_1)\rho_2}{(\rho_f - \rho_2)\rho_1}}$$

For a given flow rate, the equilibrium position of the float in a rotameter is established by a balance of three forces: (*i*) weight of float (*ii*) buoyant force of fluid on float and (*iii*) drag force on the float. Force (*i*) acts downward and forces (*ii*) and (*iii*) act upward.

For equilibrium condition,

$$F_D = V_f \rho_f g - V_f \rho g = m_f g\left(1 - \frac{\rho}{\rho_f}\right) \quad \text{(since } m_f = \rho f\, V_f\text{)}$$

where F_D = drag force

g = acceleration due to gravity

V_f = volume of float

ρ_f = desnsity of float

ρ = density of fluid

$$\text{Drag force} = \frac{C_D A_f \rho_f v^2}{2}$$

$$\text{Annular area of flow} = \frac{\pi}{4}\left(D_t^2 - D_f^2\right)$$

where D_f = float diameter

D_t = tube diameter

Pitot Tube :

It is used for the measurement of both static and impact pressure. It measures local velocity by measuring difference between impact and static pressure.

impact pressure = total pressure – static pressure

The equation for velocity is given by:

$$v = C_p\sqrt{\frac{2\Delta p}{\rho}} = C_p\sqrt{2gh}$$

where Δp = pressure drop

Cp = pitot tube coefficient

v = velocity

h = rise of fluid in tube

ρ = density of flowing fluid

Compressible Fluid Flow:

The Reynolds number is given by:

$$Re = \frac{GD}{\mu}$$

$$G = \rho v$$

where D is diameter of pipe, v is velocity, μ is viscosity of fluid and G is mass flow rate per unit area.

The density of air may be computed by:

$$\rho = \frac{PM}{RT}$$

When density of air at one pressure is given, then the density of air at another pressure can be evaluated by the equation:

$$\frac{P_1}{\rho_1} = \frac{P_2}{\rho_2}$$

Pressure Drop and Friction Factor in Flow of Gas :

When pressure drop in a gas pipe line is less than 10%, the following equation can be used to evaluate pressure at inlet or outlet of pipe line:

$$p_1^2 - p_2^2 = \frac{4fLG^2RT}{DM}$$

where D = inside diameter of pipe, m
M = molecular weight of air=28
G = mass flux of gas, kg/s.m^2
f = Fanning friction factor
T = absolute temperature, K
p_1 = pressure at inlet, *Pa*
p_2 = pressure at exit, *Pa*
R = 8314.3 J/kg mol *k*

Isothermal Compressible Flow :

The equation for isothermal compressible flow is given as:

$$p_1^2 - p_2^2 = \frac{4fG^2RT\Delta L}{DM} + \frac{2G^2RT}{M}\ln\frac{p_1}{p_2}$$

where D = diameter of pipe, m
M = molecular weight of gas
f = Fanning friction factor
p_1 = absolute pressure at inlet, Pa
p_2 = absolute pressure at exit, Pa
T = absolute temperature, K
G = mass flux, kg/sm^2

This equation can be used to calculate pressure at inlet or exit in case of compressible flow of a gas in a pipe line.

The equation for maximum velocity for compressible flow of a gas or maximum velocity of sound under isothermal flow is:

$$v_{max} = \sqrt{\frac{RT}{M}}$$

Nozzle Flow :

Nozzle flow occurs in the atomization of liquid food in spray dryer.

The equation for velocity of flow is given as:

$$v_o = \sqrt{\frac{2\gamma p}{(\gamma-1)\rho}\left[1-\left(\frac{p_o}{p}\right)^{\frac{\gamma-1}{\gamma}}\right]}$$

where v_o = velocity

p_0 = downstream pressure

p = upstream pressure

The relationship between upstream pressure and downstream pressure for maximum discharge is:

$$\frac{p_o}{p} = \left(\frac{2}{\gamma+1}\right)^{\frac{\gamma}{\gamma-1}}$$

Taking value of γ as 1.4, we get:

$$\frac{p_o}{p} = 0.528$$

This pressure ratio is known as *critical pressure ratio.*

Mass flow rate is given as:

$$\dot{m} = C_D A_o \sqrt{\frac{2\gamma p\rho}{(\gamma-1)}\left[\left(\frac{p_o}{p}\right)^{\frac{2}{\gamma}} - \left(\frac{p_o}{p}\right)^{\frac{\gamma+1}{\gamma}}\right]}$$

where C_D = discharge coefficient

A_o = area of nozzle tip, m^2.

$$A_0 = \frac{\pi}{4} d_0^2$$

where d_0 is diameter of nozzle.

Sonic Velocity :

Sonic velocity or velocity of sound in air is defined as:

$$v_s = \sqrt{\frac{K}{\rho}} = \sqrt{\frac{\gamma p}{\rho}}$$

where K is the bulk modulus of air, p is pressure and ρ is density.

Mach Number :

Mach number (Ma) is defined as the ratio of speed of fluid in conduit (v) to the speed of sound in the fluid at the actual flow condition (v_{max}).

$$Ma = \frac{v}{v_{max}}$$

where $v_{max} = \sqrt{\frac{\gamma RT}{M}}$ (maximum velocity for adiabatic flow)

where, $\gamma = \frac{C_p}{C_v}$

Cp is specific heat at constant pressure and Cv is specific heat at constant volume.

When $Ma = 1$, the flow is sonic.

When $Ma < 1$, the flow is subsonic.

When $Ma > 1$, the flow is supersonic.

Fans, Blowers and Compressors:

Fan, blower and compressors are used in food processing industry for handling gases. Fans are used flow pressure, blower for intermediate pressure and compressor for high pressure.

Fan Laws:

Fan Laws, also known as affinity laws, govern the performance of geometrically similar centrifugal fans. Relationships commonly identified as "fan laws" can be used to relate flow rate, pressure difference, and power required for geometrically similar fans. These relationships can be used to determine the effect of a change in speed for a given fan or to compare fans of the same design but different sizes. The fan law relationships are:

Case I : For constant size and density

$$Q \propto N$$
$$P \propto N^2$$
$$P_f \propto N^3$$

Case II : For constant speed and density

$$Q \propto d^3$$
$$P \propto d^2$$
$$P_f \propto d^5$$

Case III : For constant speed and size

$$Q \propto Q_1$$
$$P \propto \rho$$
$$P_f \propto \rho$$

where Q = volume of air delivered by a fan

P = pressure developed by a fan

P_f = power absorbed by a fan

d = diameter of impeller

N = impeller rotational speed

ρ = density of the air

Using above relationship we may write:

$$\frac{N_1}{N_2} = \frac{Q_1}{Q_2}$$

and

$$\frac{P_{f1}}{P_{f2}} = \left(\frac{N_1}{N_2}\right)^3$$

The percentage increase in power of a fan/blower by changing speed may be evaluated by:

$$\% \text{ increase in power} = \frac{P_2 - P_1}{P_1} = \frac{P_1\left(\frac{N_2}{N_1}\right)^3 - P_1}{P_1} = \left(\frac{N_2}{N_1}\right)^3 - 1$$

When speed of a fan increases by 100% or doubled, the power requirement may be evaluated as:

$$\frac{P_2}{P_1} = \left(\frac{N_2}{N_1}\right)^3 = \left(\frac{2N_1}{N_1}\right)^3 = 8 \quad \text{(as } N_2 = 2N_1 \text{ from given condition)}$$

Hence, $P_2 = 8 \times P_1$

Fan Power Requirements:

Fan power requirements are a function of the air flow rate, the pressure across the fan, and efficiencies of the system. Two pressure terms are used with fan operation. Static pressure (*Ps*) is simply the measured pressure difference across the fan. Fan total pressure (*Pt*) is the sum of the static pressure and the velocity pressure. The general equation for fan power can be written as:

$$P_f = \frac{Q \cdot P_t}{\eta_f \eta_m}$$

where Q = air flow rate, m^3/s

P_f = fan power input required, W

P_t = fan total pressure, Pa

η_f = fan efficiency, decimal

η_m = fan motor efficiency, decimal

Power of a fan may also be calculated by the equation:

$$P = \frac{Qh}{102}$$

where P = power, kW

Q = air flow rate, kg/s

h = air pressure, m

Efficiency of Fan :

The efficiency of fan may be referred as the ratio of energy output to input. Two commonly used fan efficiencies are fan static efficiency and fan total efficiency.

Fan static efficiency is given by:

$$\text{fan static efficiency, \%} = \frac{\text{air flow rate } (m^3/s) \times \text{fan static presure (mm)}}{\text{power input (kW)} \times 102} \times 100$$

Fan total efficiency is given by:

$$\text{fan total efficiency, \%} = \frac{\text{air flowrate } \left(m^3/s\right) \times \text{total presure (mm)}}{\text{power input (kW)} \times 102} \times 100$$

Power input at fan shaft = power drawn by motor × motor efficiency

Compressor Work Input for Adiabatic Compression:

The equation of work input given to fluid by compressor under adiabatic compression is:

$$W = \frac{\gamma R T_1}{(\gamma - 1)\, M} \left[\left(\frac{P_2}{P_1} \right)^{\frac{\gamma-1}{\gamma}} - 1 \right]$$

The adiabatic temperatures are related as:

$$\frac{T_2}{T_1} = \left(\frac{P_2}{P_1} \right)^{\frac{\gamma-1}{\gamma}}$$

where R = gas constant

M = molecular weight of gas

T_1, T_2 = initial and final absolute temperature, K

P_1 and P_2 = absolute suction pressure and discharge, Pa

Compressor Work Input for Isothermal Compression :

The equation of work input for isothermal compression is:

$$W = \frac{R T_1}{M} \ln \frac{P_2}{P_1}$$

For a given compression ratio, the work in isothermal compression is less than the work for adiabatic compression.

Fluid Flow Through Porous Media:

Many applications in food industry involve fluid flow through porous media.

The void fraction or porosity in a packed bed is defined as:

$$\varepsilon = \frac{\text{volume of voids in bed}}{\text{total volume of bed } (\text{voids + slids})} = \frac{V_v}{V_t} = \frac{V_v}{V_v + V_s}$$

Or,

$$V_v = \frac{V_s \varepsilon}{1 - \varepsilon}$$

where V_v = void volume of bed

V_t = total volume of bed (void+solid)

Vs = volune of solids

The void volume and volume of particle may also be written as:

$$\text{void volume} = \frac{\varepsilon}{1-\varepsilon} \times \text{volume of particles}$$

Interstitial Velocity :

The interstitial velocity (v') is the velocity between particles in a packed bed. The interstitial and superficial velocities (v) based on cross section of empty container are related by the bed voidage:

$$\text{interstitial velocity} = v' = \frac{\text{superficial velocity}}{\text{void fraction}} = \frac{v}{\varepsilon}$$

The velocity of approach is sometimes called the superficial velocity and is obtained by:

$$\text{suerficial velocity in a packed bed} = \frac{\text{volumetric flow rate}}{\text{cross sectional area of empty column}}$$

$$\text{Total volume of solid in a packed bed} = LA\,(1-\varepsilon)$$

where A = cross sectional area of bed

L = bed height

ε = porosity

Many particles in packed bed are often irregular in shape. For non-spherical particles, sphericity is defined as the surface-volume ratio for a sphere of diameter D_p divided by surface-volume ratio for particle whose nominal size is D_p.

Thus, $$\theta_s = \frac{S_s / V_s}{S_p / V_p}$$

where S_s = Surface area of a sphere having diameter D_p

V_s = volume of same sphere, m^3

V_p = volume of particle

S_p = surface area of particle

For a packed bed of particle volume V_p and surface area of particle S_p, the specific surface is defined as:

$$a_v = \frac{S_p}{V_p} = \frac{\pi D_p^2}{\pi D_p^3 / 6} = \frac{6}{D_p}$$

So, $$\phi_s = \frac{6 / D_p}{S_p / V_p} = \frac{6 V_p}{D_p S_p} = \frac{6}{a_v D_p}$$

where a_v = specific surface of particle (per meter)

D_p = sieve analysis diameter or nominal diameter

$$a_v = \frac{6}{\phi_s D_p}$$

So, the specific surface of non-spherical particle is given by:

$$a_v = \frac{6}{\phi_s D_p}$$

For a sphere, $\phi_s = 1$

For a cylinder having diameter equal to length,

$$\phi_s = 0.874$$

For a cube, $\phi_s = 0.806$

The effective diameter for spherical particle is given by:

$$D_p = \frac{6}{a_v} \qquad (\text{as } \phi_s = 1)$$

For flow of fluid through particles, hydraulic radius (R_H) is given by:

$$R_H = \frac{A}{P_w}$$

where A = cross sectional area of flow

P_w = wetted perimeter

It may also be defines as:

$$R_H = \frac{\text{void volume of bed}}{\text{surface area of packing}}$$

Or,

$$R_H = \frac{A \times L}{P \times L} = \frac{V_v}{S_t} = \frac{V_v / V_t}{S_t / V_t}$$

where L = length or height of bed

V_v = void volume in bed

S_t = total surface area of particles

V_t = total volume of bed

If a is total surface area available for flow in the bed (a) per unit total volume of bed (m^{-1}), then

$$a = a_v (1-\varepsilon) = \frac{6}{\phi_s D_p}(1-\varepsilon)$$

So,

$$R_H = \frac{\varepsilon}{\frac{6}{\phi_s D_p}(1-\varepsilon)} = \frac{\varepsilon \phi_s D_p}{6(1-\varepsilon)}$$

Hydraulic mean diameter for non-spherical particle is given by:

$$D_H = 4R_H = \frac{4\varepsilon \phi_s D_p}{6(1-\varepsilon)}$$

Hydraulic mean diameter for spherical particle is given by:

$$D_H = 4R_H = \frac{4\varepsilon D_p}{6\,(1-\varepsilon)}$$

When a fluid flow is taking place through a porous medium, the actual cross section available for flow is much less than empty bed cross section.

If v' is the velocity based on empty cross sectional area 'A' and v is the actual velocity through pore spaces having cross sectional area 'A' then

$$v'A = vA'$$

$$\Rightarrow \quad v' = \frac{A'}{A}v = \frac{A'L}{AL}v = \frac{V_v}{V_t}v = \varepsilon v$$

Reynolds number for the flow can be obtained by:

$$\text{Re} \approx \frac{v\rho D_H}{\mu} = \frac{\left(v'/\varepsilon\right)\rho \times \frac{4}{6} \times \varepsilon\phi_s D_p}{\mu(1-\varepsilon)} = \frac{4 \times \phi_s \times D_p \times v' \times \rho}{6 \times (1-\varepsilon) \times \mu} \approx \frac{\phi_s D_p v' \rho}{(1-\varepsilon)\mu}$$

Since based on experimental observation, it has been found that 4/6 is not necessary in the above expression, hence we may write:

$$\text{Re} \approx \frac{\phi_s D_p v' \rho}{(1-\varepsilon)\,\mu}$$

Ergun defines a Reynolds number for a bed of spherical particles of equal size as follows:

$$\text{Re}_p = \frac{D_p v' \rho}{(1-\varepsilon)\mu}$$

where D_p = particle diameter, m

v' = superficial velocity, m/s

ρ, μ = density and viscosity of the fluid, kg/m^{-3} and Pa.s respectively

ε = porosity (void fraction) of the bed.

Hagen-Poiseuille Equation for Laminar Flow:

The equation for pressure drop for laminar flow in a packed bed in given as:

$$\Delta p = \frac{32\mu L v}{D_H^2} = \frac{32\mu L\,(v'/\varepsilon)}{\left[\dfrac{4\varepsilon\phi_s D_p}{6\mu(1-\varepsilon)}\right]^2} = \frac{72\mu v' L(1-\varepsilon)^2}{\varepsilon^3 \phi_s^2 D_p^2} \approx \frac{150\mu v' L(1-\varepsilon)^2}{\varepsilon^3 \phi_s^2 D_p^2}$$

In this expression, 150 has been used instead of 72 because actual length of flow is approximately double of length of bed (2L).

This equation is called *Blake-Kozeny equation* and applicable to laminar flow where Re < 10.

Pressure Drop for Turbulent Flow in Packed Bed:

$$\Delta p = \frac{4fL\rho v^2}{2D_H} = \frac{4fL\rho\left(v'/\varepsilon\right)^2}{2\left[\frac{4\varepsilon\phi_s D_p}{6\mu(1-\varepsilon)}\right]} = \frac{3fL\rho v'^2(1-\varepsilon)}{\varepsilon^3\phi_s D_p} \approx \frac{1.75fL\rho v'(1-\varepsilon)}{\varepsilon^3\phi_s D_p}$$

(For Re>1000, 3f1.75)

This equation is called Burke-Plummer equation.

Ergun's equation for porous media flow for any value of Reynolds number is given by:

$$\Delta p = \frac{G'^2}{\rho}\frac{L}{\phi_s D_p}\frac{1-\varepsilon}{\varepsilon^3}\left[\frac{150}{\text{Re}} + 1.75\right]$$

where $G' = \rho v'$.

Fluidization:

The gas velocity based on the empty cross section of the bed at the fluidization is known as the minimum fluidization velocity (v_{mf}). The porosity or void fraction of the bed when fluidization occurs is the minimum fluidization porosity (ε_{mf}). The height of bed at the fluidization is known as minimum fluidization height (L_{mf}). At the fluidization both porosity and height increases.

Minimum fluidization height is:

$$L_{mf} = \frac{L}{1-\varepsilon_{mf}}$$

where L = compact height

Relationship between Bed Height and Porosity:

$$\frac{L_1}{L_2} = \frac{1-\varepsilon_2}{1-\varepsilon_1}$$

where L_1 is the height of bed with porosity ε_1 and L_2 is the height of bed with porosity ε_2.

Pressure Drop at Minimum Fluidization:

The pressure drop at minimum fluidization condition is given by:

$$\Delta p_{mf} = L_{mf}(1-\varepsilon_{mf})(\rho_p - \rho)\,g$$

where ρ_p = particle density or true density

ρ = fluid density

L_{mf} = minimum height of fluidized bed

Reynolds number at minimum fluidization is given by:

$$\text{Re}_{mf} = \frac{D_p\rho v_{mf'}}{\mu}$$

where v_{mf}' is minimum fluid velocity.

Minimum fluidization velocity may be calculated by:

$$1.75N_{\text{Re}}^2 + 150N_{\text{Re}} - \frac{(\varepsilon_{mf}\phi_s D_p)^3 \rho}{\left[\mu(1-\varepsilon_{mf})\right]^2}(\rho_p - \rho)g = 0$$

where, $\text{Re} = \dfrac{\phi_s D_p \rho v_{mf'}}{\mu(1-\varepsilon_{mf})}$

where v_{mf}' = minimum fluidization velocity, ρ_p = density of solid particles, ρ = density of fluid, D_p = diameter of particle, ε_{mf} = minimum fluidization porosity, μ = viscosity of fluid.

Mass of material in fluidized bed can be calculated as:

$$m = \rho V(1-\varepsilon) = \rho \times \frac{\pi}{4} d^2 h(1-\varepsilon)$$

where ρ = density of material
d = diameter of bed
h = height of fluidized bed
ε = porosity

Galileo number is given by:

$$Ga = \frac{D_p^3 g \rho_f(\rho_p - \rho)}{\mu^2}$$

where D_p = particle diameter
ρ_p = particle density
ρ = fluid density
μ = viscosity of fluid

Chapter 5

Heat Transfer

Heat transfer is the movement of energy due to a temperature difference. Heat transfer is an important operation in food processing operation such as drying, pasteurization, evaporation, sterilization, canning, freezing, etc. This chapter deals with the different modes of heat transfer, heat exchangers and their governing equations.

Basic Concepts:

Heat transfer may be classified as steady state or unsteady-state (transient) heat transfer. In steady state heat transfer, temperature does not change with time while during unsteady state heat transfer, temperature changes with time. An example of heat flow through walls is usually considered as a steady state problem. An example of unsteady state heat transfer is the heating and cooling of cans in a retort to sterilize the contents. Heat can be transferred in three ways: by conduction, by radiation and by convection.

Conduction Heat Transfer:

Conduction heat transfer occurs when heat moves through a material (usually a solid or a viscous liquid) due to molecular action only. Conduction heat transfer is guided by Fourier's law which can be written as:

$$q = -kA\frac{\Delta T}{\Delta x}$$

where q = heat transfer rate, W or J/s

A = heat transfer area, m^2

ΔT = temperature difference, K

Δx = distance, m

k = thermal conductivity, W/m-K or J/sm K

$\frac{\Delta T}{\Delta x}$ = temperature gradient i.e. the rate of change of temperature per unit length of heat-transfer path

The negative sign indicates that heat flow is always from higher temperature to lower temperature.

The above expression may be written as:

$$\text{heat flow} = \frac{\text{thermal potential difference}}{\text{thermal resistance}}$$

The unit of thermal resistance is °C/W or K/W.

$$\text{Heat conductance} = C = k/x$$

The unit of conductance is J/m^2 s K.

R-Value:

R-value used in classifying performance of insulation in commercial practice is given by:

$$R = \frac{\Delta T}{\left(\frac{q}{A}\right)}$$

The unit of R-value is m^{2}°C /W.

Convection :

Convection heat transfer is the transfer of energy due to the movement of a heated (or cooled) fluid. It is of two types: free or natural convection and forced convection. Natural convection occurs when a heated fluid moves due to the change in fluid density. Forced convection occurs when the fluid is moved by other methods (pumps, fans, etc.). Convective heat transfer between a fluid and a surface is normally written in terms of a convective heat transfer coefficient. The rate of heat transfer by convection is proportional to the temperature difference and is expressed as:

$$q = hA(T_s - T_a) = \frac{T_s - T_a}{1/hA}$$

where h is the film heat transfer coefficient, k is thermal conductivity of fluid film, δ is boundary layer thickness, A is the surface area, and Ts and Ta are the surface of wall and ambient temperatures, respectively.

Resistance due to convection is given by:

$$R = \frac{1}{hA}$$

Film Heat Transfer Coefficient:

The magnitude of the heat transfer coefficient varies in an inverse proportion to the thickness of the boundary layer. The surface or film heat transfer coefficient is a measure of the resistance to heat flow, caused by the boundary film, and is therefore equivalent to the term k/δ in the conduction equation.

The rate of heat transfer is:

$$q = \frac{k_f A(T_s - T_a)}{\delta}$$

The film coefficient of convective heat transfer or heat transfer coefficient h is defined as:

$$h = \frac{k_f}{\delta}$$

where k_f is thermal conductivity of the film and δ is the film thickness.

The rate of heat transfer by convection is then expressed by the following equation:

$$q = hA\ (T_s - T_a)$$

The SI unit of heat transfer coefficient is W/m^2 K.

The rate of heat transfer increases with increase in the value of heat transfer coefficient. The higher the value of thermal conductivity of the film and lower the value of film thickness, the higher will be the value of heat transfer coefficient.

Steady State Conduction Through a Flat Slab/Wall:

Referring Fig. 5.1 and using Fourier's law of heat conduction we may write:

$$q = \frac{kA(T_1 - T_0)}{x} = \frac{T_1 - T_0}{\frac{x}{kA}} = \frac{T_1 - T_0}{R}$$

where T_1 and T_0 are surface temperature of respective faces of slab ($T_1 > T_0$) and x is its thickness and R is the thermal resistance.

Thermal resistance is given by:

$$R = \frac{x}{kA}$$

Where x is the thickness of the layer, k is the thermal conductivity of the layer, and A is the cross-sectional area. The thermal resistance R increases as x increases, as A decreases, and as k decreases.

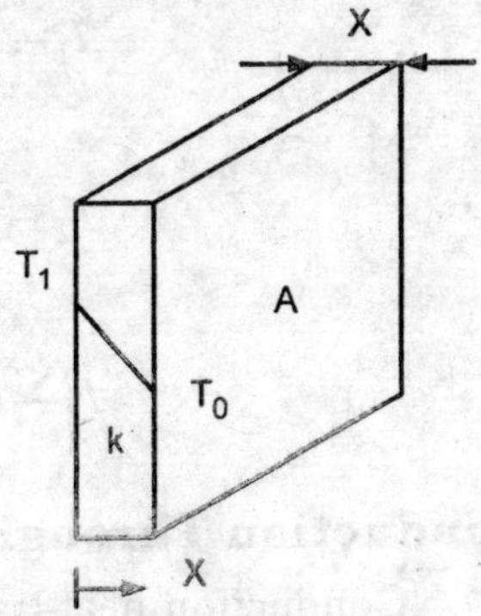

FIG. 5.1. Steady-state heat transfer through the wall

Conduction in a Composite Slab/Wall :

Under steady state conditions, since same heat flows across all slabs/walls (Fig. 5.2), so using Fourier's law we may write:

$$\frac{q}{A} = k_1 \frac{T_1 - T_2}{\Delta x_1} = k_2 \frac{T_2 - T_3}{\Delta x_2} = k_3 \frac{T_3 - T_4}{\Delta x_3}$$

The interface temperature may be evaluated using the following equations:

$$T_1 - T_2 = \frac{q}{A} \frac{\Delta x_1}{k_1}$$

$$T_2 - T_3 = \frac{q}{A} \frac{\Delta x_2}{k_2}$$

$$T_3 - T_4 = \frac{q}{A} \frac{\Delta x_3}{k_3}$$

Adding theses equations, we have:

$$T_1 - T_4 = \frac{q}{A}\left[\frac{\Delta x_1}{k_1} + \frac{\Delta x_2}{k_2} + \frac{\Delta x_3}{k_3}\right]$$

Or,
$$q = \frac{(T_1 - T_4)}{\frac{\Delta x_1}{k_1 A} + \frac{\Delta x_2}{k_2 A} + \frac{\Delta x_3}{k_3 A}} = \frac{(T_1 - T_4)}{R_1 + R_2 + R_3}$$

where, $R_1 = \frac{\Delta x_1}{k_1 A}$, $R_2 = \frac{\Delta x_2}{k_2 A}$, $R_3 = \frac{\Delta x_3}{k_3 A}$

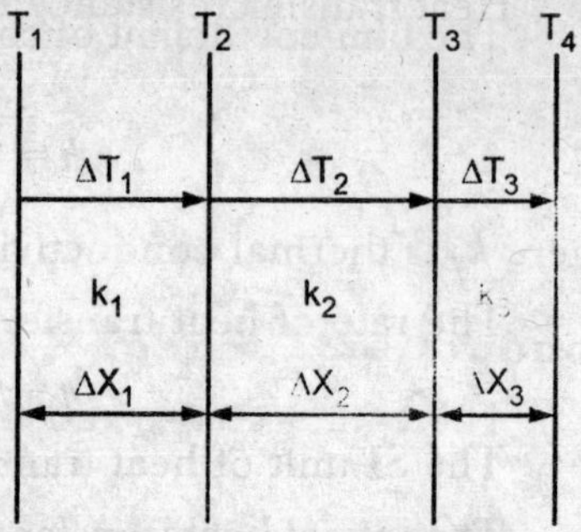

FIG. 5.2 Diagram of composite slab and temperature drop at each layer

The overall thermal resistance for three layers wall is given by:

$$R = R_1 + R_2 + R_3 = \frac{x_1}{k_1 A_1} + \frac{x_2}{k_2 A_2} + \frac{x_3}{k_3 A_3}$$

An alternative way to calculate the interface temperature is:

$$T_1 - T_2 = \frac{R_1}{R_1 + R_2 + R_3}(T_1 - T_4)$$

$$T_2 - T_3 = \frac{R_2}{R_1 + R_2 + R_3}(T_1 - T_4)$$

$$T_3 - T_4 = \frac{R_3}{R_1 + R_2 + R_3}(T_1 - T_4)$$

Conduction Through a Hollow Cylinder:

Conduction heat transfer through a cylindrical wall (Fig. 5.3) is given by:

$$q = 2\pi kL\frac{T_1 - T_2}{\left(\ln\frac{r_2}{r_1}\right)} = \frac{2\pi Lk(r_2 - r_1)(T_1 - T_2)}{(r_2 - r_1)\left(\ln\frac{2\pi r_2 L}{2\pi r_1 L}\right)} = \frac{k(A_2 - A_1)(T_1 - T_2)}{(r_2 - r_1)\ln\frac{A_2}{A_1}} = \frac{kA_{lm}(T_1 - T_2)}{x_w} \quad (T_1 > T_2)$$

where, Alm = logarithmic mean area and is given by:

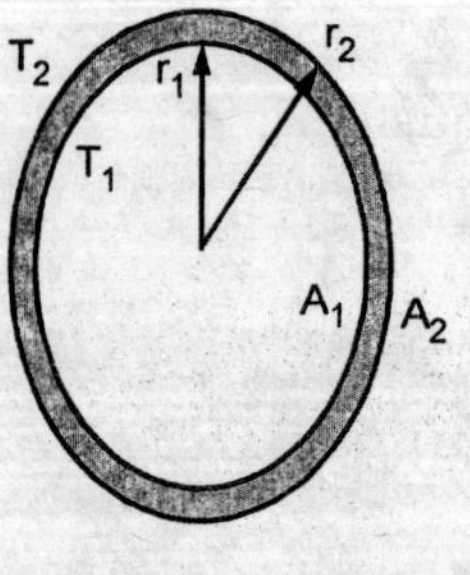

FIG. 5.3 Heat conduction in a hollow cylinder

where A_2 and A_1 are outside and inside surface areas of cylinder respectively.

r_1 = inside radius of cylinder

r_2 = outside radius of cylinder

L = length of cylinder

k = thermal conductivity of material

$xw = r_2 - r_1$ = wall thickness o the clinder

Heat transfer resistance may be written as:

$$R = \frac{\ln\left(\frac{r_2}{r_1}\right)}{2\pi kL} \quad \text{or} \quad R = \frac{x_w}{kA_{lm}}$$

Conduction Through Two Layers Cylinder:

The equation of heat transfer for two layers referring Fig. 5.4 is:

$$q = \frac{T_1 - T_3}{\frac{1}{2\pi k_1 L}\left(\ln\frac{r_2}{r_1}\right) + \frac{1}{2\pi k_2 L}\left(\ln\frac{r_3}{r_2}\right)}$$

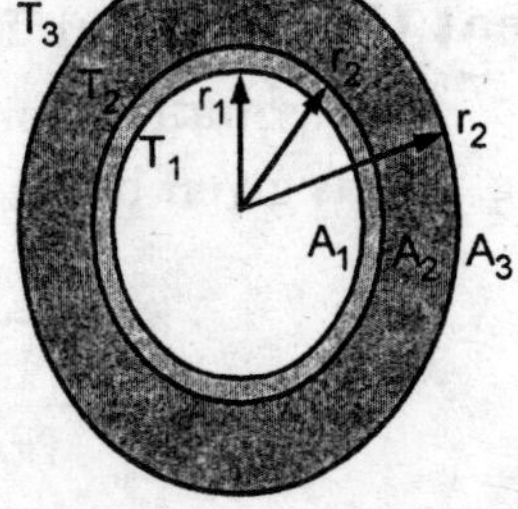

FIG. 5.4 Conduction through two layers cylinder

Equation of rate of heat loss per meter of length in case of two layers cylinder is:

$$\frac{q}{L} = \frac{T_1 - T_2}{\frac{1}{2\pi k_1}\left(\ln\frac{r_2}{r_1}\right) + \frac{1}{2\pi k_2}\left(\ln\frac{r_3}{r_2}\right)}$$

where T_1 is inside temperature and T_2 is outside temperature and $T_1 > T_2$.

The interface temperature (T_i) may be evaluated by:

$$\frac{q}{L} = \frac{T_i - T_2}{\frac{1}{2\pi k_2}\left(\ln\frac{r_3}{r_2}\right)}$$

Or

$$\frac{q}{L} = \frac{T_1 - T_i}{\frac{1}{2\pi k_1}\left(\ln\frac{r_2}{r_1}\right)}$$

Conduction Through Three Layers Cylinder:

The equation of heat transfer for three layers cylinder is:

$$q = \frac{T_1 - T_2}{\frac{1}{2\pi k_1 L}\left(\ln\frac{r_2}{r_1}\right)} = \frac{T_2 - T_3}{\frac{1}{2\pi k_2 L}\left(\ln\frac{r_3}{r_2}\right)} = \frac{T_3 - T_4}{\frac{1}{2\pi k_3 L}\left(\ln\frac{r_4}{r_3}\right)}$$

Combining these equations and eliminating T_2 and T_3, we have:

$$q = \frac{T_1 - T_4}{\frac{1}{2\pi k_1 L}\left(\ln\frac{r_2}{r_1}\right) + \frac{1}{2\pi k_2 L}\left(\ln\frac{r_3}{r_2}\right) + \frac{1}{2\pi k_3 L}\left(\ln\frac{r_4}{r_3}\right)}$$

The interface temperature T_2 and T_3 can be easily calculated by using following expressions:

$$T_1 - T_2 = \frac{q}{2\pi k_1 L}\ln\frac{r_2}{r_1} \quad \text{or} \quad T_2 = T_1 - \frac{q}{2\pi k_1 L}\ln\frac{r_2}{r_1}$$

Similarly,

$$T_3 = T_2 - \frac{q}{2\pi k_2 L}\ln\frac{r_3}{r_2}$$

$$T_4 = T_3 - \frac{q}{2\pi k_3 L}\ln\frac{r_4}{r_3}$$

Heat Conduction Through a Hollow Sphere:

The equation for the rate of conduction heat transfer through a hollow sphere (Fig. 5.5) is given by:

$$q = \frac{T_1 - T_2}{\dfrac{1}{4\pi k}\left(\dfrac{1}{r_1} - \dfrac{1}{r_2}\right)}$$

or,

$$q = \frac{4\pi k r_1 r_2 (T_1 - T_2)}{(r_2 - r_1)} = kA_{gm}\frac{(T_1 - T_2)}{x_w}$$

$$A_{gm} = \sqrt{A_1 A_2} = \sqrt{(4\pi r_1^2)(4\pi r_2^2)} = 4\pi r_1 r_2$$

where A_{gm} is geometric mean area of hollow sphere

$x_w = r_2 - r_1$ = wall thickness of the sphere

The thermal resistance is expressed as:

$$R = \frac{(r_2 - r_1)}{4\pi k r_1 r_2} \quad \text{or} \quad R = \frac{x_w}{kA_{gm}}$$

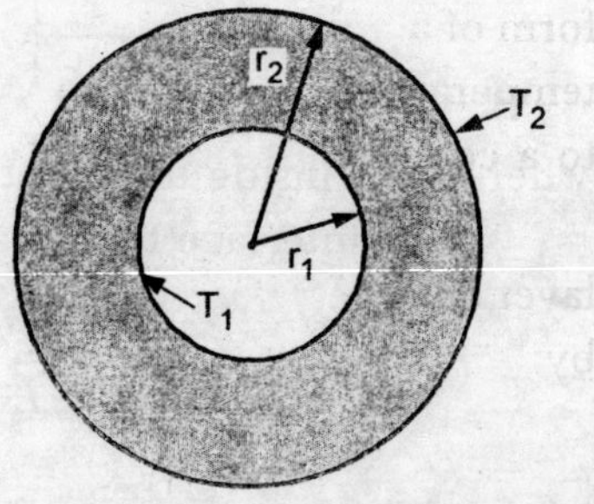

FIG. 5.5 Conduction through hollow sphere

Conduction with Internal Heat Generation:

This type of situation comes when heat is generated inside the conducting medium. The example of his is electric resistance heating. The case of heat generation in plane wall and cylinders is presented here:

Heat generation in plane wall : The equation for centre temperature in case of internal heat generation in a plane wall is given by:

$$T_0 = \frac{\dot{q}L^2}{2k} + T_w$$

where k = thermal conductivity of wall, W/m K

T_w = wall temperature

L = distance from centre to wall surface = half thickness, m

$\dot{q}$ = volumetric rate of heat generation, W/m^3

Heat Generate in Cylinder:

The centre temperature of cylindrical geometry may be calculated by:

$$T_o = \frac{\dot{q}L^2}{2k} + T_w$$

where k = thermal conductivity of wall

T_w = wall temperature

r = radius of cylinder

$\dot{q}$ = volumetric rate of heat generation, W/m^3

The heat generated per unit volume $\dot{q}$ may be calculated by following relation:

$$P = \dot{q}V = \dot{q}\pi r^2 l$$

where P is power, r is radius and l is length of cylindrical geometry.

Heat transfer area in case of cylindrical geometry is πdl.

Critical Thickness of Insulation for a Cylinder:

Consider an insulation layer of thermal conductivity (k) in the form of a hollow cylinder of length L as shown in Fig. 5.6. The inner temperature of the insulation is fixed at T_i an outer surface is exposed to a convection environment at T_0.

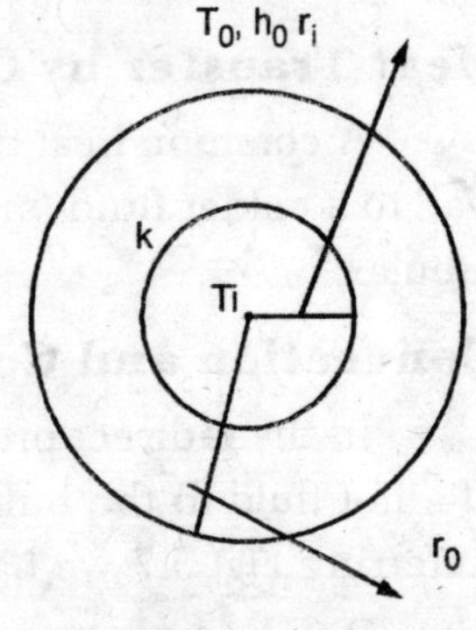

FIG. 5.6 Insulation shell surrounding a pipe

Then the equation for rate heat transfer through the insulation layer and convective boundary layer offering heat resistance is given by:

$$q = \frac{(T_i - T_0)}{\frac{1}{2\pi Lk}\left(\ln\frac{r_0}{r_i}\right) + \frac{1}{2\pi L h_0 r_0}}$$

where L = length of the cylinder

k = thermal conductivity of the insulating material

h_0 = outside convective heat transfer coefficient

r_i = inner radius of pipe

r_0 = outer radius of pipe

As r_0 increases, the first tem increases but second term decreases. Thus there must be a critical radius r_c that will allow maximum rate of heat transfer q . r_c can be obtained by

Differentiating q with respect to r_0 and equating to zero we get equation for maximum heat flow:

$$\frac{dq}{dr_o} = \frac{2\pi kL(T_i - T_0)\left(\frac{1}{r_o} - \frac{k}{r_o^2 h_o}\right)}{\left[\left(\ln\frac{r_0}{r_i}\right) + \frac{k}{h_0 r_0}\right]^2} = 0$$

$$\frac{1}{r_0} - \frac{k}{h_0 r_0^2} = 0$$

When outside radius becomes equal to the critical radius, then we get:

$$r_0 = r_c = \frac{k}{h_0}$$

This radius is critical radius or critical thickness r_c when rate of heat transmission is maximum. In practice, thickness of insulation used must exceed critical thickness if the rate of heat loss is to be reduced. This equation can be used for calculation of thickness of critical insulation for a cylinder having insulation thermal conductivity (k) and heat transfer coefficient (h_o).

The critical thickness of insulation for a sphere having insulation thermal conductivity (k) and heat transfer coefficient (h_o) is:

$$r_c = \frac{2k}{h_0}$$

Heat Transfer by Conduction and Convection:

A common heat transfer application involves heat flow from a hot fluid, through a solid wall to a colder fluid on the other side. In some cases, the wall can be flat, but it is frequently tubular.

Convection and Conduction Heat Transfer Through Plane Wall:

In the indirect process, there are three resistances to the transfer of heat from the bulk of a hot fluid to the bulk of a cold fluid, two due to convection and one due to conduction. Referring Fig. 5.7 we have:

Rate of heat transfer from inner fluid to wall:

$$q = h_i A (T_i - T_1)$$

Heat transfer by conduction through wall is:

$$q = \frac{kA(T_1 - T_2)}{x}$$

Heat transfer by convection from outer wall surface to outer fluid is:

$$Q = h_o A (T_2 - T_o)$$

Since thermal resistance is additive hence

$$Q = \frac{A(T_i - T_o)}{\frac{1}{h_o} + \frac{x}{k} + \frac{1}{h_i}} = \frac{A(T_i - T_o)}{1/U} = US\ (T_i - T_o)$$

$$\frac{1}{U} = \frac{1}{h_o} + \frac{x}{k} + \frac{1}{h_i}$$

where A = heat transfer area, m^2

x = thickness of the wall, m

k = thermal conductivity of the wall, w/m.K.

T_i = inner fluid temperature

T_o = outer fluid temperature

h_i = inside convective heat transfer coefficient

h_o = outside convective heat transfer coefficient

U = overall heat transfer coefficient

The higher the value of U, the more efficient is the heat exchange system.

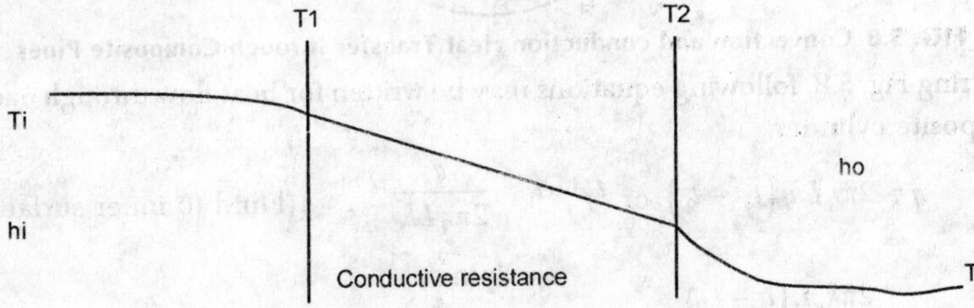

FIG. 5.7 Convection and conduction heat transfer in plane wall

Convection and Conduction Heat Transfer Through Three Layers Plane Wall:

The rate of heat transfer for combined convection and conduction through three layers plane wall is:

$$q = \frac{t_o - t_i}{\frac{1}{h_o A} + \frac{x_1}{k_1 A} + \frac{x_2}{k_2 A} + \frac{x_3}{k_3 A} + \frac{1}{h_i A}} = \frac{t_o - t_i}{\frac{1}{A}\left(\frac{1}{h_o} + \frac{x_1}{k_1} + \frac{x_2}{k_2} + \frac{x_3}{k_3} + \frac{1}{h_i}\right)} \quad (t_o > t_i)$$

The overall heat transfer by combined conduction and convection is expressed in term of an overall heat transfer coefficient U defined by:

$$q = UA\Delta T_{overall}$$

where $\frac{1}{U} = \frac{1}{h_o} + \frac{x_1}{k_1} + \frac{x_2}{k_2} + \frac{x_3}{k_3} + \frac{1}{h_i}$

t_o = outside temperature

t_i = inside temperature

$\Delta T_{overall} = t_o - t_i$

Convection and Conduction Heat Transfer Through Composite Pipes:

Heat is transferred from a fluid at a temperature of t_f through the materials a, b, and c to ambient air at a temperature of t_o.

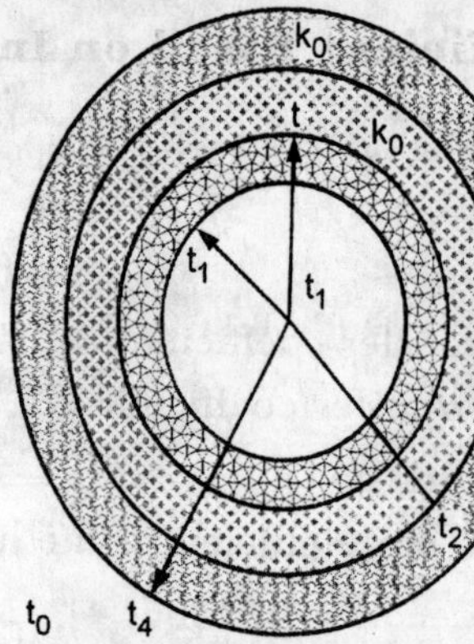

FIG. 5.8 Convection and conduction Heat Transfer through Composite Pipes

Referring Fig. 5.8, following equations may be written for heat flow through each element of the composite cylinder:

$$q = 2\pi r_1 L h_i \left(t_f - t_1\right) \text{ or } t_f - t_1 = \frac{q}{2\pi r_1 L h_i} \qquad \text{(Fluid to inner surface)}$$

$$q = \frac{2\pi k_a L (t_1 - t_2)}{\ln \frac{r_2}{r_1}} \text{ or } t_1 - t_2 = \frac{q \ln \frac{r_2}{r_1}}{2\pi k_a L} \qquad \text{(Through material } a\text{)}$$

$$q = \frac{2\pi k_b L (t_2 - t_3)}{\ln \frac{r_3}{r_2}} \text{ or } t_2 - t_3 = \frac{q \ln \frac{r_3}{r_2}}{2\pi k_b L} \qquad \text{(Through material } b\text{)}$$

$$q = \frac{2\pi k_c L (t_3 - t_4)}{\ln \frac{r_4}{r_3}} \text{ or } t_3 - t_4 = \frac{q \ln \frac{r_4}{r_3}}{2\pi k_c L} \qquad \text{(Through material } c\text{)}$$

$$q = 2\pi r_4 L h_o (t_4 - t_o) \text{ or } t_4 - t_o = \frac{q}{2\pi r_4 L h_o} \qquad \text{(Outside to surrounding)}$$

Solving these equations we have:

$$q = \frac{(t_f - t_o)}{\frac{1}{2\pi r_1 L h_i} + \frac{\ln \frac{r_2}{r_1}}{2\pi k_a L} + \frac{\ln \frac{r_3}{r_2}}{2\pi k_b L} + \frac{\ln \frac{r_4}{r_3}}{2\pi k_c L} + \frac{1}{2\pi r_4 L h_o}}$$

$$= \frac{(t_f - t_o)}{\frac{1}{2\pi L}\left(\frac{1}{r_1 h_i} + \frac{\ln \frac{r_2}{r_1}}{k_a} + \frac{\ln \frac{r_3}{r_2}}{k_b} + \frac{\ln \frac{r_4}{r_3}}{k_c} + \frac{1}{r_4 h_o}\right)}$$

Overall Heat Transfer Coefficient Based on Inside and Outside Area of Cylindrical Pipe:

$$q = U_i A_i (T_i - T_o)$$

where T_i and T_o are hot fluid temperature on the inside surface and cold fluid temperature on the outside surface, U_i = overall heat transfer coefficient based on inside area and expressed as:

$$\frac{1}{U_i} = \frac{1}{h_i} + \frac{d_i \ln(d_2/d_i)}{2k_1} + \frac{d_i \ln(d_o/d_2)}{2k_2} + \frac{d_i}{h_o d_o}$$

where k_1 = thermal conductivity of first cylinder

k_2 = thermal conductivity of second cylinder

$$q = U_o A_o (T_i - T_o)$$

where U_o is overall heat transfer coefficient based on outside area and expressed as:

$$\frac{1}{U_o} = \frac{d_o}{h_i d_i} + \frac{d_o \ln(d_2/d_i)}{2k_1} + \frac{d_o \ln(d_o/d_2)}{2k_2} + \frac{1}{h_o}$$

Or,
$$\frac{1}{U_o} = \frac{r_o}{r_i h_i} + \frac{r_o \ln \frac{r_2}{r_1}}{k_1} + \frac{r_o \ln \frac{r_3}{r_2}}{k_2} + \frac{1}{h_o}$$

$$\frac{1}{U_i} = \frac{r_i}{r_o h_o} + \frac{r_i \ln \frac{r_2}{r_1}}{k_1} + \frac{r_i \ln \frac{r_3}{r_2}}{k_2} + \frac{1}{h_i}$$

$$q = \frac{T_i - T_o}{\frac{1}{h_i \times 2\pi r_1 L} + \frac{1}{2\pi k_1 L}\left(\ln \frac{r_2}{r_1}\right) + \frac{1}{2\pi k_2 L}\left(\ln \frac{r_3}{r_2}\right) + \frac{1}{h_o \times 2\pi r_3 L}}$$

Correlation for Prediction of Heat Transfer coefficient:

The convective heat transfer coefficient is predicted from empirical correlation. It is influenced by velocity of flow, physical properties of fluid, temperature difference and geometry of system under consideration. The empirical correlations useful in prediction of convective heat transfer coefficient are presented in the following section for both forced and free convection:

Forced convection heat transfer : For forced convection heat transfer, the three dimensionless numbers which are used are Reynolds number (*Re*), Prandtl number (*Pr*) and Nusselt number (*Nu*) which are given below:.

Reynolds number : It is expressed by:

$$Re = \frac{\rho v d}{\mu}$$

where, ρ is the density of the fluid (kg/m³), v is the fluid velocity (m/s), μ is the dynamic viscosity (kg/ms) and d is the characteristic dimension (diameter for pipe).

Prandtl number : Prandtl number is defined by:

$$Pr = \frac{\mu C_p}{k}$$

where C_p = specific heat of fluid
μ = dynamic viscosity of fluid
k = thermal conductivity of fluid

It may also be expressed as:

$$Pr = \frac{\nu}{\alpha} = \frac{\text{kinematic viscosity}}{\text{thermal diffusivity}}$$

It may be considered as the ratio of rate of momentum exchange between molecules and the rate of energy exchange between molecules that lead to the transfer of heat.

When $Pr = 1$, then thickness of hydrodynamic and thermal boundary layer will be exactly same.

When $Pr < 1$, then molecular diffusivity of heat will be much larger than that of momentum

Nusselt number : The heat transfer coefficient is calculated from the Nusselt number which is given by:

$$Nu = \frac{hD}{k} = \frac{\text{convective heat transfer}}{\text{convective heat transfer}}$$

where h = convective heat transfer coefficient of fluid, W/m^2 K
k = thermal conductivity of fluid, W/mK
D = equivalent diameter of conduit, m

This dimensionless expression may be considered as the ratio of the characteristic dimension of a system and the thickness of the boundary layer of fluid that would transmit heat by conduction at the same rate as that calculated using the heat transfer coefficient. The Nusselt number is also called dimensionless heat transfer coefficient.

$$Nu = \frac{hD}{k} = \frac{k}{\delta} \cdot \frac{D}{k} = \frac{D}{\delta} \quad (\text{as } h = k/\delta)$$

where δ = film thickness

The Nusselt number may also be expressed by:

$$Nu = \frac{h_i D}{k}$$

In forced convection, heat transfer equation is:

$$q = \dot{m} C_p (T_0 - T_i) = A h_i \left[T_w - \frac{(T_0 + T_i)}{2} \right]$$

$$A = \pi d L \text{ for tubular pipe.}$$

The film coefficient h_i is the average value over the length of the pipe and is calculated as follows for the case of constant wall temperature:

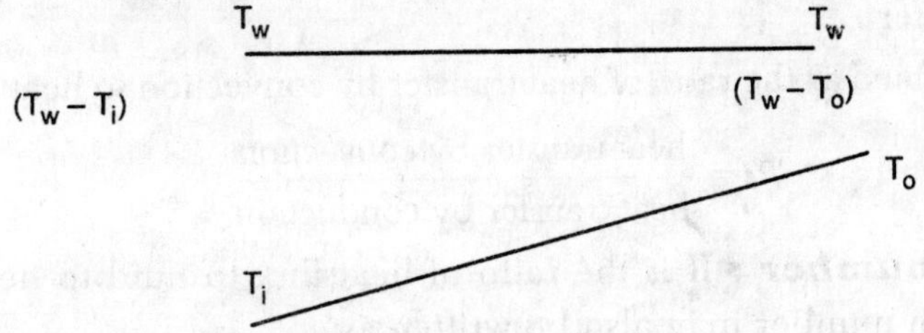

Let T_w = constant wall temperature

T_i = inlet temperature

T_o = outlet temperature

When a fluid through a tube is heated by condensing steam at a particular temperature, then following equation may be used:

Heat gained by fluid = heat given out by tube

$$h_i \pi D L \Delta T_{LMTD} = \dot{m} C_p (T_0 - T_i)$$

$$\Delta T_{LMTD} = \frac{(T_w - T_i) - (T_w - T_o)}{\ln \dfrac{T_w - T_i}{T_w - T_o}}$$

$$h_i \pi D L \frac{T_o - T_i}{\ln \dfrac{T_w - T_i}{T_w - T_o}} = \dot{m} C_p (T_0 - T_i)$$

or

$$h_i = \frac{\dot{m} C_p}{\pi D L} \ln \frac{T_w - T_i}{T_w - T_o}$$

$$Nu = \frac{h_i D}{k} = \frac{\dot{m} C_p}{\pi D L} \frac{D}{k} \ln \frac{T_w - T_i}{T_w - T_o} = \frac{\dot{m} C_p}{\pi k L} \ln \frac{T_w - T_i}{T_w - T_o} = \frac{Gz}{\pi} \ln \frac{T_w - T_i}{T_w - T_o}$$

The length of tube can be estimated by the equation:

$$L = \frac{\rho v D C_p (T_o - T_i)}{4 h_i \Delta T_{LMTD}}$$

where D is diameter, v is velocity, ρ is density of fluid, C_p is specific heat.

Other important relevant dimensionless numbers are given below:

Peclet number **:** The product of *Re* and *Pr* which occurs in the laminar flow correlation is called the Peclet number and is given by:

$$Pe = Re\,Pr = \frac{\rho v D}{\mu} \times \frac{\mu Cp}{k} = \frac{\rho v D Cp}{k} = \frac{vD}{k/\rho Cp} = \frac{vD}{\alpha}$$

where D = diameter

It is also defined as the ratio of heat transfer by convection to heat transfer by conduction.

$$Pe = \frac{\text{heat transfer by convection}}{\text{heat transfer by conduction}}$$

Stanton number **:** It is the ratio of heat flux to fluid to heat transfer capacity of fluid flow. Stanton number may also be written as:

$$St = \frac{\text{wall heat transfer rate}}{\text{heat transfer by convection}}$$

Stanton number, Reynolds number, Prandtl number and Nusselt number are related as:

$$St = \frac{Nu}{Re\,Pr} = \frac{\frac{hD}{k}}{\frac{\rho v D}{\mu} \times \frac{\mu C_p}{k}} = \frac{h}{\rho v C_p} = \frac{h}{GCp}$$

where St = Stanton number

v = velocity of fluid

ρ = density of fluid

C_p = specific heat of fluid

h = heat transfer coefficient

$G = rv$

where G is mass velocity.

Also, $St = \frac{f}{2}$ where f is friction factor

The Nu can be expressed in term of Re, Pr and St by the following equation:

$$Nu = St \cdot Re \cdot \cdot Pr = \frac{h}{CpG} \cdot \frac{GD}{\mu} \cdot \frac{\mu Cp}{k} = \frac{hD}{k}$$

Dean number **:** It is a non dimensional number that characterizes the flow in a coiled tube and is given by:

$$De = Re\sqrt{d/D}$$

where D = diameter of tube

d = diameter of helical coil

For forced convection, the general form is:

$$Nu = f(Re,\ Pr)$$

Heat transfer coefficient for fully developed laminar flow inside a pipe : For laminar flow of fluids inside a horizontal tubes or pipes, the following equation can be used:

$$N_{Nu} = 1.86\left(Re\,Pr\frac{D}{L}\right)^{0.33}\left(\frac{\mu_b}{\mu_w}\right)^{0.14}$$

where $N_u = \frac{hD}{k}$

D = diameter

L = length of pipe

k = thermal conductivity

μ = viscosity

h = heat transfer coefficient

μb = viscosity at bulk mean temperature

μw = viscosity at wall temperature

This equation is called Sieder-Tate equation and is applicable for Re < 2100.

All fluid properties are evaluated at arithmetic mean bulk temperature ie arithmetic mean of inlet and outlet temperature and except μ_w which is evaluated at wall temperature.

The =arithmetic mean of the inlet and outlet temperatures is:

$$T_b = \frac{T_{in} + T_{out}}{2}$$

Heat transfer coefficient for fully developed turbulent flow inside a pipe : Rate of heat transfer is greater in turbulent flow than in laminar flow. Forced convective transfer is extremely common in engineering applications such as heat exchangers, evaporation, convective drying, blast freezing, agitated vessels etc. Dittus-Boelter equation is commonly used for turbulent flow in pipe and is given by:

$$Nu = 0.023Re^{0.8}Pr^n$$

where n = 0.4 when the fluid is heated

n = 0.3 when the fluid is cooled

One of the most widely quoted correlations is Sieder-Tate equation for turbulent heat transfer between the walls of a cylindrical duct (pipe) and a fluid fl owing inside.

$$Nu = 0.023Re^{0.8}Pr^n\left(\frac{\mu}{\mu_w}\right)^{0.14} \qquad \text{(for } Re > 10000\text{)}$$

Or,

$$\frac{h_i D}{k} = 0.023Re^{0.8}Pr^n\left(\frac{\mu}{\mu_w}\right)^{0.14}$$

The exponent (n) of Pr is 0.3 for heating and 0.4 for cooling. The dimension D is the inside diameter of the pipe. The fluid properties are taken at the average temperature, except for μ_w which is the viscosity at the wall temperature.

For circular annulus where heat flow is across the inner wall, D is given by:

$$D = \frac{4\,(\text{cross sectional area})}{\text{wetted perimeter}} = \frac{4A}{P}$$

where A = cross sectional area of flow

P = heat transfer perimeter

For heat transfer, the heat transfer perimeter is the outer circumference of inner pipe.

Hence,
$$D = \frac{4 \times \frac{\pi}{4}\left(D_2^{\,2} - D_1^{\,2}\right)}{\pi D_1} = \frac{\left(D_2^{\,2} - D_1^{\,2}\right)}{D_1}$$

where D_1 and D_2 are inner and outer diameter.

For non-circular tube (in case of annulus), the heat flow is across both inner and outer surface and hence D is replaced by the equivalent diameter which is defined as:

$$D = \frac{4 \times \frac{\pi}{4}\left(D_2^{\,2} - D_1^{\,2}\right)}{\pi\left(D_2 + D_1\right)} = D_2 - D_1$$

where D_1 and D_2 are inside and outside diameter respectively.

Heat transfer coefficient for fluid flow parallel to flat plate : The flow fluid parallel to flat late occurs in case of tray drying of food materials. If a plate of length L is placed parallel to the fluid flow, then following equation is used for laminar flow:

$$Nu = 0.664 Re^{0.5} Pr^{0.33} \qquad \text{(Valid for } Re < 3 \times 105 \text{ and } Pr > 0.7\text{)}$$

$$Re = \frac{\rho v L}{\mu}$$

where v = average velocity of undisturbed free stream

For turbulent flow, the following equation may be used:

$$Nu = 0.0366\; Re^{0.8}\; Pr^{0.3} \qquad \text{(Valid for } Re > 3 \times 105 \text{ and } Pr > 0.7\text{)}$$

All fluid properties are evaluated at film temperature (T_f) which is computed as:

$$T_f = \frac{T_b + T_w}{2}$$

where T_b = bulk fluid temperature = $(T_1 + T_2)/2$

T_w = wall or surface temperature

T_1 and T_2 = fluid temperature at inlet and outlet

Flow Past a Sphere:

For heat transfer between a sphere and a fluid in turbulent flow (*e.g.* drying of liquid droplets), the following equation is used to predict average heat transfer coefficient:

$$Nu = 2 + 0.6Re^{0.5}Pr^{0.33} \quad \text{(valid for } 1 < Re < 70000 \text{ and } 0.6 < Pr < 400)$$

All fluid properties are evaluated at film temperature (T_f) which is computed as:

$$T_f = \frac{T_b + T_w}{2}$$

where T_b = bulk fluid temperature = $(T_1 + T_2)/2$

T_w = wall or surface temperature

T_1 and T_2 = fluid temperature at inlet and outlet

Flow Past a Sphere:

For heat transfer between a sphere and a fluid in turbulent flow (eg. drying of liquid droplets), the following equation is used to predict average heat transfer coefficient:

$$Nu = 2 + 0.6Re^{0.5}Pr^{0.33} \quad \text{(valid for } 1 < Re < 70000 \text{ and } 0.6 < Pr < 400)$$

All fluid properties are evaluated at film temperature (T_f) which is computed as:

$$T_f = \frac{T_b + T_w}{2}$$

where T_b = bulk fluid temperature = $(T_1 + T_2)/2$

T_w = wall or surface temperature

T_1 and T_2 = fluid temperature at inlet and outlet

Free Convection Heat Transfer:

The important useful numbers in free convention heat transfer are given below:

Grashof Number : Grashof Number is the ratio of the buoyancy forces to the viscous forces in the fluid, which is used for natural or free convection and plays a role similar to that of the Reynolds number in forced convection. This number is useful for determining whether a flow over an object is laminar or turbulent.

$$Gr = \frac{\text{buoyant force}}{\text{viscous force}}$$

Mathematically, it is expressed as:

$$Gr = \frac{g\beta\Delta T\rho^2 L^3}{\mu^2}$$

where β is coefficient volumetric expansion for the fluid, ΔT is the difference of temperature, g is the gravity acceleration, μ is viscosity, ρ is density and L is length.

The coefficient of thermal expansion β is a property of the fluid defined as the fractional increase in volume at constant pressure of the fluid per degree of temperature change.

$$\beta = \frac{\left(\frac{\partial V}{\partial T}\right)_P}{\nu}$$

where υ = specific volume of fluid

$\left(\frac{\partial V}{\partial T}\right)_P$ = rate of change of specific volume with temperature at constant pressure

The coefficient of thermal expansion of an ideal gas equals the reciprocal of the absolute temperature.

i.e. $$\beta = \frac{1}{T}$$

Rayleigh number (Ra): The product of the Grashof number and Prandtl number is called the Rayleigh number and is given by the relation:

$$Ra = Gr.Pr = \frac{g\beta \Delta T L^3 C_p \rho^2}{\mu k}$$

where L = length

k = thermal conductivity

C_p = specific heat

ΔT = temperature difference between wall and bulk fluid

The values of all properties are estimated at the average film temperature

$$T_f = (T_w + T_b)/2$$

Graetz number : This is similar to the Peclet number. For combined free and forced convection, Graetz number is defined as:

$$Gz = \frac{\pi}{4}\left[\text{Re}\cdot \text{Pr}\cdot\left(\frac{d}{L}\right)\right] = \frac{\dot{m}C_p}{kL}$$

where $\dot{m}$ = mass rate of flow

d = diameter of pipe

L = length of pipe

The Graetz number may also be defined by the equation:

$$Gz = \frac{\dot{m}C_p}{kL} = \frac{\pi}{4}d^2\rho v\frac{C_p}{kL} = \frac{\pi}{4}d\cdot\frac{1}{L}\cdot\frac{\rho v d C_p}{k} = \frac{\pi d}{4L}\cdot Pe \qquad (\text{as } \dot{m} = \rho A v)$$

where Pe is Peclet number.

In natural convection, average natural convection heat transfer coefficient can be expressed by the following general equation:

$$Nu = a(Gr, Pr)^m$$

where Nu = Nusselt number

Gr = Grashof number

= Prandtl number

a, = constant

Natural Convection Empirical Equations :

The equation suitable for the calculation of the heat transfer coefficient in free convection is:

$$\text{Nu} = 0.53Gr^{0.25}\,Pr^{0.25} \qquad (\text{for } 10^4 < (Pr.Gr) < 10^9)$$

$$\text{Nu} = 0.13(Pr.Gr)^{0.33} \qquad (\text{for } 10^9 < (Pr.Gr) < 10^{12}\ )$$

The characteristic dimension to be used in the calculation of Nu and Gr in these equations is the length of the vertical plane or cylinder, diameter in the case of a horizontal cylinder and radius in the case of a sphere. The physical properties must be calculated at the film temperature T_f (average of air temperature and contact surface temperature).

Reynolds analogy between fluid friction and heat transfer:

$$St\ .\ Pr^{2/3} = \frac{f}{8}$$

where f is Fanning friction factor, Pr is Prandtl number and St is Stanton number.

Boiling and Condensation Heat Transfer:

Film heat transfer coefficient for condensation on vertical tubes or plane surfaces is given by:

$$h = 1.13\left[\frac{\rho_l\left(\rho_l-\rho_v\right)k_l^{\,3}\,gh_{fg}}{\mu_l L\left(T_s-T_w\right)}\right]^{0.25}$$

Film heat transfer coefficient for condensation on a horizontal tube or surface is:

$$h = 0.725\left[\frac{\rho_l\left(\rho_l-\rho_v\right)k_l^{\,3}\,gh_{fg}}{\mu_l d_o\left(T_s-T_w\right)}\right]^{0.25}$$

where L = height of the plate or tube

d_o = external tub diameter

h_{fg} = latent heat of the condensation at T_s in and the other symbols have their usual meanings

$ñ_l$ = liquid density

$ñ_v$ = density of saturated vapour

μ_l = viscosity of liquid

k_l = thermal conductivity of liquid

T_s = steam temperature

T_w = wall temperature

All physical properties of liquid are evaluated at the mean film temperature

$$T_f = \frac{(T_w + T_s)}{2}$$

The flow behaviour (laminar /turbulent) of condensate may be estimated by:

$$Re = \frac{4\dot{m}}{\pi d \mu_l} \quad \text{(for vertical tube)}$$

where d is diameter of vertical tube.

and $$Re = \frac{4\dot{m}}{w \mu_l} \quad \text{(for vertical plate)}$$

where w is width of plate.

Total heat transferred may be computed by:

$$q = hA(T_s - T_w)$$

This must be equal to heat obtained by condensation of steam hence, we may write:

$$q = \dot{m} h_{fg} = hA(T_s - T_w)$$

where $\dot{m}$ is condensate flow rate in kg/s.

Heat Transfer Coefficient for Non-Newtonian Fluids :

Laminar Flow : For laminar flow inside circular tubes of power law fluids, the equation of Metzner and Gluck can be used with highly viscous non-Newtonian fluids:

$$Nu = 1.75\delta^{\frac{1}{3}} (Gz)^{\frac{1}{3}} \left(\frac{\gamma_b}{\gamma_w} \right)^{0.14} \quad (Gz > 20 \text{ and } n > 0.1)$$

where, $\delta = \frac{3n+1}{4n}$

$$Gz = \frac{\dot{m} C_p}{kL} = \frac{\pi}{4} \frac{\rho v D}{\mu} \frac{\mu C_p}{k} \frac{D}{L} = \frac{\pi}{4} \text{Re} \, \text{Pr} \frac{D}{L}$$

where $\dot{m}$ = mass flow rate

Gz = Graetz number

n = flow behaviour index

L = length of heating section

D = inside diameter

The Graetz number is similar to Peclet number.

γ_b and γ_w are generalized coefficient of viscosity at bulk mean and wall temperature respectively.

$$\gamma = K'8^{n-1} = k\left(\frac{3n+1}{4n}\right)^n 8^{n-1}$$

$$\frac{\gamma_b}{\gamma_w} = \frac{K_b}{K_w}$$

where k is consistency index.

$$\mu_w = k(\gamma_w)^{n-1}$$

The equation of heat transfer rate is:

$$q = hA\Delta T_a = h(\pi dl)\Delta T_a = \dot{m}C_p\Delta T$$

$$\Delta T_a = \text{arithmetic mean temperature difference} = \frac{(T_w - T_{bi}) + (T_w - T_{bo})}{2}$$

Where T_w = wall temperature

T_{bi} = inlet bulk temperature

h = heat transfer coefficient

T_{bo} = outlet bulk temperature

$\Delta T = T_{bo} - T_{bi}$

The shear rate at the wall γ_w is calculated using the following equation:

$$\gamma_w = \frac{8v}{D}\left[\frac{3n+1}{4n}\right] = \frac{2v}{D}\left[\frac{3n+1}{n}\right]$$

and $$\mu_w = k\left(\frac{2v}{D}\right)^{n-1}\left[\frac{3n+1}{n}\right]^{n-1}$$

These equations are used in the correlation equations of heat transfer coefficients.

Turbulent Flow:

For turbulent flow in tubes following equation is used:

$$Nu = 0.0041 Re_{gen} Pr_{gen}^{0.4} \quad \text{where } Re_{gen} = \frac{v^{2-n} D^n \rho}{\gamma}$$

$$Pr_{gen} = \frac{CpK'}{k}\left(\frac{8v}{D}\right)^{n-1}$$

where k is thermal conductivity of fluid.

Reynolds number for non-Newtonian fluid:

$$Re_{gen} = \frac{8\rho v^{2-n} R^n}{k\left(\frac{3n+1}{n}\right)^n}$$

Heat Exchanger :

Heat exchangers are widely used in the food industry for heating (e.g. pasteurizers), cooling (chilled water generators) and heat induced phase change (freezing, evaporation). The primary objective in using a heat exchanger is to transfer thermal energy from one fluid to another. Two popular types of heat exchangers are parallel flow heat exchanger and counter flow heat exchanger. In parallel flow heat exchanger, both fluids flow in same direction while in counter flow heat exchanger, both fluids flow in opposite direction.

Parallel flow Heat Exchanger :

Referring Fig. 9 for parallel flow heat exchanger, we may write:

$$q = \dot{m}_h C_{ph}\left(T_{hi} - T_{ho}\right) = \dot{m}_c C_{pc}\left(T_{co} - T_{ci1}\right)$$

where $\dot{m}_h$ and $\dot{m}_c$ are mass flow rate of hot and cold fluid respectively, C_{ph} is the specific heat of the hot fluid, C_{pc} is the specific heat of the cold fluid, T_{hi} and T_{ho} are the inlet and outlet temperature of hot fluid, T_{ci} and T_{co} are inlet and outlet temperature of cold fluid respectively.

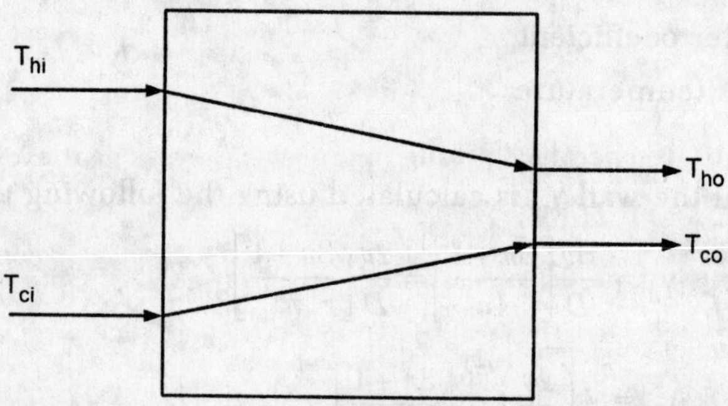

FIG. 5.9 Temperature profile for parallel current heat exchanger

This equation is useful to determine the inlet and exit temperatures of the two fluid streams, and to determine the mass flow rate of either fluid stream, provided all other conditions are known

Also, $$q = UA\Delta t_{LMTD}$$

$$\Delta T_{LMTD} = \frac{\left(T_{hi} - T_{ci}\right) - \left(T_{ho} - T_{co}\right)}{\ln \dfrac{T_{hi} - T_{ci}}{T_{ho} - T_{co}}}$$

$$\Delta T_{LMTD} = \frac{\Delta T_i - \Delta T_o}{\ln \dfrac{\Delta T_i}{\Delta T_o}}$$

where $\Delta Ti = T_{hi} - T_{ci}$

$\Delta To = T_{ho} - T_{co}$

The concept of a logarithmic mean temperature difference is useful in the analysis of heat exchangers.

Counter Flow Heat Exchanger:

Referring Fig. 10, the heat balance for cold (*c*) and hot (*h*) fluid for counter flow heat exchanger may be written as:

$$q = \dot{m}_h Cph\left(T_{hi} - T_{h0}\right) = \dot{m}_c Cpc\left(T_{ci} - T_{co}\right)$$

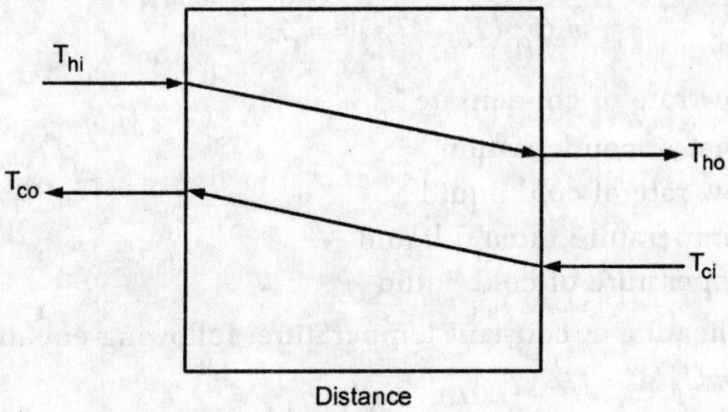

FIG. 5.10 Temperature profile for counter current heat exchanger

Also, $q = UA\Delta t_{LMTD}$

The total heat transfer area for *n* number of circular tubes may be given as:

$$A = n\pi DL$$

where L = length of tube
d = diameter of tube
n = number of tubes

$$\Delta T_{LMTD} = \frac{\left(T_{hi} - T_{co}\right) - \left(T_{ho} - T_{ci}\right)}{\ln \dfrac{T_{hi} - T_{co}}{T_{ho} - T_{ci}}}$$

$$\Delta T_{LMTD} = \frac{\Delta T_i - \Delta T_o}{\ln \dfrac{\Delta T_i}{\Delta T_o}}$$

where $\Delta T_i = T_{hi} - T_{co}$
$\Delta T_o = Th_o - T_{ci}$

The *LMTD* is a logarithmic average of the temperature difference between the hot and cold streams at each end of the exchanger. The *LMTD* approach to H.E analysis is useful when inlet and outlet temperature are known

When $\Delta Ti = \Delta To$, then $\Delta T_{LMTD} = 0$

Under this situation, arithmetic mean temperature difference (*AMTD*) is used which is as given below:

$$AMTD = \frac{\Delta T_i + \Delta T_o}{2}$$

When one of the two fluids undergoes phase change (at constant temperature and pressure) as in condensation and evaporation, ΔT_{LMTD} is same for parallel flow and counter flow.

For a condenser, the following heat balance equation can be used:

$$q = m_c C_{pc}\left(T_{c0} - T_{ci}\right) = \dot{m}_s \lambda$$

where, $\dot{m}_s$ = mass flow rate of condensate

λ = latent heat of condensation

$\dot{m}_c$ = mass flow rate of cold liquid

T_{co} = outlet temperature of cold liquid

T_{ci} = inlet temperature of cold liquid

For cooling or heating at constant temperature, following equation can be used:

$$\dot{m} C_p \Delta t = UA\Delta T_{LMTD}$$

Effectiveness of a Heat Exchanger:

It is defined as the ratio of actual rate of heat transfer to the maximum possible rate of heat transfer for a given heat exchanger.

Effectiveness of heat exchanger is given by:

$$\text{heat exchanger effectiveness} = \frac{\text{actual heat transfer}}{\text{maximum possible heat transfer}}$$

The actual heat transfer may be computed by calculating either the energy lost by the hot fluid or the energy gained by the cold fluid.

For parallel heat exchanger:

Heat lost by hot fluid = heat gained by cold fluid

$$\dot{m}_h C_{ph}\left(T_{hi} - T_{h0}\right) = \dot{m}_c C_{pc}\left(T_{c0} - T_{ci}\right) = q$$

Or
$$q = C_h\left(t_{hi} - t_{ho}\right) = C_c\left(t_{co} - t_{ci}\right)$$

$$q_{\max} = C_{\min}\left(t_{hi} - t_{ci}\right)$$

$$\varepsilon_p = \frac{C_h\left(t_{hi} - t_{ho}\right)}{C_{\min}\left(t_{hi} - t_{ci}\right)} = \frac{C_c\left(t_{co} - t_{ci}\right)}{C_{\min}\left(t_{hi} - t_{ci}\right)}$$

$$= \frac{1 - \exp\left(-\frac{UA}{C_{\min}}\left(1 + \frac{C_{\min}}{C_{\max}}\right)\right)}{1 + \frac{C_{\min}}{C_{\max}}}$$

When temperature of fluids leaving the heat exchanger is not known, then heat exchanger effectiveness (ε) is used.

For counter flow heat exchanger:

$$q = \dot{m}_h C_{ph}\left(T_{hi} - T_{h0}\right) = \dot{m}_c C_{pc}\left(T_{ci} - T_{co}\right)$$

$$\varepsilon_c = \frac{C_h\left(t_{hi} - t_{ho}\right)}{C_{\min}\left(t_{hi} - t_{ci}\right)} = \frac{Cc\left(t_{co} - t_{ci}\right)}{C_{\min}\left(t_{hi} - t_{ci}\right)}$$

$$\varepsilon_c = \frac{1 - \exp\left(-\frac{UA}{C_{\min}}\left(1 - \frac{C_{\min}}{C_{\max}}\right)\right)}{1 - \frac{C_{\min}}{C_{\max}}\exp\left(\frac{UA}{C_{\min}}\left(1 - \frac{C_{\min}}{C_{\max}}\right)\right)}$$

The ration $\frac{UA}{C_{\min}}$ is termed as *NTU* (Number of Transfer Unit).

$$NTU = \frac{UA}{C_{\min}}$$

The *NTU* is indicative of the size of a heat exchanger.

The effectiveness of a countercurrent heat exchanger is:

$$\varepsilon_c = \frac{\frac{UA}{C_{\min}}}{1 + \frac{UA}{C_{\min}}} = \frac{NTU}{1 + NTU}$$

Heat Balance for Mixing Chamber in Direct Heat Exchanger :

Milk is sterilized at Ultra High Temperature in direct heat exchanger where steam and milk is mixed (Fig. 5.11). Referring Fig. 5.10 we may write the heat balance equation as given below:

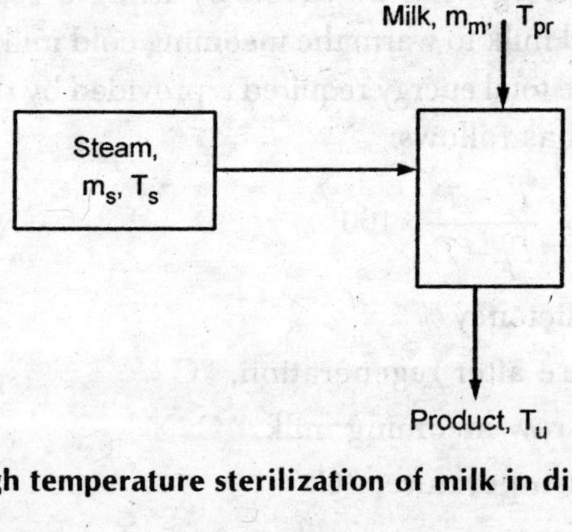

FIG. 5.11 Ultra high temperature sterilization of milk in direct heat exchanger

Heat in with milk and steam = Heat out with milk and condensate

$$\dot{m}_m C_m T_{pr} + \dot{m}_s H_s = \dot{m}_m C_m T_u + \dot{m}_s C_c T_u$$

Solving this, we have the following equation:

$$\frac{\dot{m}_s}{\dot{m}_m} = \frac{C_m\left(T_u - T_{pr}\right)}{H_s - C_c T_u}$$

where T_u = ultra high temperature (UHT) sterilization temperature of milk

T_{pr} = preheated temperature of milk

$\dot{m}_m$ = mass flow rate of milk

$\dot{m}_s$ = mass flow rate of steam

H_s = enthalpy of steam

C_m = specific heat of milk

C_c = specific heat of condensate

This equation can be used for calculation of mass flow rate of steam used in direct heat exchanger for heating of any liquid foods.

Heat Balance for Expansion Vessel in Direct Heat Exchanger:

In expansion vessel both milk and condensate gets separated. The heat balance equation may be written as:

$$\dot{m}_m C_m T_u + \dot{m}_s C_c T_u = \dot{m}_m C_m T_e + \dot{m}_s H_{ve}$$

Dividing both sides by $\dot{m}_m C_m$ we have:

$$T_e = T_u + \frac{\dot{m}_s C_c}{\dot{m}_m C_m} T_u - \frac{\dot{m}_s H_{ve}}{\dot{m}_m C_m}$$

where T_e = temperature of milk in expansion chamber

H_{ve} = enthalpy of saturated vapour after expansion at temperature T_e

Regeneration Efficiency:

Heating and cooling energy can be saved by using a regenerator which utilizes the heat content of the pasteurized milk to warm the incoming cold milk. The regeneration efficiency is a measure of how much of the total energy required is provided by regeneration. The regeneration efficiency may be calculated as follows:

$$\eta_{reg} = \frac{T_r - T_i}{T_p - T_i} \times 100$$

where η_{reg} = regenerative efficiency %

T_r = milk temperature after regeneration, °C

T_i = temperature of raw incoming milk, °C

T_p = pasteurization temperature, °C

Heat Transfer in Agitated Vessel:

Correlation for the heat transfer coefficient from agitated Newtonian liquid inside the vessel to the jacket walls of the vessel have the following form:

$$\frac{hD_t}{k} = a\left(\frac{D_a^2 \rho N}{\mu}\right)^b \left(\frac{\mu C_p}{k}\right)^{1/3} \left(\frac{\mu}{\mu_w}\right)^m$$

where D_t = inside diameter of vessel

D_a = diameter of agitator

k = thermal conductivity of liquid

N = rotational speed

ρ = density of liquid

C_p = specific heat of liquid

μ = viscosity of liquid

All liquid physical properties are evaluated at the bulk liquid temperature except μw which is evaluated at wall temperature T_w.

Radiation Heat Transfer:

Radiation heat transfer is the transfer of heat energy by electromagnetic radiation. Radiation often occurs in combination with conduction and convection. Radiation operates independently of the medium through which it occurs and depends upon the relative temperatures, geometric arrangements and surface structures of the materials that are emitting or absorbing heat. Electromagnetic radiation can be visualized as waves traveling at the speed of light. The two prominent characters of the wave are the wavelength (λ) and frequency (ν). The frequency is related to wavelength by the following expression:

$$\nu = \frac{c}{\lambda}$$

where c is the speed of light, approximately equal to 3×10^8 m/s in vacuum. The wavelength is measured in units of length, and the frequency is given in cycles per second (hertz, Hz).

The propagation of thermal radiation takes place in the form of discrete quanta each quantum having an energy of $E = h\nu$ where h = Plank's constant and ν is frequency. The value of h is 6.625×10^{-34} J . s.

Radiation Properties:

When radiant energy strikes on a material, part of the radiation is reflected, some part is absorbed and rest is transmitted. The fraction of the radiation falling on a body that is reflected is called the reflectivity (ρ). The fraction that is absorbed is called the absorptivity (α). The fraction that is transmitted is called the *transmissivty* (τ). Figure 5.12 shows these processes graphically.

$$\text{reflectivity} = \frac{\text{reflected radiation}}{\text{incident radiation}} = \rho$$

$$\text{absorptivity} = \frac{\text{absorbed radiation}}{\text{incident radiation}} = \alpha$$

$$\text{transmissivity} = \frac{\text{transmitted radiation}}{\text{incident radiation}} = \tau$$

The sum of absorptivity, reflectivity and transmissivity of a surface is always equal to one i.e.

$$\alpha + \rho + \tau = 1$$

and

$$0 \le \rho \le 1$$
$$0 \le \alpha \le 1$$
$$0 \le \tau \le 1$$

For most cases in process engineering:

$$\alpha + \rho = 1$$

A gray body is one for which $\alpha = \varepsilon$ where

$$0 < \alpha < 1 \quad \text{and} \quad 0 < \varepsilon < 1$$

Real bodies are normally approximated as gray bodies.

For an opaque body, $\alpha + \rho = 1$

For an gray body, $\varepsilon + \rho = 1$

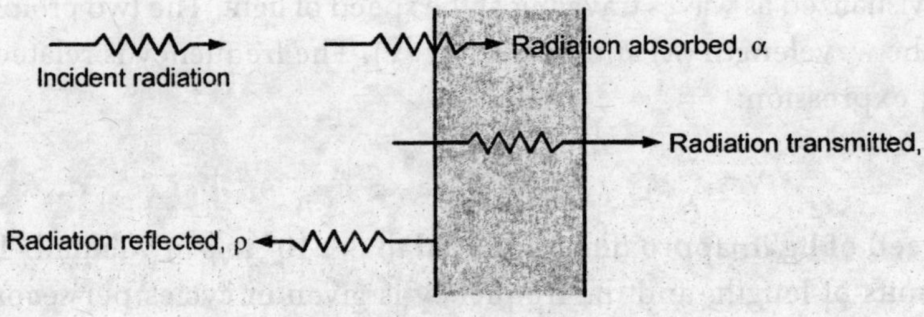

FIG.5.12 Radiation surface properties

The irradiance and radiosity are expressed as:

$$\text{irradiation} = \frac{\text{energy incident on surface}}{\text{area} \times \text{time}}$$

$$\text{radiosity} = \frac{\text{energy leaving surface}}{\text{area} \times \text{time}}$$

Kirchoff's Law:

A body at constant temperature is in equilibrium with its surroundings, and the amount of energy absorbed by radiation is exactly the same as that emitted. Thus, the absorptivity of a surface (α) is exactly the same as the emissivity (ε)

i.e. $\alpha = \varepsilon$

This relation holds good for any black or non-black solid surface. A brightly polished surface has a low absorptivity and low emissivity.

Wein's Displacement Law:

The wavelength for maximum energy flux from a body shifts with a change in temperature. The product of the wavelength for maximum flux intensity and absolute temperature is a constant and is given by:

$$\lambda_{max} \cdot T = 2.884 \times 10^{-3} \ m.K$$

Stefan-Boltzmann Law:

The total energy emitted by a gray body, regardless of the wavelengths, is given by:

$$q = \varepsilon A \sigma T^4$$

where ε is the emissivity of the body, A is the surface area, T is the temperature, and σ is the Stefan-Boltzmann constant, equal to 5.67 × 10–8 W/m^{2}K^4.

Emissivity is a material property, ranging from 0 to 1, which measures how much energy a surface can emit with respect to an ideal emitter ($\varepsilon = 1$) at the same temperature.

Black Body:

A body that absorbs all incident radiation is called a ***black body***. The absorbtivity of a black body is unity and its reflectivity and transmissivity are both zero.

The ratio of the emissive power of a surface to that of a black body is called ***emissivity*** ε and it is 1 for a black body. The substances that have emissivity of less than 1 are called ***grey bodies*** when emissivity is independent of the wavelength. All real materials have an emissivity less than 1.

Black Body Radiation:

Emissive power is defined as the total emitted radiant thermal energy leaving a surface per unit time per unit area. The emissive power of a perfect black body with an emissivity 1 depends on 4th power of its absolute temperature and is given by:

$$q = A \sigma T^4$$

where q = heat flow rate, W
T = absolute temperature, K
A = surface area of a body, m^2

Radiation to a Small Body from Surrounding:

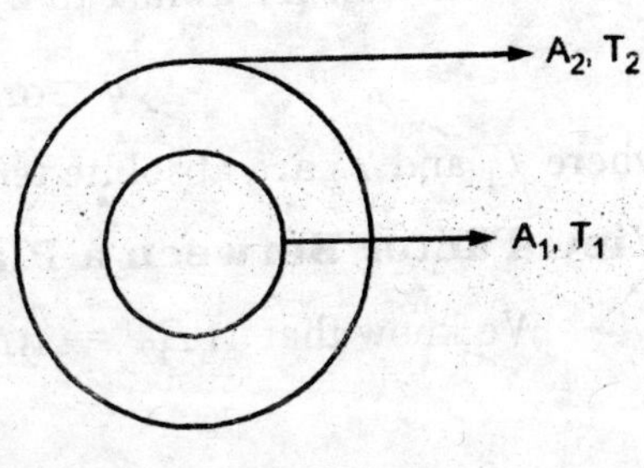

When a relatively small body completely surrounded by a surface at a uniform temperature, the net exchange of heat be radiation is given by:

$$q = \sigma \varepsilon A_1 \left(T_1^4 - T_2^4\right)$$

where A_1 is surface area of the smaller gray body (m^2), ε is emissivity of the body, T_1 is absolute temperature of the body (K) and T_2 is the absolute temperature of the surrounding (K). This equation can be used to calculate rate of heat transfer in infrared ovens or in other similar situations.

Radiation View Factor :

It is defined as the fraction of energy reaching a particular surface compared to the total energy emitted from another surface. Radiation shape factor is also called view factor, angle factor and configuration factor.

Radiation shape factor (F_{mn}) = fraction of energy leaving surface m and arriving at surface n.

Similarly,

$F_{1\text{-}2}$ = fraction of energy leaving surface 1 which reaches surface 2

$F_{2\text{-}1}$ = fraction of energy leaving surface 2 which reaches surface 1

If surface A_1 can see only surface A_2, the $F_{12} = 1$

If surface A_1 sees a number of surfaces A_2, A_3, ... and all the surface form an enclosure then the enclosure relationship is $F_{11} + F_{12} + F_{13} + ... = 1$

If a surface A_1 can not see itself, the $F_{11} = 0$.

View factor F_{12} for a small surface A_1 completely enclosed by a large surface A_2 is 1 since all the radiation leaving A_1 is intercepted by A_2.

Reciprocity Relation:

The reciprocity relation in radiation heat transfer is given by:

$$A_1 F_{12} = A_2 F_{21}$$

Radiation heat transfer from surface with area A_1, emissivity ε_1 and temperature $T_1(K)$ to large enclosure at temperature T_2 (K) is:

$$q_{12} = \sigma A_1 \varepsilon_1 \left(T_1^4 - T_2^4\right)$$

where surface 1 is relatively small compared to surface 2.

When two perfectly two black surfaces 1 and 2 are exchanging radiation between them, the net heat transfer from 1 to 2 is given by:

$$q = \sigma A_1 \left(T_1^4 - T_2^4\right)$$

where T_1 and T_2 are absolute temperature of two black bodies.

View Factor Between a Plane A_1 Covered by a Hemisphere A_2:

We know that $A_1 F_{12} = A_2 F_{21}$

Since surface A_1 sees only A_2 hence $F_{12} = 1$

Area of plane $A_1 = \pi r^2$

Area of hemisphere $A_2 = 2\pi r^2$ where r is radius of plane and hemisphere.

$$A_1F_{12} = A_2F_{21}$$

Or, $$F_{21} = \frac{F_{12}A_1}{A_2} = \frac{1 \times \pi r^2}{2\pi r^2} = \frac{1}{2}$$

For surface A_1, we may write: $F_{11} + F_{12} = 1$

$$F_{11} = 1 - 1 = 0$$

For surface A_2, we may write: $F_{22} + F_{21} = 1$

$$F_{22} = 1 - 0.5 = 0.5$$

View Factor for Gray Bodies:

Radiation heat transfer from plane 1 to plane 2 is:

$$q_{12} = \sigma A_1 F_{12} \varepsilon_1 \left(T_1^4 - T_2^4\right)$$

$$F_{12} = \frac{1}{\frac{1}{\bar{F}_{12}} + \frac{A_1}{A_2}\left(\frac{1}{\varepsilon_2} - 1\right) + \left(\frac{1}{\varepsilon_1} - 1\right)}$$

where A_1 and A_2 are two gray bodies having emissivities ε_1 and ε_2 respectively.

$\bar{F}_{12}$ = interchange factor

F_{12} = overall interchange factor

When refractory (radiating) walls are not present, then $\bar{F}_{12} = F_{12}$

$\bar{F}_{12}$ is used for two black surfaces A_1 and A_2 connected by refractory walls.

When A_2 is very large as compared to A_1, the $A_1/A_2 = 0$

The view factor for an small cold object having an area A_1, emissivity ε_1 at temperature T_1 placed in a warm room with walls at temperature T_2 and emissivity $\varepsilon_2 = \varepsilon_1$.

View Factor for Infinite Parallel Black Planes:

Net radiation from plane 1 to 2 when all radiation from 1 to is intercepted by 2 is:

$$q_{12} = F_{12}\sigma A_1 \left(T_1^4 - T_2^4\right)$$

Similarly, $$q_{12} = F_{21}\sigma A_2 \left(T_1^4 - T_2^4\right)$$

Where F_{12} is view factor or geometric view factor which is the fraction of radiation leaving 1 and intercepted by 2 and F_{12} is view factor or geometric view factor which is the fraction of radiation leaving 2 and intercepted by 1.

In case of parallel planes, $F_{12} = F_{21} = 1$ hence view factor is omitted.

Radiation Heat Transfer between two Infinite Gray Parallel Planes:

Radiation heat transfer between two infinite parallel planes from 1 to 2 is:

$$q_{12} = \frac{\sigma A_1 \left(T_1^4 - T_2^4\right)}{\frac{1}{\varepsilon_1} + \frac{1}{\varepsilon_2} - 1}$$

where A_1 = area of plane 1

T_1 = temperature of plane1

ε_1 = emissivity of plane 1

T_2 = temperature of plane 2

ε_2 = emissivity of plane 2

The view factor for two very large (infinite) parallel gray plane surfaces is:

$$F_{1-2} = \frac{1}{\frac{1}{\varepsilon_1} + \frac{1}{\varepsilon_2} - 1}$$

For black bodies, $\varepsilon_1 = \varepsilon_2 = 1$ and hence the above equation becomes:

$$q_{12} = \sigma A_1 \left(T_1^4 - T_2^4\right)$$

Radiation Heat Transfer between two Infinite Gray Concentric Cylinders:

Radiation heat transfer between two infinite gray concentric cylinders is:

$$q = \frac{\sigma A_1 \left(T_1^4 - T_2^4\right)}{\frac{1}{\varepsilon_1} + \frac{A_1}{A_2}\left(\frac{1}{\varepsilon_2} - 1\right)}$$

Since, $A = 2\pi r L = \pi d L$

Hence,
$$q = \frac{\sigma A_1 \left(T_1^4 - T_2^4\right)}{\frac{1}{\varepsilon_1} + \frac{r_1}{r_2}\left(\frac{1}{\varepsilon_2} - 1\right)}$$

Or,
$$q = \frac{\sigma A_1 \left(T_1^4 - T_2^4\right)}{\frac{1}{\varepsilon_1} + \frac{d_1}{d_2}\left(\frac{1}{\varepsilon_2} - 1\right)}$$

where d_1 and d_2 are diameters of two concentric cylinders respectively.

Radiation Heat Transfer between two Infinite Gray Concentric Spheres:

Radiation heat transfer between two concentric spheres is:

$$q = \frac{\sigma A_1\left(T_1^4 - T_2^4\right)}{\frac{1}{\varepsilon_1} + \frac{A_1}{A_2}\left(\frac{1}{\varepsilon_2} - 1\right)}$$

Since, $A = 4\pi r^2$

Hence, $$q = \frac{\sigma A_1\left(T_1^4 - T_2^4\right)}{\frac{1}{\varepsilon_1} + \left(\frac{r_1}{r_2}\right)^2\left(\frac{1}{\varepsilon_2} - 1\right)}$$

where r_1 and r_2 are radius of two concentric spheres respectively.

In all above cases, $F_{12} = 1$

Combined Radiation and Convection Heat Transfer:

Heat transfer by a combination of convection and radiation is very common. For example, in a baking oven, heat is transferred to the product both from hot air by convection and from hot bodies by radiation.

Rate of heat transfer by convection is:

$$q_c = A_1 h_c \left(T_1 - T_2\right)$$

where h_c = natural or forced convection heat transfer coefficient

T_1 = temperature of surface

T_2 = temperature of enclosure

Rate of heat transfer by radiation is:

$$q_r = A_1 h_r \left(T_1 - T_2\right)$$

where h_r = radiation heat transfer coefficient

Hence total rate of heat transfer = $q = q_c + q_r = \left(h_c + h_r\right) A_1 \left(T_1 - T_2\right)$

Comparing equation $q_r = \sigma \varepsilon_1 A_1 \left(T_1^4 - T_2^4\right)$ and $q_r = A_1 h_r \left(T_1 - T_2\right)$ we have:

$$h_r = \varepsilon\sigma \frac{T_1^4 - T_2^4}{T_1 - T_2}$$

where h_r is radiation heat transfer coefficient.

Unsteady (Transient) State Heat Transfer:

The governing equation for unsteady-state heat transfer may be written as:

$$\frac{\partial T}{\partial t} = \frac{k}{\rho Cp}\left[\frac{\partial^2 T}{\partial x^2} + \frac{\partial^2 T}{\partial y^2} + \frac{\partial^2 T}{\partial z^2}\right]$$

where t = time, s

ρC_p = thermal storage capacity, J/m^3 K

$$\frac{k}{\rho Cp} = \alpha = \text{thermal diffusivity} = \frac{\text{conducting ability}}{\text{storage capacity}}, \ \text{m}^2/\text{s}$$

This equation represents Fourier's second law of heat transfer. The rate of change of temperature with time at any position within a solid conducting heat is proportional to the second derivative of the temperature with respect to distance at that particular point.

Lumped System Analysis:

A common approximation in transient conduction, which may be used whenever heat conduction within an object is much faster than heat conduction across the boundary of the object, is Lumped system analysis. Lumped system analysis is applicable for situation when Biot number, Bi is less than 0.1. One example is of a hot steel ball immersed in a cool pan of water. The governing equation is:

$$\ln\frac{T_m - T}{T_m - T_0} = -\frac{hAt}{V\rho Cp}$$

where T_m = cooling or heating medium temperature

The quantity $\frac{\rho CpV}{hA}$ is called time constant of the system because it has the dimension of time.

Some useful dimensional numbers relevant to unsteady state heat transfer are presented below:

Biot number **:** The ratio of the internal resistance to heat transfer in solid to the external resistance to heat transfer in the fluid is defined as Biot number.

$$Bi = \frac{\text{internal heat transfer resistance}}{\text{external heat transfer resistance}} = \frac{hL}{k}$$

where k is thermal conductivity of solid.

$$L = \text{characteristic dimension} = \frac{\text{volume}}{\text{surface area}} = \frac{V}{A}$$

The characteristic length depends on the shape of the system.

For a sphere having radius (r) and diameter (d), characteristic dimension is given by:

$$\frac{V_{sphere}}{A_{sphere}} = \frac{\frac{4}{3}\pi r^3}{4\pi r^2} = \frac{r}{3} = \frac{d}{6}$$

For a long cylinder having radius (r) and diameter (d), characteristic dimension is given by:

$$\frac{V_{cylinder}}{A_{cylinder}} = \frac{\pi r^2 h}{2\pi rh} = \frac{r}{2} = \frac{d}{4}$$

For a long square rod of thickness t and length l, characteristic dimension is given by:

$$L = \frac{V}{A} = \frac{t^2 l}{4(lt)} = \frac{t}{4}$$

High Biot number greater than 40 indicates that external resistance is negligible and Biot number less than 0.2 indicate that internal resistance is negligible.

Lumped thermal capacitance is given by:

$$C_L = \rho C_p V \text{ where } V \text{ is volume of body.}$$

The SI unit is J/K.

Fourier number **:** Fourier number is the ratio of rate of conduction of heat across a characteristic length to the rate of storage of heat in a volume. The Fourier number (Fo) is defined as follows:

$$Fo = \frac{\text{rate of heat conduction}}{\text{rate of heat storage}}$$

Mathematically, $$Fo = \frac{\alpha t}{L^2} = \frac{kt}{\rho C_p L^2}$$

where L is a characteristic length of the system and t is time. The characteristic length is the shortest distance from the surface to the centre of the object and is equal to one half of the thickness of a plate or slab and equal to radius of a sphere or cylinder.

Fourier number can be expressed in term of Graetz number as follows:

$$Fo = \frac{\alpha t}{r^2} = \frac{\alpha t}{(D/2)^2} = \frac{4\alpha t}{D^2} = \frac{4kt}{\rho C p D^2} = \frac{4kL}{\rho v C p D^2} = \frac{\pi}{Gz}$$

where r is radius and D is diameter of tube and L is length.

Time of Cooling and Heating of Liquid in a Steam Jacketed Vessel (Batch Process):

Predicting the heating and cooling times (batch process) involves unsteady state heat transfer and illustrates the exponential nature of the heat transfer process. The heating time is determined by equating the rate of heat transfer from the heating medium to the rate at which the fluid absorbs energy. Thus:

$$UA(T_h - T) = mC_p \frac{dT}{dt}$$

On integration gives:

$$t = \frac{mC_p}{UA} \ln\left[\frac{(T_h - T_i)}{(T_h - T_f)}\right]$$

Where m is mass (kg), C_p is specific heat (J/kgK), A is surface area (m^2), U is overall heat transfer coefficient (W/m^{2}K), t is the heating time (s) required to raise the temperature from T_i (initial temperature) to T_f (final temperature) using a heating medium temperature T_h.

This equation can be written separately for both heating and cooling of liquid foods in a pan as follows:

$$t_c = \frac{mCp}{UA}\ln\frac{T_i - T_c}{T_f - T_c} \quad \text{where } t_c \text{ is cooling time.}$$

$$t_h = \frac{mCp}{UA}\ln\frac{T_h - T_i}{T_h - T_f} \quad \text{where } t_h \text{ is heating time.}$$

where m = mass, kg

C_p = specific heat of fluid, J/kg °C

T_i = initial temperature, °C

T_f = final temperature, °C

T_c = temperature of cooling medium temperature, °C

T_h = temperature of heating medium temperature, °C

A = surface area, m^2

U = Over all heat transfer coefficient, W/m^2 °C

These equations are also applicable for low Biot number (negligible internal resistance to heat transfer).

The heat transfer area and volume for hemispherical steam jacketed vessel may be computed as:

$$A = \frac{\pi d^2}{2} \text{ and } V = \frac{4}{3}\pi r3 \times \frac{1}{2} = \frac{4}{3}\pi \times \frac{d^3}{8} \times \frac{1}{2} = \frac{\pi d^3}{12}$$

where r is radius and d is diameter.

Equation for time of heating or cooling of slab of known thickness from both sides by a medium at constant surface temperature as:

$$t = \frac{1}{\alpha}\left(\frac{2x}{\pi}\right)^2 \ln\frac{8(T_s - T_0)}{\pi^2 (T_s - T)}$$

where T_s = constant average temperature of surface of slab

T_0 = initial temperature of slab

T = temperature after time t

α = thermal diffusivity

x = one-half slab thickness when slab is heated from both

x = slab thickness when slab is heated from one side only

Chapter 6

Mass Transfer

Mass Transfer:

Mass transfer is a very important phenomenon in food process engineering. It is concerned with the movement of material in fluid system both in gases and liquids under the influence of a concentration gradient. In food processing, mass transfer occurs in distillation, drying, absorption, liquid-liquid extraction, adsorption and membrane process. This chapter describes the governing equations relevant to mass transfer.

Basic Transport Equation:

The rate of transport (i.e. quantity transported per unit time) is proportional to the driving force and inversely proportional to the resistance of the medium to the transport. For mass transfer we may write:

$$\text{mass transfer rate} = \frac{\text{driving force}}{\text{resistance}}$$

For mass transfer by molecular diffusion, the driving force is the concentration difference. Molecular diffusion or molecular transport can be defined as the transfer of individual molecules through a fluid by means of the random individual movements of molecules.

Fick's Law for Molecular Diffusion:

The basic mechanism of mass transfer is the movement of molecules. The law which describes the molecular diffusion is known as Fick's law which is given by:

$$N_{az} = -D_{AB}\frac{dC_A}{dz}$$

where N_{Az} = molar flux of component A in z direction, kgmole/m^{2}s

D_{AB} = molecular diffusivity of molecule A in B, m^2/s

C_A = concentration of A, kgmole/m^3

z = distance along direction of diffusion, m

The molar concentration of species A (CA) is defined as the number of moles of A present per unit volume of the mixture. Applying ideal gas law, the molar concentration is given by:

$$C_A = p_A/RT$$

where p_A = partial pressure of the species A in the mixture
T = absolute temperature
R = gas constant.

The mole fraction for liquid or solid mixtures (x_A) and for gaseous mixtures (y_A) are the molar concentrations of species A divided by the total molar concentration and are related as:

$$x_A = \frac{C_A}{C} \quad \text{(For solids and liquids)}$$

$$y_A = \frac{C_A}{C} \quad \text{(For gases)}$$

For a gaseous mixture that obeys the ideal gas law, the mole fraction (y_A) can be written in terms of pressures as:

$$y_A = \frac{C_A}{C} = \frac{p_A}{P}$$

Molecular Diffusion of Gases:

Equation of flux of A from point1 to point 2 is expressed as:

$$N_{Az} = -D_{AB}\frac{dC_A}{dz} = -D_{AB}\frac{C_{A2}-C_{A1}}{z_2-z_1} = D_{AB}\frac{C_{A1}-C_{A2}}{z_2-z_1}$$

Since we may write: $C_{A1} = p_{A1}/RT$ and $C_{A2} = p_{A2}/RT$

Hence,
$$N_{Az} = \frac{D_{AB}(p_{A1}-p_{A2})}{RT(z_2-z_1)}$$

Similarly equation of flux of B from point 2 to point 1 is given by:

$$N_{Bz} = D_{BA}\frac{dC_B}{dz} = D_{BA}\frac{C_{B1}-C_{B2}}{z_1-z_2} = D_{BA}\frac{(p_{B1}-p_{B2})}{RT(z_1-z_2)}$$

where D_{AB} and D_{BA} are the diffusion coefficients of A in B and B in A respectively.

Equimolar Counter Diffusion in Gas Phase:

For equimolar counter diffusion in gases,

$$D_{AB} = D_{BA} \text{ and } N_A = -N_B$$

The diffusivity coefficient D_{AB} is for A diffusing in B and D_{BA} for B diffusing into A.

N_A = molar flux of component A, kg mol/s m^2
N_B = molar flux of component B, kg mol/s m^2

Diffusion of Liquid (*A*) Through Stagnant Non-diffusing Air (B):

This type of situation comes when water (A) kept in a container evaporates into stagnant air (B). The equation of flux may be written as:

$$N_A = \frac{D_{AB}P}{RT(z_2 - z_1)} \ln \frac{(P - p_{A2})}{(P - P_{A1})}$$

where T = absolute temperature
P = total pressure (absolute)
$z_2 - z_1$ = path length
p_{A1} & p_{A2} = partial pressure of component 'A' at point 1 and 2

This equation can be expressed in another form as follows:

Since, $P = p_{A1} + p_{B1} = p_{A2} + p_{B2}$

Hence, $p_{B1} = P - p_{A1}$

$p_{B2} = P - p_{A2}$

A logarithmic mean partial pressure of *B* is defined as:

$$P_{BM} = \frac{p_{B2} - p_{B1}}{\ln \frac{p_{B2}}{p_{B1}}} = \frac{p_{A1} - p_{A2}}{\ln \frac{p - p_{A2}}{p - p_{A1}}}$$

Hence above equation of flux may be written as:

$$N_A = \frac{D_{AB}P}{RT(z_2 - z_1)p_{BM}}(p_{A1} - p_{A2})$$

When the value of p_{B1} and p_{B2} are close to each other, then

$$P_{BM} = (p_{B1} + p_{B2})/2$$

Total amount of water evaporated = mass flux × area × time.

Diffusion in a Tube with Change in Path Length:

Diffusion of water vapour from a tube filled with water to surrounding is an example of this case. Equation for the time t_F for the level to drop from starting point z_0 at $t = 0$ to t_F at $t = t_F$ is given by:

$$N_A = \frac{\rho_A\left(z_F^2 - z_0^2\right)RTP_{BM}}{2M_A D_{AB} P(P_{A1} - P_{A2})}$$

where M_A = molecular weight of component A
p_{A1} & p_{A2} = partial pressure of component 'A' at point 1 and 2
ρ_A = density of component 'A'

Diffusion Through a Varying Cross Sectional Area:

Evaporation of a droplet of liquid is an appropriate example of diffusion through a varying cross sectional area. The equation for the rate of evaporation from a sphere to surrounding medium may be given as:

$$N_A = \frac{D_{AB}P}{RTr_1 p_{BM}}(P_{A1} - P_{A2})$$

where r_1 is original radius of sphere.

The equation for the time for sphere to evaporate completely to the surrounding medium is given as:

$$t_F = \frac{\rho_A r_1^2 RTP_{BM}}{2M_A D_{AB} P(P_{A1} - P_{A2})}$$

Where r_1 is original radius of sphere, ρ_A is the density of the sphere and M_A is the molecular weight.

Molecular diffusion in liquids:

Diffusion of solutes in liquid is important in many industrial processes such as liquid-liquid extraction or solvent extraction.

Diffusion of solute (*A*) through non-diffusing solvent (*B*):

This type of situation comes when solute *A* diffuses and solvent *B* remains stagnant ($N_B = 0$). The equation flux is given by:

$$N_A = \frac{D_{AB} C_{avg}(x_{A1} - x_{A2})}{(z_2 - z_1)x_{BM}}$$

where $C_{avg} = \dfrac{\left(\dfrac{\rho_1}{M_1} + \dfrac{\rho_2}{M_2}\right)}{2}$

and $x_{BM} = \dfrac{x_{B2} - x_{B1}}{\ln \dfrac{x_{B2}}{x_{B1}}}$

where N_A = flux of *A* in kg mol A/s m^2

D_{AB} = diffusivity of *A* in *B* in m^2/s.

C_{avg} = average total concentration of *A* + *B* in kg mol/m^3

M_1 = molecular weight of solution at point 1 in kg mass/kg mol

M_2 = molecular weight at point 2

ρ_1 = average density of solution in kg/m^3 at point 1

ρ_2 = average density of solution in kg/m^3 at point 2

$x_{A1} + x_{B1} = x_{A2} + x_{B2} = 1$

x_{A2} = mole fraction of *A* at point 2

x_{A1} = mole fraction of *A* at point 1

$z_2 - z_1$ = thickness

When x_{B1} and x_{B2} are close to each other, then $x_{BM} = (x_{B1} + x_{B2})/2$

For dilute solution, x_{BM} is close to 1 and c is constant and hence the equation becomes:

$$N_A = \frac{D_{AB}(C_{A1} - C_{A2})}{z_2 - z_1}$$

Mass Transfer by Convection:

For mass transfer by convection, the driving force is the concentration difference expressed in mol/m^3 or mol fraction or pressure, and the resistance R is equal to $1/K_cA$, where K_c is mass transfer coefficient and A is surface area (m^2) perpendicular to the direction of transfer.

Convective Mass Transfer Coefficient:

The equation for mass transfer coefficient is given by:

$$N_A = K_c(C_{A1} - C_{A2})$$

where N_A = molar flux of component A, kg mol/s m^2

K_c = convective mass transfer coefficient, m/s

For gases, it may be written as:

$$N_A = K_G(p_{A1} - p_{A2})$$

where C_{A1} and C_{A2} are concentration through which diffusion occurs, kg mol A/m^3.

The unit of K_G is kg mol/s m^2 Pa.

The mass transfer coefficient is similar to heat transfer coefficient and is a function of the system geometry, fluid properties and flow velocity.

The convective mass transfer coefficient may also be expressed in another form. The expression for convective mass transfer coefficient K_m is defined as:

$$K_m = \frac{\dot{m}_B}{A(C_{As} - C_{A\infty})}$$

where K_m is the rate of mass transfer per unit area per unit concentration differences, $\dot{m}_B$ is the mass flow rate (kg/s), C_{As} is concentration under saturated condition, $C_{A\infty}$ is concentration of water in free stream of air (kg/m^3), A is area, m^2. The unit of K_m is m/s.

This equation can be used to calculate evaporation rate of water from a tray full of water.

$$A = \text{area} = \text{length} \times \text{width (in case of rectangular tray)}$$

The mass transport due to convection process may be expressed as:

$$\dot{m}_B = \frac{K_m A M_B}{RT}(p_{B1} - p_{B2})$$

where p_{B1} = vapour pressure of water at saturation

p_{B2} = partial pressure of water vapour in air

R = 8314.4 m^{3}Pa/kg mol K

M_B = molecular weight of water = 18

T = absolute temperature of water

The partial pressure of water vapour in air can be computed by:

$$p_{B2} = \frac{RH \times p_{B1}}{100}$$

where RH is relative humidity in percentage.

This expression can be used to estimate the water evaporated from a tray of water.

Following equation can be used to compute convective transport of water vapour in air based on humidity ratio gradient in the region of convective mass transport:

$$\dot{m}_B = \frac{K_m A M_B P}{0.622 RT}(H_1 - H_2)$$

where A = area, m^2

P = total pressure, 101.325 kPa

R = 8314.4 m^3Pa/kg mol K

M_B = molecular weight of water = 18

T = absolute temperature of water, K

H_1 = humidity ratio of water vapor at water surface

H_2 = humidity ratio of water vapor in air

Relationship Between Mass Transfer Coefficients:

Mass transfer coefficient for steady state diffusion of A while B is stagnant and non-diffusing:

$$N_A = \frac{D_{AB}P}{RTzP_{BM}}(p_{A1} - p_{A2}) = k_g(P_{A1} - P_{A2})$$

$$\Rightarrow \quad kg = \frac{D_{AB}P}{RTzP_{BM}}$$

$$N_A = \frac{D_{AB}c_{av}}{zc_{BM}}(c_{A1} - c_{A2}) = k_c(c_{A1} - c_{A2})$$

$$\Rightarrow \quad k_c = \frac{D_{AB}c_{av}}{zc_{BM}}$$

The unit of mass transfer coefficient k_g and k_c are kg mol/m^2 s Pa and m/s respectively.

Correlation for Mass Transfer Coefficient:

The film mass transfer coefficient can be correlated with physical properties and process variables in a manner which is analogous to that for heat transfer. The relevant dimensionless groups used in mass transfer are Sh, Re and Sc.

The most commonly used equation for predicting mass transfer coefficient is of the form:

For forced convection:

$$Sh = f(Re, Sc)$$

For natural convection:

$$Sh = f\ (Gr, Sc)$$

Schmidt number **:** (Sc) is the ratio of kinematic viscosity (momentum diffusivity) to mass diffusivity. This number is analogous to Prandtl number in convection heat transfer.

$$Sc = \frac{\text{momentum diffusivty}}{\text{mass diffusivity}} = \frac{\text{thickness of hydrodynamic layer}}{\text{thickness of mass transfer boundary layer}}$$

Mathematically, $$Sc = \frac{\nu}{D_{AB}} = \frac{\mu}{\rho D_{AB}}$$

where μ = fluid viscosity, Pa s

ρ = fluid density, kg/m^3

Sherwood number **:** Sherwood number is the ratio of convective mass transfer to diffusivity. Sherwood number in mass transfer is equivalent to Nusselt number in heat transfer. Sherwood number is given by:

$$Sh = \frac{K_c D}{D_{AB}}$$

Or, $$Sh = \frac{\text{concentration gradient at boundary}}{\text{concentration gradient across the fluid to the boundary}}$$

where K_c = mass transfer, m/s

D = characteristic dimension, m

D_{AB} = diffusion coefficient, m^2/s

Grashof number **:** Grashof number in mass transfer is given by:

$$Gr_M = \frac{gD^3\ \rho\Delta\rho_A}{\mu^2}$$

where ρ = mass density of fluid

μ = viscosity of fluid

g = acceleration due to gravity

$\Delta\rho_A$ = mass density difference

D = characteristic length

Peclet number **:** The Peclet number, defined as is the ratio of bulk mass transport to diffusive mass transport. Peclet number in mass transfer (P_{eM}) is the product of the Reynolds and Schmidt numbers while Peclet number in heat transfer (P_{eH}) is the product of the Reynolds and Prandtl numbers.

$$Pe_M = Re\ Sc$$

$$Pe_H = RePr$$

Lewis number **:** It is ratio of thermal diffusivity and mass diffusivity. It plays an important role in processes where simultaneous convective transfer of energy and mass occurs. Lewis number is the ratio of Schmidt number and Prandtl number.

$$Le = \frac{\alpha}{D_{AB}} = \frac{k/\rho Cp}{D_{AB}} = \frac{Sc}{Pr}$$

Stanton number in mass transfer is given by:

$$St = \frac{Sh}{ReSc}.$$

Graetz number : The Graetz number is defined as the product of the Reynolds and Schmidt numbers. It includes the effects of forced and free convection.

$$Gz = \frac{\dot{m}}{D_{AB} L \rho} = \frac{\pi}{4} Re \cdot Sc \cdot \frac{D}{L}$$

where, L = length of pipe or tube

Empirical Mass Transfer Equations:

Equation for laminar flow mass transfer in a pipe is given by:

$$Sh = \frac{K_m d}{D_{AB}} = 1.86 \left(\frac{Re \cdot Sc}{L/d} \right)^{1/3} \qquad \text{(for } Re < 10000\text{)}$$

where d is diameter of pipe.

For the turbulent flow inside a tube, the following equation can be used:

$$Sh = \frac{K_m d}{D_{AB}} = 0.023 \left(\frac{\rho v d}{\mu} \right)^{0.8} \left(\frac{\mu}{\rho D_{AB}} \right)^{1/3} \qquad \text{(for } Re > 10000\text{)}$$

where, d = inside diameter

D_{AB} = diffusion coefficient

v = average velocity in the tube

ρ = density of fluid

μ = viscosity of fluid

K_m = mass transfer coefficient

Equation for turbulent flow mass transfer to pipe wall is:

$$Sh = 0.023 Re^{0.8} Sc^{1/3} \left(\frac{\mu}{\mu_w} \right)^{0.14}$$

where μ_w is viscosity at pipe wall.

Mass Transfer for Flow Over Spherical Objects:

The Ranz-Mashall equation is often used to describe mass transfer from free falling droplets produced by atomization in pressure or twin fluid nozzles for example in spray drying. The equation used is:

$$Sh = \frac{K_m d}{D_{AB}} = 2 + 0.6 Re^{0.5} Sc^{0..33}$$

where d is diameter of spherical droplet.

This equation can be used for calculating mass transfer coefficient in case of flow around a single sphere.

Mass Transfer Coefficient for Laminar Flow Past a Flat Plate:

For gas having $Re_L = \frac{\rho L v}{\mu} < 15000$, the following equation can be used:

$$Sh = 0.664 Re_L^{0.5} Sc^{0.33}$$

$$Sh = \frac{K_m L}{D_{AB}}$$

L = length of plate in the direction of gas flow

Turbulent Flow Past a Flat Plate:

The equation used to determine the convective mass transfer coefficient during turbulent flow is:

$$Sh = 0.036 Re_L^{0.8} Sc^{0.33}$$

$$Sh = \frac{K_m L}{D_{AB}}$$

In this equation, the characteristic dimension is the total length of the plate.

Gilliland and Sherwood Equation:

This equation is suitable for air flowing parallel to the surface of a bed of particles.

$$Sh = 0.023 Re^{0.81} Sc^{0.44}$$

The equation for mass transfer to small bubbles is:

$$Sh = 2 + 0.31\, Gr^{1/3}\, Sc^{1/3}$$

Analogies Among Momentum, Heat and Mass Transfer:

The most widely used analogy is the Chilton and Colburn J-factor Analogy which is related as:

$$\frac{f}{2} = J_H = \frac{h}{C_p \rho v} Pr^{2/3} = J_M = \frac{K_c}{v} Sc^{2/3} = \frac{Sh}{\left(Re Sc^{\frac{1}{3}}\right)}$$

where f = Fanning friction factor

K_c = mass transfer coefficient, m/s

v = velocity, m/s

This is most widely used analogy between dimensionless numbers in momentum, mass and heat transfer. The numbers involved in the analogy are Fanning friction factor, Pr, Sh and Sc. We can use the values obtained in any two transfer process to estimate a value for the third process.

The Reynolds analogy for mass transfer is:

$$\frac{K}{v}Sc^{2/3} = \frac{f'}{8}$$

The Reynolds analogy for heat transfer is:

$$\frac{h}{v\rho Cp}Pr^{2/3} = \frac{f'}{8}$$

Or

$$St = \frac{Nu}{Re \times Pr} = \frac{f'}{8}$$

Or

$$Nu = Re.Pr.\frac{f'}{8}$$

where f' is Darcy or Blasius friction factor and h is heat transfer coefficient and K is mass transfer coefficient.

Darcy or Blasius friction factor (f') = 4 × Fanning friction factor (f)

Fluid Friction Analogy:

$$St \cdot Pr^{2/3} = \frac{f'}{8}$$

$$St = \frac{h}{\rho v Cp}$$

Solving these two equations we may write:

$$\frac{h}{K} = \rho Cp\left(\frac{Sc}{Pr}\right)^{2/3} = \rho Cp\left(\frac{\alpha}{D}\right)^{2/3} = \rho Cp(Le)^{2/3}$$

This expression gives a relationship between heat and mass transfer when both heat and mass transfer occur simultaneously.

Prediction of Diffusivity in Liquids:

The diffusivity D of a spherical solute molecule, with a molecular radius r, in a liquid of viscosity μ is given by Einstein-Stokes equation is:

$$D = \frac{kT}{6\pi r\mu}$$

where κ is the Boltzmann's constant (1.38×10^{-23} J/K) and T is the absolute temperature.

Prediction of Diffusivities for Biological Solutes in Liquid:

The equation of prediction of diffusivity for biological solutes in dilute liquid is:

$$D_{AB} = \frac{9.40 \times 10^{-15}\,T}{\mu M_A^{1/3}}$$

where M_A is the molecular weight of the large molecule A, μ is viscosity of solvent and T is absolute temperature.

The diffusivity of a solute in a liquid medium at a particular temperature can also be estimated using following mathematical correlations (Stokes-Einstein correlation):

$$D_{AB} = \frac{9.96 \times 10^{-16} T}{\mu V_A^{1/3}}$$

where T is absolute temperature and μ is viscosity of liquid medium in *Pa s*, *Va* is the solute molar volume at its normal boiling point in m^3/kg mol.

Molecular Diffusion in Solids:

Diffusion of gases through polymer films used in packaging is an example of this case.

For solids, $D_{AB} \neq D_{BA}$

The equation for flux is:

$$N_A = \frac{D_{BA}(C_{A1} - C_{A2})}{z_1 - z_2}$$

Diffusion of Gases in Porous Solids and Capillaries:

Diffusion of gases occurs through very fine pores of porous structure and diffusion of gases depend on the diameters of pores. The mean free path λ which is the average distance a gas molecule travels before collides with another gas molecule is defined as:

$$\lambda = \frac{3.2\mu}{P}\sqrt{\frac{RT}{2\pi M}}$$

where λ = mean free path, *m*

μ = viscosity, *Pa.s*

P = pressure, *Pa*

T = absolute temperature, *K*

M = molecular weight in kg/kg mol

For liquid, λ is small and hence diffusion follows Fick's law.

Knudsen Diffusion of Gases:

Knudsen diffusion occurs when mean free path λ is large compared to the diameter *d*. The Knudsen diffusivity is independent of pressure and is calculated from following equation:

$$D_{KA} = \frac{2}{3}\bar{r}\ \bar{v}_A$$

where D_{KA} is diffusivity in m^2/s, $\bar{r}$ is average pore radius in *m*, and $\bar{v}_A$ is the average molecular velocity for component *A* in m/s.

Diffusion of Solutes in Porous Solid:

The steady state equation for unhindered diffusion of a solute from point 1 and 2 within a slab of porous solid filled with water is given by:

$$N_A = \frac{\varepsilon D_{AB}(C_{A1} - C_{A2})}{\tau(z_2 - z_1)}$$

where D_{AB} = diffusivity of the solute in the liquid within the pores (m^2/s)

ε = porosity of medium

τ = tortuosity of the medium

C_{A1} & C_{A2} are concentration of solute in water at point 1 and 2.

In porous solids, the bulk of mass transfer occurs through the gas or liquid filling the pores and not through the solid matrix. The effective diffusivity D_{eff} through a porous solid is related to the molecular diffusivity D through the medium in the pores as follows:

$$D_{eff} = \frac{\varepsilon D_{AB}}{\tau}$$

where ε (dimensionless) is the fractional porosity, i.e. the void volume fraction of the porous solid. τ (dimensionless) is the tortuosity factor , a consequence of the tortuous path of the diffusing molecule through the porosity of the solid.

The tortuosity is defined as the ratio of the pore actual length to the length if the pore were straight in the direction of diffusion.

Knudsen number **:** For binary mixtures diffusing inside porous solids, a dimensionless ratio called the Knudsen number is used which is defined as

$$Kn = \frac{\lambda}{d}$$

where λ = mean free path of the diffusing molecules

d = pore diameter

For liquids, the mean free path is commonly very less and hence the Knudsen number is almost always very small and there by diffusion inside the pores is usually only by ordinary molecular diffusion.

For gases, the molecular mean free path is much larger than the diameter of the channel in which the diffusing molecules reside and hence the Knudsen number is large. In this case, the molecules bounce from wall to wall rather than colliding with other molecules and diffuses independently. This mode of transport is known as Knudsen diffusion.

The effective diffusivity is smaller than the molecular diffusivity. The hindered diffusion of a solute through a porous solid from point 1 to 2 is given by:

$$N_{AB} = \varepsilon D_{eff} \frac{(C_{A1} - C_{A2})}{\tau(z_2 - z_1)}$$

where D_{eff} = effective hindered diffusivity (m^2/s)

The effective hindered diffusivity of a solute in a pore can be obtained by:

$$D_{eff} = D\left(1 - \frac{d_s}{d_p}\right)^4$$

where d_s = solute diameter (m)

d_p = pore diameter(m)

Chapter 7

Cleaning, Size Reduction and Mixing

Cleaning, size reduction and mixing have many applications in food processing industry. Cleaning is carried out to remove the undesirable matters from raw materials while size reduction is usually carried out to increase the surface area of the material. The aim of mixing operation is to obtain a uniform mixture from two or more components in a food material. This chapter presents the governing equations used in cleaning, size reduction for solid and liquid, and mixing.

Cleaning:

Cleaning in agricultural processing refers to the removal of undesirable materials from the desired materials. This operation can be accomplished by washing, screening, etc.

Screen Effectiveness:

It is defined as the ratio of actual amount of oversize material in the overflow to the amount of oversize material entering with feed.

Let F = mass flow rate of feed

O = mass flow rate of oversize

U = mass flow rate of undersize

x_F = mass fraction of material in feed

x_O = mass fraction of material in overflow

x_U = mass fraction of material in underflow

Now we have:

$$F = O + U$$

$$F \cdot x_F = O \cdot x_O + U \cdot x_U$$

Mass flow rate ratio of overflow to feed is given by:

$$\frac{O}{F} = \frac{x_F - x_U}{x_O - x_U}$$

Mass flow rate ratio of underflow to feed is given by:

$$\frac{U}{F} = \frac{x_O - x_F}{x_O - x_U}$$

By definition:

$$\text{Effectiveness of overflow} = E_O = \frac{O \cdot x_O}{F \cdot x_F}$$

$$\text{Effectiveness of underflow} = E_U = \frac{U \cdot (1 - x_U)}{F \cdot (1 - x_F)}$$

Hence, overall effectiveness of screen is given by:

$$E = E_O \times E_U = \frac{OUx_O(1 - x_U)}{F^2 x_F (1 - x_F)}$$

Putting the values of O/F and U/F we get:

$$E = \frac{x_O(x_O - x_F)(x_F - x_U)(1 - x_U)}{x_F(1 - x_F)(x_O - x_U)^2}$$

This equation can be solved on the basis of screen analysis data.

Cleaning Efficiency:

The cleaning efficiency for an air screen grain cleaner as suggested by the Bureau of Indian Standard (BIS) is given by:

$$\eta_c = \frac{E(E - F)(F - G)(1 - G)}{F(1 - F)(E - G)^2} \times 100$$

where η_c = cleaning efficiency in percentage
E = fraction of clean seed at clean seed outlet
F = fraction of clean seed in feed
G = fraction of clean seed at foreign matters outlets

Cyclone Separator:

Cyclone separator (Fig. 7.1) is widely used for the separation of solid particles from gases. In a cyclone separator, particles are acted upon by the centrifugal force and gravitational force. The centrifugal force that acts on the particle in a cyclone separator is given by:

$$C_f = \frac{mv^2}{r}$$

where v = linear or tangential velocity (m/s),
r = radius of rotation (m),
m = mass of particle (kg).

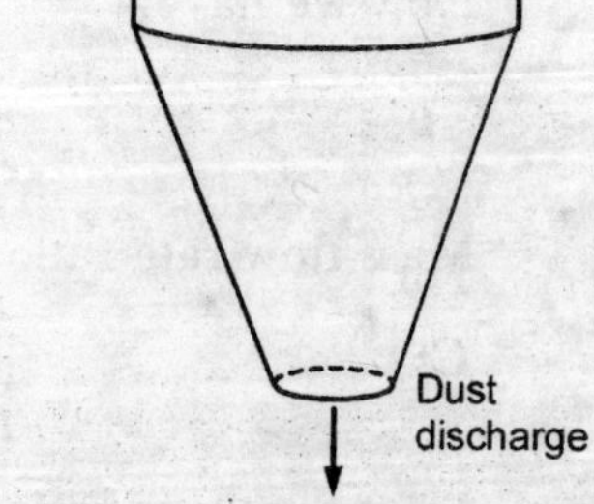

FIG. 7.1 Diagram of a cyclone

The gravitational force that acts on the particle in a cyclone separator is given by:

$$F_g = mg$$

where g is acceleration due to gravity (m/s^2).

The performance factor (S) of cyclone separator is the ratio of centrifugal force (F_c) and gravitational force (F_g) and is given by:

$$S = \frac{F_c}{F_g} = \frac{mv^2/r}{mg} = \frac{v^2}{gr}$$

The pressure drop through the cyclone may be estimated by the equation:

$$\Delta p = \frac{12wh}{KE^2\left(\frac{lH}{d^2}\right)^{1/3}}$$

where Δp = pressure head
d = cylinder diameter, m
l = cylinder height, m
H = cone height, m
w = entry width, m
h = entry height, m
E = exit duct diameter, m
K = vane constant, 0.5-0.7

The smallest particle size that can be removed by a cyclone may be estimated by the following equation:

$$d_p = \sqrt{\frac{9\mu E}{2\pi N v(\rho_p - \rho_a)\left(\frac{4R}{E}\right)^K}}$$

where d_p = smallest particle diameter, m
μ = viscosity of air, kg/ms
E = exit duct diameter, m
K = vane constant, 0.5-0.7
N = number of effective turns of air stream in inner spiral
v = entrance velocity of particle, m/s
ρ_p = density of particle, kg/m^3
ρ_a = density of air, kg/m^3
R = radius at which the spiral velocity equal to v = cyclone diameter/2

For commonly used cyclone, the number of effective turns is taken to be two.

Cyclone collection (particle removal) efficiency is given by:

$$\eta = \frac{1}{1 + \left(\frac{d_{pc}}{d_p}\right)^2}$$

where d_{pc} = diameter of particle collected with 50% efficiency
dp = diameter of particle of interest
η = fractional particle collection efficiency

Cyclone effective number of turns approximation:

$$Ne = \frac{1}{H}\left[L_b + \frac{L_c}{2}\right]$$

where Ne = number of effective turns gas makes in cyclone
H = inlet height of cyclone (m)
L_b = length of body cyclone (m)
L_c = length of cone of cyclone (m)

Cyclone 50% collection efficiency for particle diameter:

$$d_{pc} = \left[\frac{9\mu w_i}{2\pi N e v_i\left(\rho_p - \rho_g\right)}\right]^{0.5}$$

where d_{pc} = diameter of particle that is collected with 50% efficiency
μ = viscosity of gas (kg/m .s)
wi = inlet width of cyclone (m)
Ne = number of effective turns gas makes in cyclone
vi = inlet velocity into cyclone (m/s)
ρ_p = density of particle (kg/m^3)
ρ_g = density of gas (kg/m^3)

At terminal velocity of particle in a cyclone separator, the basic force balance around particle falling in a centrifugal force field is:

$$F_g - F_b = F_d$$

where F_g = gravity force
F_b = buoyant force
F_d = drag force

The resisting force due to fluid friction acting on a sphere when relative motion produces laminar flow (Stoke's Law) is:

$$F_d = 3\pi d_p \mu v$$

Putting the values of all forces, we have:

$$mg - m\frac{\rho}{\rho_s}g = 3\pi d_p \mu v$$

$$\frac{m}{\rho_s}(\rho_s - \rho)g = 3\pi d_p \mu v$$

The radial acceleration g in a cyclone depends on the radius of the path being followed by the gas and is given by the equation:

$$g = \omega^2 r$$

where ω is angular velocity and r is radius.

Hence, $$\frac{m}{\rho_s}(\rho_s - \rho)\omega^2 r = 3\pi d_p \mu v$$

Putting the value of mass of particle and replacing v by v_r (radial velocity of particle), we have:

$$\frac{\rho_s \times \pi d_p^{\ 3}}{6\rho_s}(\rho_s - \rho)\omega^2 r = 3\pi d_p \mu v_r$$

Since, $$\omega = \frac{v_{\tan}}{r}$$

where v_{tan} is tangential velocity of particle at radius r.

Hence, $$\frac{\pi d_p^{\ 3}}{6}(\rho_s - \rho)\left(\frac{v_{\tan}}{r}\right)^2 r = 3\pi d_p \mu v_r$$

Or, $$v_r = \left[\frac{d_p^{\ 2}(\rho_s - \rho)}{18\mu}\right] \times \frac{v_{\tan}^{\ 2}}{r} = \frac{v_t}{g} \times \frac{v_{\tan}^{\ 2}}{r} \qquad \left(\text{as } v_t = \frac{d_p^{\ 2}(\rho_s - \rho)g}{18\mu}\right)$$

where v_t = gravitational terminal settling velocity

Size Reduction:

The size reduction is a very common operation in food processing industry. It is used for both solid dry material and liquid material. It improves eating quality or suitability of material for further processing. The energy (E) required to reduce the size of particulate solids depend on the energy absorbed by solids and the mechanical efficiency of the process which takes account of frictional losses.

Mechanical Efficiency:

Mechanical efficiency (ηm) of a size reduction device is defined as the ratio of the energy absorbed (E_a) by the material to the total energy consumption or input energy (E) of the equipment per unit mass of material treated and is given by:

$$\eta_m = \frac{\text{energy absorbed by material}}{\text{total energy}} = \frac{E_a}{E}$$

Crushing Efficiency:

Crushing efficiency (η_c) is defined as the ratio of the increment in surface energy to the total energy absorbed by the material and is expressed as:

$$\eta_c = \frac{e_s\left(A_p - A_f\right)}{E_a}$$

where e_s = surface energy per unit area, J/m^2

A_p = surface area per unit mass of product, m^2/kg

A_f = surface area per unit mass of feed, m^2/kg

Since, $$\eta_m = \frac{E_a}{E}$$

where E = input energy per unit mass, J/kg

Hence input energy (E) and can be expressed as:

$$E = \frac{E_a}{\eta_m} = \frac{e_s\left(A_p - A_f\right)}{\eta_m \eta_c} \qquad \left(\text{since, } E_a = \frac{e_s\left(A_p - A_f\right)}{\eta_c}\right)$$

Since, $$P = E \times f$$

Hence, $$P = \frac{e_s f\left(A_p - A_f\right)}{\eta_m \eta_c}$$

Or $$P = \frac{6 f e_s}{\rho_p \eta_m \eta_c}\left(\frac{1}{\phi_p X_p} - \frac{1}{\phi_f X_f}\right) \qquad \left(\text{as } S_p = \frac{6m}{\phi \rho_p D_p}\right)$$

where P = power required by grinding machine, W

f = feed rate, kg/s

X_f, X_p = surface-volume mean particle sizes of the feed and product

ϕ_f, ϕ_p = sphericity of feed and product

ρ_p = density of particle

f = feed rate

Theoretical considerations suggest that the energy required to produce a small change in the size of unit mass of material can be expressed as a power function of the size of the material:

$$\frac{dE}{dx} = -Kx^{-n}$$

where dE is the change in energy, dx is the change in size, K is a constant, n is the power value and x is the particle size.

This equation is referred to as the general law of size reduction and has been used by a number of workers to derive more specific laws depending on the application.

Kick's Law:

Kick's law states that the energy required to reduce the size of particles is proportional to the ratio of the initial size of a typical dimension to the final size of that dimension.

i.e. $n = 1$

Hence, $$\frac{dE}{dx} = -Kx^{-1}$$

On integration we get:

$$\int_0^E dE = -K \int_{X_f}^{X_p} x^{-1} dx = -K \int_{X_f}^{X_p} \frac{dx}{x} = -K [\ln x]_{X_f}^{X_p}$$

$$= -K\left[\ln X_p - \ln X_f\right] = K\left[\ln X_f - \ln X_p\right]$$

Or, $$E = K \ln \frac{X_f}{X_p}$$

Replacing K by K_K we have:

Or, $$\frac{P}{f} = K_K \ln \frac{X_f}{X_p}$$

where K_K = Kick's Constant.

The Kick's coefficient depends on the equipment and operating conditions.

Kick's Law is best suited to coarse grinding where there is relatively little change in surface area is required.

Size Reduction Ratio:

The size reduction ratio (RR) is defined as:

$$RR = \frac{X_f}{X_p}$$

The size reduction ratio (RR) is used to evaluate the relative performance of different types of grinding equipments. Coarse grinding has RR below 8:1 whereas in fine grinding ratios can exceed 100:1.

Rittinger's Law:

Rittinger's Law states that the energy required to reduce the size of particles is proportional to the change in surface area of the particles.

i.e. $n = 2$

Hence, $$\frac{dE}{dx} = -Kx^{-2}$$

On integration we get:

$$\int_0^E dE = -K \int_{X_f}^{X_p} x^{-2} dx$$

Or, $$E = -K\left[\frac{x^{-2+1}}{-2+1}\right]_{X_f}^{X_p} = K\left[\frac{1}{x}\right]_{X_f}^{X_p}$$

$$E = K\left(\frac{1}{X_p} - \frac{1}{X_f}\right)$$

Replacing K by K_R we have:

Or, $$\frac{P}{f} = K_R\left(\frac{1}{X_p} - \frac{1}{X_f}\right) \quad (\text{as } P = E \times f)$$

where X_f = average initial size of feed particles, m

X_p = average size of product particles, m

K_R = Rittinger's constant

The Rittinger's coefficient depends on the operating conditions and equipments.

Rittinger's Law gives better results for fine grinding where there is a much greater change in surface area is required.

Bond's Law:

According to Bond's law, energy required for grinding a large size feed is directly proportional to square root of surface to volume ratio of product.

i.e. $$n = 1.5 = 3/2$$

Hence, $$\frac{dE}{dx} = -Kx^{-3/2}$$

On integration we get:

$$\int_0^E dE = -K\int_{X_f}^{X_p} x^{-3/2}\,dx = -K\left[\frac{x^{\frac{-3+2}{2}}}{\frac{-3+2}{2}}\right]_{X_f}^{X_p} = 2K\left[\frac{1}{\sqrt{x}}\right]_{X_f}^{X_p} = 2K\left[\frac{1}{\sqrt{X_p}} - \frac{1}{\sqrt{X_f}}\right]$$

Or, $$E = 2K\left[\frac{1}{\sqrt{X_p}} - \frac{1}{\sqrt{X_f}}\right]$$

Replacing K by K_B we get:

$$\frac{P}{f} = 2K_B\left[\frac{1}{\sqrt{X_p}} - \frac{1}{\sqrt{X_f}}\right]$$

where K_B = Bond's Constant

The Bond's coefficient depends on the equipment and operating conditions.

Bond's law holds reasonably well for a variety of materials undergoing coarse, medium and fine size reduction.

The energy required for size reduction by Bond's law may also be predicted by the expression:

$$E = 0.3162Wi\left(\frac{1}{\sqrt{D_p}} - \frac{1}{\sqrt{D_f}}\right)$$

Or,

$$\frac{P}{f} = 0.3162Wi\left(\frac{1}{\sqrt{D_p}} - \frac{1}{\sqrt{D_f}}\right)$$

where P = power, kW

f = feed rate, t/h

Wi = bond work index

D_p = 80% of product passes through mesh of diameter D_p, mm

D_f = 80% of feed passes through mesh of diameter D_f, mm

It is suitable for materials undergoing coarse, intermediate and fine grinding.

Critical Speed of Ball in Ball Mill:

The ball mill is used for dry and wet grinding of matter. The critical speed may be determined by the following expression:

$$n_c = \frac{1}{2\pi}\sqrt{\frac{g}{R-r}}$$

where n_c = critical speed, revolution per second (rps)

R = radius of cylinder, m

r = radius of ball, m

g = acceleration due to gravity, m/s^2

The rotational speed of ball mills are kept at 65 to 80% of their critical speed with the lower value for wet grinding in viscous suspension while higher value for solid matter grinding.

Crushing Rolls:

It is also used widely used in food industry for size reduction application. The following formula relates the coefficient of friction (μ), angle of nip (α), diameter of rolls (D_r), average diameter of feed particles (D_f) and average diameter of product particles (D_p):

$$\cos\alpha/2 = \frac{D_r + D_p}{D_r + D_f}$$

Angle of Nip:

It is the angle formed by the tangents to the roll faces at the points of contact with the particle.

$\alpha/2$ is related to the coefficient of friction by the relation:

$$\mu = \tan\alpha/2$$

where μ = coefficient of friction between the particle and the rolls

Capacity of Crushing Roll:

The theoretical capacity of crushing roll depends on speed, nip, diameter and length of the rollers. The theoretical capacity is the volume of continuous ribbon of product discharged from the rolls and is given by:

$$Q = \pi D_r N D_p L$$

where, D_r is roll diameter (m), D_p is nip (distance between the surfaces of the rollers) (m), N is roll speed (*rps*) and L is length of face (m) and Q is in m^3/s.

The peripheral velocity of roll (m/s) is given by:

$$v = \pi D_r N$$

The mass flow rate is given by:

$$\dot{m} = Q \times \rho, \text{ kg/s}$$

where ρ = bulk density of product, kg/m^3

In practice, the actual capacity is usually between 0.1 and 0.3 of the theoretical capacity.

Degree of Grinding:

The degree of grinding is defined as the ratio of the overall surface area of the ground product to the overall surface area of the feed and is given by the relation:

$$dg = \frac{S_p}{S_f}$$

where S_p = overall surface area of product, m^2

S_f = overall surface area of feed, m^2

Fineness Modulus:

The fineness modulus (*FM*) indicates the uniformity of ground product. It is determined by adding the weight fractions retained above each sieve and dividing the sum by 100.

i.e. $$FM = \frac{\sum \text{cumulative percentage retained}}{100}$$

If five consecutive sieves and pan retains w_1 %, w_2 %, w_3 %, w_4 %, w_5% and w_6 % of ground material respectively then fineness modulus is calculated as:

$$FM = \frac{w_1 \times 5 + w_2 \times 4 + w_3 \times 3 + w_4 \times 2 + w_5 \times 1 + w_6 \times 0}{100}$$

Fineness Modulus of Blended Ground Product:

Fineness modulus of blended ground product can be estimated by the following equation:

$$FM_{blend} = FM_A \frac{w_A}{100} + FM_B \frac{w_B}{100}$$

where FM_A, FM_B = fineness modulus of component A and B

w_A, w_B = % weight of component A and B in the blended ground product

The average size of ground particle of diameter D in mm and fineness modulus number (F.M) are related as:

$$D = 0.135\,(1.366)^{F.M}$$

This relation can be used to predict the average particle size.

Milling:

The meaning of milling varies with crops. In rice, industry, milling refers to production of milled rice. The shelling and polishing are commonly used unit operations in rice mill.

Shelling:

The main aim of shelling is to remove husk from the paddy grain to get brown rice. It is also known as *hulling*. The machine used is huller or sheller. The rubber roller sheller is widely used in rice milling industry.

The linear speed of rubber roll sheller may be given as:

$$v = \pi DN$$

where v = linear speed, m/s

D = diameter of roll, m

N = speed of rotation, revolution per second (rps)

Length of Husking Zone:

The length of husking zone (l_h) in a rubber roll sheller is given by:

$$l_h = \frac{2\pi D_r}{360}\cos^{-1}\left(\frac{D_r + D_p}{D_r + D_f}\right)$$

where D_r = diameter of roll, m

D_f = average diameter of feed particle (grain), m

D_p = average diameter of product particle, m

Polishing:

Polishing is used to remove bran from brown rice. It is carried out by polishers. One example of polisher is vertical whitening cone. The number of brakes (n) in vertical whitening cone is given by the relation:

$$n = \frac{D}{100} - 2$$

where D = cone diameter, mm

Coefficient of Hulling:

The coefficient of hulling is expressed as:

$$\text{coefficient of hulling} = \frac{\text{weight of brown rice}}{\text{weight of paddy fed to machine}}$$

Milling Degree:

Milling degree is computed based on the amount of bran removed from the brown rice. The percent milling degree can be estimated using the equation:

$$\%\ \text{milling degree} = \frac{\text{weight of milled rice}}{\text{weight of brown rice}} \times 100$$

Milling Recovery:

The milling recovery can be computed by dividing the weight of milled rice recovered by the weight of the paddy sample. Mathematically,

$$\%\ \text{milling recovery} = \frac{\text{weight of milled rice}}{\text{weight of paddy sapmples}} \times 100$$

The percentage head rice and broken rice may be computed by the following expressions:

$$\%\ \text{head rice} = \frac{\text{weight of whole rice}}{\text{weight of paddy sapmples}} \times 100$$

$$\%\ \text{broken rice} = \frac{\text{weight of broken rice}}{\text{weight of paddy sapmples}} \times 100$$

Homogenization:

It is used for size reduction in liquid food such as milk. Milk is homogenized to break fat globules present in milk.

During homogenization, pressure head and velocity head are related as:

$$\frac{P}{\rho g} = \frac{v^2}{2g}$$

Or, $$v = \sqrt{\frac{2P}{\rho}}$$

where P = homogenization pressure, *Pa*

ρ = density of milk, kg/m^3

v = velocity, m/s

The mean globule size of fat globule can be estimated by the following Phipps formula:

$$\bar{d} = \frac{w\sigma}{v\rho\nu}\left(\frac{1}{\text{Re}}\right)^{1/3}$$

where w = width of slit, m
v = velocity at slit aperture, m/s
σ = interfacial tension, N/m
ρ = density of continuous phase, kg/m^3
ν = kinematic viscosity of continuous phase, m^2/s
Re = mean Reynolds number in the slit

The increase in temperature during homogenization in flowing liquid having a density of ρ (kg/m^3) and specific heat of C_p(J/kg °C) can be found out by the following expression:

$$\Delta T = \frac{P}{\rho C_p} \ ^\circ\text{C}$$

where P is pressure in Pa or N/m^2.

The temperature rise (°C) of milk during homogenization may also be found by the following equation:

$$\Delta T = \frac{P}{40}$$

where P = homogenization pressure, kg/cm^2

Power Consumption in Homogenization:

Power consumption in homogenization is given by:

$$P_o = QP$$

where P_o is in W and Q is volumetric flow rate (m^3/s) and P is homogenizing pressure in Pa.

Mixing:

Mixing is the dispersing of components, one throughout the other. The fundamental objective of mixing is to increase the homogeneity of material in bulk Mixing of liquid, solids and gases are one of the commonest of all operation in the food processing industry.

Power Consumption in Liquid Mixing:

An important consideration in the design of an agitated vessel is the power requirement to drive the impeller.Most commonly, the mixing power correlations comprise the following dimensionless groups:

$$\text{Power number} = P_0 = \frac{P}{\rho N^3 D^5}$$

$$\text{Reynolds number} = Re = \frac{\rho N D^2}{\mu}$$

$$\text{Froude number} = Fr = \frac{N^2 D}{g}$$

where D = impeller diameter, m
N = rotational speed, rps
ρ = density of liquid, kg/m^3
μ = viscosity of liquid, *Pa* s
P = power consumed by the impeller
g = gravitational acceleration, m/s^2

The characteristic length is the impeller diameter and relevant velocity is that at the tip of impeller blade equal to ND.

For mixing vessels, following types of flow occurs based on Reynolds number:

Laminar flow	:	$Re < 10$
Transitional flow	:	$10 < Re < 10^4$
Turbulent flow	:	$Re > 10^4$

Apart from above dimensionless numbers, other important numbers related to mixing are flow number and Weber number.

Flow number **:** It is given by the relation:

$$N_Q = \frac{q}{ND^3}$$

where N is rotational speed (*rps*), D is diameter of impeller (m) and q is flow rate through impeller (m^3/s).

Weber number **:** It is the ratio of kinetic energy of the fluid at the impeller tip speed to a surface tension stress based on D and is given as:

$$We = \frac{N^2 D^3 \rho_c}{\sigma} = \rho_c \frac{(ND)^2}{\sigma/D}$$

where, ρ_c = density of continuous liquid phase, kg/m^3
σ = interfacial tension, N/m
N = impeller speed, *rps*

The power consumed in liquid mixing can be expressed by a relationship of the form:

$$P_o = K\,(Re)^n\,(Fr)^m$$

The coefficient K and the exponents m, n are determined experimentally and depend on the geometry of mixer.

The density of a mixture is found by addition of component densities of the continuous and dispersed phases:

$$\rho_m = V_1\rho_1 + V_2\rho_2$$

where V = volume fraction and the subscript 1 and 2 refers to the continuous and dispersed phase respectively.

Dough Mixing:

The increase in dough temperature during dough mixing can be calculated by:

$$\Delta T_d = \frac{q}{(\dot{m}_d \times Cp_d)}$$

where $\dot{m}_d$ is mass flow rate of dough (kg/s) and C_{pd} is specific heat of dough (J/kg K) and q is heat transfer rate (W).

When water is used for cooling the dough, then mass flow rate of water can be calculated by:

$$q = \dot{m} Cp \Delta T$$

where $\dot{m}$ is mass flow rate of water (kg/s), ΔT temperature increase of the water and C_p specific heat of water (J/kg K).

Measurement of Particle Mixing:

The deviation of the sample compositions from the mean composition of the overall mixture represents a measure of the mixing process. This deviation decreases as mixing progresses and this deviation is measured by standard deviation. It is given by:

$$S^2 = \frac{1}{n}\left[(x_1 - \bar{x})^2 + (x_2 - \bar{x})^2 + ... + (x_n - \bar{x})^2\right]$$

where S is the standard deviation, n is the number of samples taken, x_1, x_2, ... xn , are the fractional compositions of component X in the 1, 2, ... n samples and is the mean fractional composition of component X in the whole mixture. The values of S can be calculated from the measured sample compositions, taking the n samples at some stage of the mixing operation.

Quality of Mixing:

The quality of good mixing is very important in food processing industry. Improper mixing may lead to poor quality products. Assessing the extent of mixing is of great interest for both equipment manufacturers and food powder processors. Mixing indices intend to provide a measure of the performance of a piece of equipment.

Consider a two-component mixture consisting of a fraction p of component P and a fraction q of component Q placed in a mixer. In the beginning, when the components are totally separated, a sample would consist of either pure P or pure Q. The variance of the totally unmixed system would be:

$$S_0{}^2 = q(1-q) = pq \qquad \text{(Since } p + q = 1\text{)}$$

The variance of samples taken from a perfectly randomized mixture is:

$$S_R{}^2 = \frac{qp}{N} = \frac{p(1-p)}{N} = \frac{S_o^2}{N}$$

where N is the number of particles in the samples.

The subscripts *o* and *R* have been used to denote the initial and the random values of S^2. The quality of mixing of a real mixture would be between that of the totally unmixed (segregated) and that of the perfectly mixed (random) mixtures.

A mixing index or index of mixedness (*M*) may be defined as follows:

$$M = \frac{S_0^2 - S^2}{S_0^2 - S_R^2}$$

where S^2 is the variance of the real mixture.

When the samples are fairly large, then above equation becomes:

$$M = 1 - \frac{S^2}{S_0^2}$$

The mixing index *M* of a real mixture lies between 0 (totally segregated) and 1 (totally randomized). This measure can be used for mixtures of particles and also for the mixing of heavy pastes.

Rate of Mixing:

A mixing index (*M*) may be related to the time of mixing (*t*) by:

$$1 - (M) = e^{-Kt}$$

where k = rate constant representing the rate at which mixing proceeds

This equation can be used to predict the time required to attain a given degree of mixing.

Chapter 8

Thermal Processing of Foods

Thermal processing is carried out to preserve food by destroying the microbes/ enzymes and minimizing chemical reactions. An understanding of reaction mechanisms coupled with quantification of rate constants is essential for the selection of the best conditions of a process or storage to maintain the desired quality characteristics in the product. This chapter presents the concept of deteriorative reaction in foods, microbial growth and thermal death of microorganisms.

Deteriorative Reaction in Foods:

Degradation of food occurs during processing and storage. To optimize the process and storage condition, quantification of rate constants is essential.

General Equation of Rate of Food Deteriorative Reaction:

The quality loss can be represented in term of power of concentration of the reactant or product.

i.e. $$-\frac{dC}{dt} = kC^n$$

where t = time, s

k = rate constant, s^{-1}

n = order of reaction

dC/dt = change in concentration of C with time

Reaction Order:

The order of a reaction is the sum of the exponents of reactant concentration terms in the rate equation. For most quality changes in foods, the reaction order n is either 0 or 1.

Zero-Order Reactions:

For zero order reaction, n = 0 and hence above equation becomes:

$$-\frac{dC}{d\theta} = k$$

This equation implies that the rate of loss of C is constant with time and independent of concentration of C.

Integrating between C_0 at t = 0 and C_e at time t_s we have:

$$\int_{C_0}^{C_e} dC = -k \int_0^{t_s} dt$$

Or, $$C_e - C_o = -kt_s$$

Or, $$C_e = C_o - kt_s$$

where C_e = concentration of C at the end of shelf life

t_s = shelf life

Shelf life of food (t_s) is the time for the concentration (C) to reach an undesirable level (C_e).

During thermal processing as in *UHT* sterilization, browning reaction occurs which is due to reaction between lysine and lactose present in milk.

For browning reaction in a given food products with time, following equation may be used:

$$k = \frac{B - B_0}{t}$$

where B = concentration of browning at time t

B_0 = concentration of browning at time $t = 0$

k = rate constant

Based on concentration of browning in a given food products, shelf life may be estimated using the equation:

$$t_s = \frac{B_e - B_0}{k}$$

where B_e = concentration of browning at the end of shelf life

First Order Reaction:

Most of the reactions involved in the processing of foods are first order reactions. A first-order reaction is characterized by a logarithmic change in the concentration of a reactant with time. Most of the reactions involved in the processing of foods are first order reactions.

For first order reaction, $n = 1$

Hence $$-\frac{dC}{dt} = kC$$

Integrating between C_0 at $t = 0$ and C_e at time t_s we have:

$$\ln \frac{C_e}{C_0} = -kt_s$$

or $$\frac{C_e}{C_o} = e^{-kt_s}$$

or $$C_e = C_0 e^{-kt_s}$$

Shelf life of a food product can be evaluated from the following equation:

$$t_s = \frac{\ln C_0 - \ln C_e}{k}$$

where k = first order reaction rate constant (time^{-1})

C_0 = initial concentration like concentration of vitamin C at time $\theta = 0$

C_e = concentration at the end of shelf life

Reaction Rate Constant:

The reaction rate constant defines the reaction rate. There are several ways in which the speed of a chemical reaction can be reported for first order reactions which predominate in food systems. The rate constant k has unit of reciprocal time.

Half Life:

The half life is the time required for the reactant to lose half of its original concentration. The half life is related to k as follows:

$$t_{0.5} = \frac{0.693}{k}$$

Growth of Bacterial Population:

Bacteria multiply by division. Every cell division yields two new bacterial cells. The multiplication is a geometrical progression ($2^0 \rightarrow 2^1 \rightarrow 2^2 \rightarrow 2^3 \ldots \rightarrow 2^n$) (where n = number of generations). This is called *exponential growth*. The rate of exponential growth of a bacterial culture is expressed as generation time, also known as the *doubling time of the bacterial population*.

Generation time (G) is defined as the time (t) per generation and is given by:

$$G = \frac{t}{n}$$

where n = number of generations

Generation Time:

The generation time is the time interval required for the cells (or population) to divide.

$$G = \frac{t}{n}$$

Let t = time interval

N_0 = number of bacteria at the beginning of a time interval

N = number of bacteria at the end of the time interval

n = number of generations (number of times the cell population doubles during the time interval)

By definition of exponential growth of bacteria we have:

$$N = N_0 \times 2^n$$

Taking log on both sides we get:

$$\log N = \log N_0 + n\log 2$$

$$n = \frac{\log N - \log N_0}{\log 2} = \frac{\log N - \log N_0}{0.301}$$

$$n = 3.3\log\frac{N}{N_0}$$

$$\frac{t}{G} = 3.3\log\frac{N}{N_0} \qquad \text{(as } G = t/n\text{)}$$

$$G = \frac{t}{3.3\log\frac{N}{N_0}}$$

The rate of growth of bacteria may also be expressed in the form:

$$N = N_o 2^{G/1}$$

where N = number of bacteria/ml at time t

N_0 = number of bacteria/ml at time 0

t = time of growth in s

G = generation time in s

The generation time or doubling time (t_{double}) and rate constant k are related as follows:

$$k = \frac{0.693}{t_{double}}$$

Or,
$$t_{double} = \frac{0.693}{k}$$

Thermal Death Kinetics of Microorganisms:

The rate of destruction (dN/dt) is directly proportional to the number of viable micro-organisms (N).

i.e.
$$\frac{dN}{dt} = -kN$$

where, N = number of viable organisms at a given time t.

k = first-order rate constant for microbial inactivation, time^{-1}

After integration using the initial condition, $N = N_0$ at $t = 0$ we have:

$$\ln\frac{N}{N_0} = -kt$$

where No = number of micro-organisms initially presents in the food at $t = 0$

N = number of micro-organisms at time t.

Decimal Reduction Time:

It is defined as the duration of heating time at a constant lethal temperature required for the reduction of the number of living cells by a factor of 10 (i.e. by one log factor). It also represents a heating time that results in 90 % destruction of the original number of microbial population. It may be noted that one log cycle reduction represents a 90% decrease (100 to 10, 10 to 1, 1 to 0.1, etc.). Thus, a 2*D* reduction is a 99 % reduction; a 3*D* reduction is a 99.9% reduction, etc. Fig. 8.1 is a graphical representation of the logarithmic reduction model.

Applying decimal reduction time *D* and replacing *t* by *D* we have:

$$N = \frac{N_0}{10} = 0.1N_0$$

$$\ln\frac{0.1N_0}{N_0} = -kD$$

or $$\ln(1) - \ln(10) = -kD$$

or $$\ln(10) - \ln(1) = kD$$

or $$\ln 10 = kD$$

or $$D = \frac{\ln 10}{k} = \frac{2.303}{k}$$

Hence, $$\log\frac{N_0}{N} = \frac{kt}{2.303} = \frac{t}{D}$$

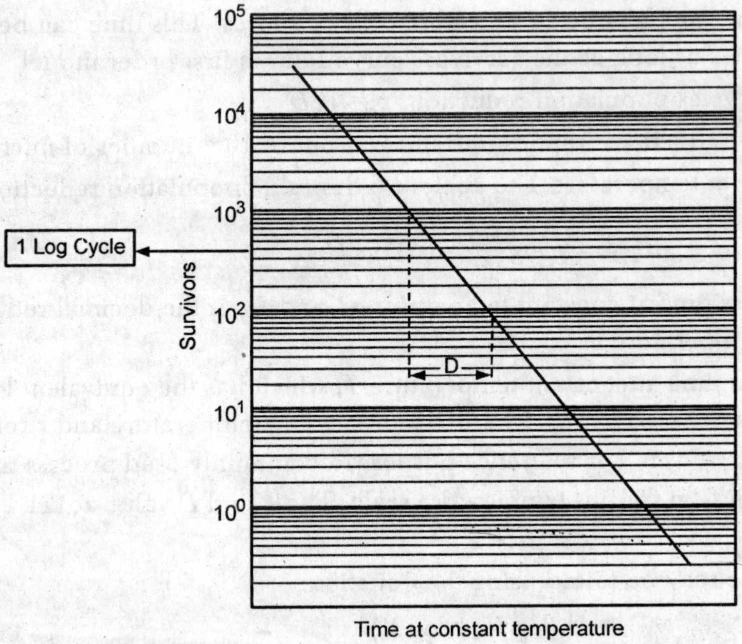

FIG. 8.1 Log-linear model of thermal reduction of microorganisms

Or, $$t = \log\frac{N_0}{N}\cdot D = SV \times D$$

where, $SV = \log\frac{N_0}{N}$

SV = sterilization value

The equation $\log\frac{N_0}{N} = \frac{kt}{2.303} = \frac{t}{D}$ may be written in the form $y = mx + c$ as:

$$\log N = \log N_0 - \frac{kt}{2.303}$$

where slope = $m = -k/2.303$

constant = $c = \log N_0$

N = number of survivors after treatment time t

Plotting graph between log N and t, and knowing the slope, k may be calculated.

Sterilizing Value or Lethality of a Process

The sterilization value (SV) of a process is defined in term of the number of decimal reduction in the microbial population. The sterilization value is also called log cycle reduction. The following equation may be used as means of expressing the sterilizing value of a process:

$$SV = \text{number of decimal reduction} = \log\frac{N_0}{N} = \frac{F}{D}$$

where F is thermal death time F which is defined as the total time required to accomplish a stated reduction in a population of vegetable cells or spores. This time can be expressed as multiple of D values as long as the survivors curve follows first order model

For 12 log cycles population reduction, $F = 12D$

12 log cycle reductions implies one survival out of 10^{12} number of microorganisms.

The F value at temperature T to achieve a desirable population reduction is given by:

$$F_T = D_T \log\frac{N_0}{N} = (SV) \times D_T$$

where F_T is process time at constant temperature T and D_T is the decimal reduction time of the organism at temperature T.

F_T is process time at constant temperature T, which has the equivalent lethality of the given process. It is denoted by F_T^z where T is processing temperature and z refers to z-value for a given microorganism. For reference purpose, a commonly used process time is F_{250}^{18} in Frenheit scale or F_{121}^{10} in Celsius temperature scale. The F and D value at 121.1°C are F_0 and D_0, respectively.

The F_0 value may be found using the equation:

$$F_0 = D_0(\log N_0 - \log N)$$

where N_0 is initial number of micro-organisms and N is final number of micro-organisms.

$$\% \text{ inactivation} = \frac{N_0 - N}{N_0} \times 100$$

$$\frac{N}{N_0} = \text{fraction of viable organisms survived thermal treatment at time } t.$$

A 99.99 % reduction in microbial population is equivalent to 4 log cycles reduction

or $F = 4D$.

A 99.999% inactivation indicates 5 decimal reductions (one survivor from 100,000)

or $F = 5D$.

Determination of *D* Values Using the Partial Sterilization Technique:

This technique allows the determination of *D* values by using survivor data at two different heating times. The following equation may be used to determine the *D* value:

$$D = \frac{t_2 - t_1}{\log N_1 - \log N_2}$$

where N_1 and N_2 represent the survivor counts following heating for t_1 and t_2 time respectively.

Z-Value:

Z-value is defined as the number of degrees (Celsius or Fahrenheit) required to change a *D*-value by one factor of 10. It is a measure of the change in death rate with change in temperature. *Z* value indicates the sensitivity of the rate of thermal inactivation to temperature. The reaction that has small *z* value is highly temperature dependent whereas reaction with large *z* value is less influenced by temperature. The *Z*-value can be found by plotting *D*-values against temperatures on a semi-logarithmic scale and adding a line that best fits the data. The absolute value of the reciprocal of the slope of this line gives the *Z*-value. Referring Fig. 8.2 we may write:

$$m = \frac{\Delta \text{ Dvalue}}{\Delta \text{ Temperature}} \Rightarrow \frac{\Delta D}{\Delta T}$$

For 1 log cycle reduction in *D*-value, $\Delta D = 1$

Since, $\Delta T = $ Z-value.

Hence, $m = \frac{1}{z}$

and $z = \left|\frac{1}{m}\right|$ (as z-value always should be a positive value)

The *z*-value may also be expressed as:

$$z = \frac{(T_2 - T_1)}{[\log(D_1) - \log(D_2)]}$$

where D_1 and D_2 are *D*-values at T_1 and T_2 respectively.

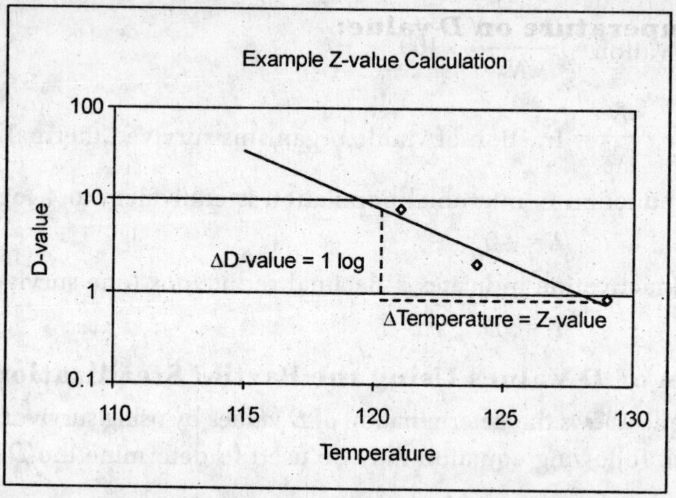

FIG. 8.2 Calculating a Z-value graphically

Thermal Death Time Model Equations:

A semi-logarithmic plot of heating time for inactivation against temperature is called the *thermal death time plot* (Fig. 3) and equations based on this linear semi-logarithmic plot are called the thermal death time model equations for microbial inactivation at different temperatures.

$$\log \frac{F}{F_0} = \frac{T_0 - T}{z} \quad \text{or} \quad \log \frac{F_1}{F_2} = \frac{T_2 - T_1}{z}$$

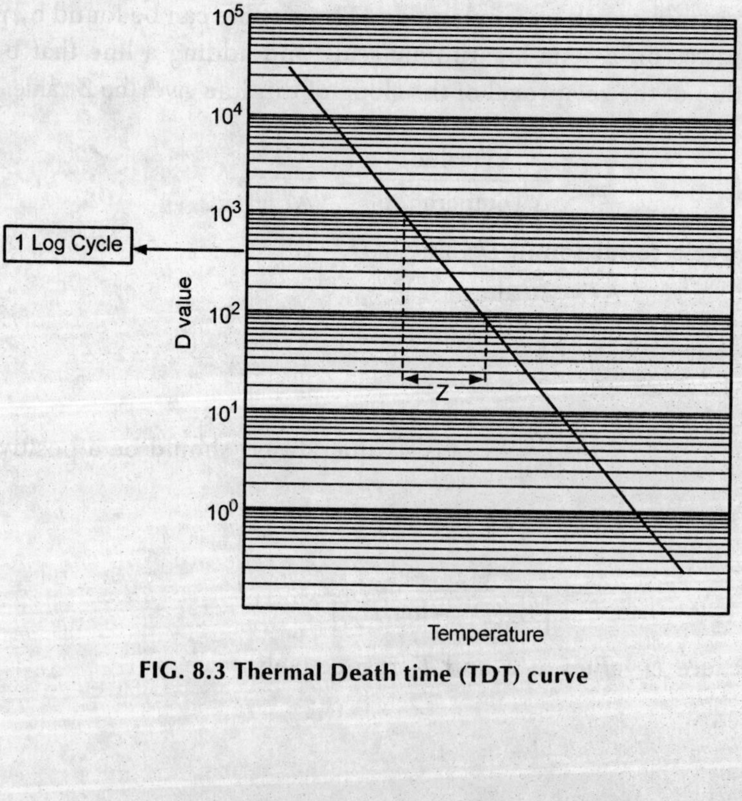

FIG. 8.3 Thermal Death time (TDT) curve

Effect of Temperature on *D*-value:

The relationship between *D* values at two different temperatures and *z* value is given by:

$$\log\frac{D_1}{D_2} = \frac{T_2 - T_1}{z}$$

Or,
$$\log\frac{D}{D_0} = \frac{T_0 - T}{z}$$

Since $D \propto 1/k$

Hence
$$\log\frac{k_1}{k_2} = \frac{T_1 - T_2}{z}$$

Or,
$$\log\frac{k_0}{k} = \frac{T_0 - T}{z}$$

where T_0 is reference temperature and T is any temperature.

D_1 and D_2 are the decimal reduction time at temperatures T_1 and T_2 respectively.

This equation can be rewritten, replacing decimal reduction time (D) by the processing time (t), as:

$$\log\frac{t_1}{t_2} = \frac{T_2 - T_1}{z} \quad \text{or} \quad \frac{t_1}{t_2} = 10^{\frac{T_2 - T_1}{z}} \qquad (\text{as } t \propto D)$$

Temperature Dependence of Reaction Rates:

Arrhenius relationship **:** The effect of temperature on the reaction rate constant k may be expressed by Arrhenius equation:

$$k = Ae^{-\frac{E_a}{RT}}$$

where k = rate constant for deteriorative reaction (s^{-1})

A = collision number or frequency factor

E_a = activation energy, J/mol

R = ideal gas constant, 8.314 J/K mol or 1.987 cal/K mol

T = absolute temperature, K

The negative sign is placed on the exponent of the Arrhenius equation in order that a positive activation energy will indicate an increasing reaction rate constant with increasing temperature. The value of k is much higher for vegetative form than for spore forms. The value of activation energy is a measure of the temperature sensitivity of a reaction.

Taking natural log on both sides of this equation we have:

$$\ln k = \ln A - \frac{E_a}{RT}\ln e \quad (\ln e = 1)$$

or, $$\ln k = \ln A - \frac{E_a}{RT} \qquad (\ln e = 1)$$

A graphical representation of the Arrhenius equation is shown in Fig. 4.

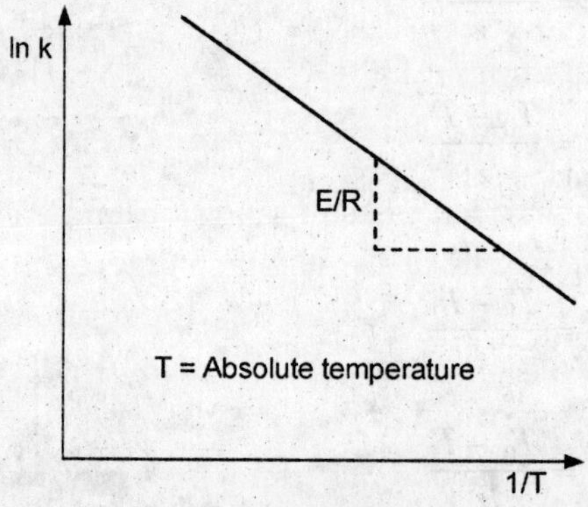

FIG. 8.4 Graphical representation of the Arrhenius law

Since k is function of temperature, hence we may write:

$$\ln k_1 = \ln A - \frac{E_a}{RT_1}$$

$$\ln k_2 = \ln A - \frac{E_a}{RT_2}$$

Solving these two equations we have:

$$\ln \frac{k_1}{k_2} = \frac{E_a}{R}\left(\frac{1}{T_2} - \frac{1}{T_1}\right) = \frac{E_a}{R}\frac{(T_1 - T_2)}{T_1 T_2}$$

or, $$2.303 \log \frac{k_1}{k_2} = \frac{E_a}{R}\frac{(T_1 - T_2)}{T_1 T_2}$$

$$\log \frac{k_1}{k_2} = \frac{E_a}{2.303R}\frac{(T_1 - T_2)}{T_1 T_2}$$

where k_1 and k_2 are the rate constants at temperatures T_1 and T_2 respectively.

$$\log \frac{D_2}{D_1} = \frac{E_a}{2.303R}\frac{(T_1 - T_2)}{T_1 T_2} \qquad \left(\text{as } k \propto \frac{1}{D}\right)$$

Hence, $$\frac{T_1 - T_2}{z} = \frac{E_a}{2.303R}\frac{(T_1 - T_2)}{T_1 T_2} \qquad \left(\text{as } \log \frac{D_2}{D_1} = \frac{T_1 - T_2}{z}\right)$$

Or $$z = \frac{2.303 R T_1 T_2}{E_a}$$

When temperatures T_1 and T_2 are not too far apart, then we may write:

$$z = \frac{2.303RT_m^{\ 2}}{E_a}$$

where T_m = average absolute temperature = $\frac{T_1 + T_2}{2}$

Temperature Quotient (Q_{10}):

The Q_{10} value of a reaction is often used for reporting temperature dependence of biological reactions. It is a factor by which the rate of a reaction changes for a 10 °C change in temperature. If a reaction rate doubles with a 10°C change in temperature, then Q_{10} = 2. For reactions such as enzymatically induced color or flavor change in foods, degradation of natural pigments, nonenzymatic browning, and microbial growth rate, the Q_{10} is usually around 2.

The dependence of rate of a reaction on temperature is expressed as temperature quotient. Let k_1 and k_2 are rate constant at T_1 and T_2.

So by definition of the Q_{10}:

$$k_2 = k_1 [Q_{10}]^{\frac{T_2 - T_1}{10}}$$

Q_{10} can also be expressed as:

$$Q_{10} = \frac{k_{T+10}}{k_T}$$

The Q_{10} approach is often used for estimation of the temperature acceleration of shelf life. For a given extent of deterioration and reaction order, the rate constant is inversely proportional to the time to reach some degree of quality loss. Thus by taking the ratio of shelf life between any two temperature 10°C apart, the Q_{10} of the reaction can be found.

Rate of deteriorative reaction at two temperatures is related to shelf life at these two temperatures as:

$$Q_{10} = \frac{k_{T+10}}{k_T} = \frac{t_{ST}}{t_{ST+10}}$$

where t_{ST} = shelf life at temperature T °C

t_{ST} + 10 = shelf life at temperature (T + 10) °C

$$\therefore \quad Q_{10} = \frac{t_{ST}}{t_{ST+10}}$$

Since, $\quad D \propto \frac{1}{k}$

Hence, $\quad Q_{10} = \frac{k_{T+10}}{k_T} = \frac{D_T}{D_{T+10}}$

From Arrhenius model, we may write:

$$\log\frac{k_{T+10}}{k_T} = \frac{E_a}{2.303R}\left(\frac{1}{T}-\frac{1}{T+10}\right)$$

or,
$$\log\frac{k_{T+10}}{k_T} = \frac{E_a}{2.303R}\left(\frac{10}{T(T+10)}\right)$$

or,
$$\frac{k_{T+10}}{k_T} = 10^{\frac{E_a}{2.303R}\left(\frac{10}{T(T+10)}\right)}$$

$$Q_{10} = 10^{\frac{E_a}{2.303R}\left(\frac{10}{T(T+10)}\right)}$$

Since,
$$Q_{10} = 10^{\frac{10}{z}} \qquad \left(\text{as } z = \frac{2.303RT_1T_2}{E_a}\right)$$

$$10^{10/z} = 10^{\frac{10E_a}{2.303RT(T+10)}}$$

$$\frac{10}{z} = \frac{10E_a}{2.303RT(T+10)}$$

$$z = \frac{2.303RT(T+10)}{E_a} \qquad \left(\begin{array}{l}\text{as } \ln(x) = 2.303\log(x),\\ \ln 2 = 0.693, \ln 10 = 2.303\end{array}\right)$$

$$E_a = \frac{RT(T+10)\ln(10)}{z}$$

Ea may also be expressed as:

$$Ea = \frac{\ln(10)RT_1T_2}{z}$$

$$\Rightarrow \qquad Ea \propto \frac{1}{z}$$

From this expression, z value and Ea value may be calculated for a given condition.

The above model used to describe how much faster/slower a reaction will go if the product is held at some other temperature. It is also used to predict the expected product shelf life. The z-value measures the effect of temperature on the reaction rate constant.

For $10°C$ reduction in storage temperature of food, shelf life increases by a factor of 2.

Q_{10} may also be expressed as:

$$\therefore \qquad Q_{10} = 10^{\left(\frac{10Ea}{RT(T+10)}\right)} = \frac{t_{ST}}{t_{ST+10}}$$

Also, z may be expressed in term of Q_{10} as:

$$z = \frac{10\ln(10)}{\ln(Q_{10})} = \frac{10}{\log Q_{10}}, \ ^{\circ}\mathrm{C} \qquad (\text{as } Q_{10} = 10^{10/z})$$

Or

$$z = \frac{18}{\log Q_{10}}, \ ^{\circ}\mathrm{F}$$

Lethal Rate (*LR*):

It is a measure of the rate of inactivation of the microorganisms at any given time is given by the following equation:

$$LR = 10^{\left(\frac{T-121}{z}\right)} = \frac{D_{121}}{D_T}$$

When process temperature changes, F_0 value is used to calculate the total lethal rate.

$$F_0 = \int_0^t (LR)dt = \int_0^t 10^{\left(\frac{T-121}{z}\right)} dt \approx \sum_0^t 10^{\frac{T-121}{10}} \Delta t$$

The effects of different sterilization process in a given material are additive. Hence for several different temperatures T_1, T_2, ... each having different treatment time t_1, t_2,....., the F_0 value of each stage are added to give total value F_0. The total F_0 is given by:

$$F_0 = t_1 \times 10^{(T_1-121)/z} + t_2 \times 10^{(T_2-121/z)} + ...$$

This value of F_0 is then compared with the standard value of F for the organism to check the adequacy of the sterilization process.

The lethality of a process is the ratio of F value of the process divided by the F value required for commercial sterility and is given by:

$$\text{Process lethality} = \frac{\left(F_{Tref}^{z}\right)_{\text{process}}}{\left(F_{Tref}^{z}\right)_{\text{required}}}$$

Process lethality must be greater than one to have an acceptable process.

Continuous Flow Sterilization:

The specified process for sterilization in continuously flowing systems is a time of residence in a holding tube, an unheated section of the piping system that leads the fluid from the heat exchangers for heating to the heat exchangers for cooling. The time of residence is set by the volume of the holding tube and the rate of fluid flow delivered by a positive displacement pump.

$$t_{avg} = \frac{AL}{Q}$$

where $t_{avg.}$ is average fluid residence time (s), A is cross-sectional area of the holding tube (m^2), L is length of the holding tube (m), and Q is volumetric rate of flow (m^3/s).

The average velocity in the holding tube may be computed by:

$$\bar{v} = \frac{Q}{A}$$

The average residence time based on average velocity is given by:

$$t_{avg} = \frac{L}{\bar{v}}$$

where L is tube length.

The maximum velocity for Newtonian fluids and power flow fluids in laminar flow are:

$$v_{max} = 2 \times \bar{v}$$

and $$v_{max} = \left(\frac{3n+1}{n+1}\right)\bar{v}$$

where n is flow behaviour index.

Minimum residence time based on maximum velocity is given by:

$$t_{min} = 0.5 \times t_{avg}$$

In thermal process calculation, the residence time of fastest flowing portion of the fluid is used as required holding time.

Minimum residence time (t_{min}), length of holding tube (L) and maximum velocity (v_{max}) is related as:

$$t_{min} = \frac{L}{v_{max}}.$$

Required holding tube length of a heat exchanger may be computed by the relation:

$$L = v_{max} \times \text{residence time}$$

The maximum velocity for turbulent flow of Newtonian fluid is given by:

$$v_{max} = \frac{\bar{v}}{0.00332 \log(\text{Re}) + 0.662}$$

where v_{max} = maximum velocity (m/s),
L = length of holding tube (m),
t_{min} = minimum residence time (s)

In turbulent flow, the velocity profile is much flatter and the maximum and minimum residence time is given by:

$$v_{max} = 1.2\bar{v}$$

$$t_{min} = 0.83 \times t_{avg}$$

The lethality accomplished in the hold tube is the product of the lethal rate at the hold tube temperature and the minimum residence time.

$$F = \text{lethality} = \text{lethal rate} \times t_{\min} = 10^{\frac{Th-121}{z}} \times t_{\min}$$

where F = lethality, T_h = temperature at the exit of hold tube

Nutrient Degradation:

Nutrient degradation can be calculated the same way as for microbial inactivation. Nutrient retention with increasing processing temperature can be derived by simultaneously solving the rate equations for microbial inactivation and nutrient degradation. Using the subscript c and m to signify parameters for nutrient degradation and microbial inactivation respectively, equation used to determine the heating time at various temperatures for microbial inactivation is:

For microbial death, we may write:

$$t = D_{m0}\left[\log\frac{N}{N_0}\right](10)^{\frac{T_0-T}{z_m}}$$

A similar expression can be formulated for nutrient degradation.

or $$t = D_{c0}\left[\log\frac{C}{C_0}\right](10)^{\frac{T_0-T}{z_c}}$$

Solving these equations and putting $SV = \log(N_0/N)$ we have:

$$\log\left(\frac{C}{C_0}\right) = -\left[\frac{D_{m0}}{D_{c0}}Sv\right](10)^{(T_0-T)\left[\frac{1}{z_m}-\frac{1}{z_c}\right]}$$

This equation is based on constant temperature processes and is applicable for estimating nutrient retention in holding tubes of aseptic processing systems.

$$\%\ \text{vitamin loss} = \frac{C_0 - C}{C_0}\times 100$$

where Co = initial concentration of vitamin

C = final concentration of vitamin

C/C_0 = fraction of vitamin retained

Equation for nutrient degradation during thermal processing can be derived as:

The equation for microbial death kinetics is:

$$\ln\frac{N}{N_0} = -k_m t$$

Or, $$t = \frac{\ln {N_0}/{N}}{k_m}$$

where k_m = thermal death rate constant for microorganism

Since deterioration of any nutrient is also of first order, hence we may write:

$$\ln \frac{V}{V_0} = -k_v t$$

$$t = \frac{\ln V_0/V}{k_v}$$

where V = amount of nutrient retained after processing time t

V_0 = amount of nutrient initially present

k_v = rate constant for nutrient

Equating both equations we may write:

$$\frac{\ln V_0/V}{k_v} = \frac{\ln N_0/N}{k_m}$$

$$\frac{\log V_0/V}{k_v} = \frac{\log N_0/N}{k_m}$$

Or, $$\log \frac{V_0}{V} = \frac{k_v}{k_m} \log \frac{N_0}{N} = (SV) \times \frac{k_v}{k_m}$$

Or, $$\frac{V}{V_0} = 10^{-(SV)\times\frac{k_v}{k_m}} = 10^{-(SV)\times\frac{D_m}{D_v}}$$

This equation can be used for % vitamin loss calculation for a given condition.

The above equation may also be written as:

$$\frac{V_0}{V} = 10^{(SV)\times\frac{k_v}{k_m}}$$

From Arrhenius Relationship, we may write:

$$k_v = \alpha_v e^{-\frac{E_v}{RT}}$$

$$k_m = \alpha_m e^{-\frac{E_m}{RT}}$$

α = frequency factor

Since, $$\frac{k_v}{k_m} = \frac{\alpha_v}{\alpha_m} e^{\frac{E_m - E_v}{RT}}$$

Hence, $$\frac{V_0}{V} = 10^{(SV)\times\frac{k_v}{k_m}} = 10^{(SV)\left[\frac{\alpha_v}{\alpha_m} e^{\frac{E_m - E_v}{RT}}\right]}$$

Or, $$\frac{V_0 - V}{V_0} \times 100 = \left[1 - 10^{-(SV)\left[\frac{\alpha_v}{\alpha_m} e^{\frac{E_m - E_v}{RT}}\right]}\right] \times 100$$

This equation can be used for calculation of % nutrient loss (*e.g.*: % Vitamin loss) during thermal processing.

To achieve same degree of sterility at two different time and temperature condition (*e.g.* pasteurization of milk), *z* value can be estimated from the following expression:

$$\left(\frac{t_1}{D_{121}}\right) 10^{\frac{T_1 - 121}{z}} = \left(\frac{t_2}{D_{121}}\right) 10^{\frac{T_2 - 121}{z}} \qquad \left(\text{as } \log\frac{N_0}{N} = \left(\frac{t}{D_{121}}\right) 10^{\frac{T - 121}{z}}\right)$$

Where t_1 processing time at temperature T_1 and t_2 is processing time at temperature T_2.

Extruder Throughput:

An extruder is a device which is used to produce extruded food products. The volumetric throughput (m^3/s) of a single-screw extruder is given by:

$$Q = \frac{(\pi DN \cos\theta) WH}{2} - \frac{WH^3}{12\mu}\left(\frac{p_2 - p_1}{L}\right)$$

where D = screw diameter, m

N = rotation speed, s^{-1}

θ = angle of the helix.

W, H = width and height of the flow channel

μ = apparent viscosity of the mass

P_1 and P_2 = pressure, at the feed end and exit end respectively

L = length of the extruder

Microwaves Heating of Foods:

The microwave is widely used for processing of solid and liquid foods due faster rate of heating and improvement in quality.

The rate of heat generation per unit volume (Q) at a location inside the food during microwave heating can be characterized by:

$$Q = 2\pi f \varepsilon_0 \varepsilon'' E^2$$

where f is the frequency, ε_0 is the dielectric constant of free space and ε is the dielectric loss factor, and E is the electric field.

Dielectric constant (ε_0) is the ability of a material to store microwave energy and dielectric loss factor (ε'') is the ability of a material to dissipate microwave energy into heat.

Conversion of Microwave Energy into Heat:

The power absorbed by food during microwave and dielectric heating is given by:

$$P = 55.61 \times 10^{-14} E^2 f \varepsilon''$$

where P = power per unit volume (W/m^3)
E = electric field strength (V/m)
f = frequency (Hz or cps)
ε'' = dielectric loss factor

The dielectric loss factor (ε'') for a given material which expresses the degree to which an externally applied electric field will be converted to heat is given by:

$$\varepsilon'' = \varepsilon' \tan \delta$$

where $\tan \delta$ = loss tangent
ε' = Dielectric constant

The loss tangent tand provides an indication of how well the material can be penetrated by an electrical field and how it dissipates electrical energy as heat.

The depth of penetration of microwaves is found from the loss factor and the frequency of the microwaves:

$$d = \frac{\lambda}{2\pi\sqrt{(\varepsilon' \tan \delta)}}$$

where d = depth of penetration (m)
λ = wavelength (m)
$\tan \delta$ = loss tangent or loss factor or dissipation constant
ε' = constant

Unsteady Heating of Semisolid Food Inside a Retort:

The general equation for unsteady heating of semisolid food (kept in tin can) inside a retort is given by:

$$T_r - T = ae^{-bt}$$

where T_r = retort chamber temperature
T = temperature of food after time t inside retort
t = heating time

Chapter

9

Refrigeration and Freezing

Refrigeration is a process of removing heat from an enclosed space or substance. It is used to keep the product at low temperature to enhance the shelf life of foods by minimizing growth of microbes and biochemical reaction. Freezing further improves the shelf life of food materials as free water becomes unavailable for growth of microbes and biochemical reaction. Proper freezing retains food color, texture, and nutrient quality for long time periods provided storage temperatures are maintained sufficiently low. This chapter describes the governing equations used in refrigeration and freezing.

Refrigeration

Refrigeration Load : Refrigeration systems are widely used for cooling, freezing, and refrigerated storage of food and other products. Total heat load on a refrigeration system required includes sensible heat removal from initial temperature to freezing temperature, latent heat removal during phase change, and sensible heat removal from initial freezing temperature to final storage temperature.

Mathematically total amount of heat required can be represented as:

$$Q = mC_p\left(T_1 - T_f\right) + m\lambda_f + mC'_p\left(T_f - T_2\right)$$

where C_p, C'_p = specific heat values above and below freezing, respectively, J/kg ºC

λf = latent heat of fusion, J/kg

m = mass of product being frozen, kg

Q = total amount of heat removed in the cooling operation, J

T_1, T_2, T_f = the initial, final and freezing point temperatures, respectively, ºC

Heat of Respiration:

Fruits and vegetables generate heat during respiration and this heat of respiration adds to the refrigeration load. The heat of respiration of fruits and vegetables is a function of temperature and can be calculated using the expression:

$$q = a(e)^{bT}$$

where q is the rate of heat generation (W/kg) and the values of a and b are different for different fruits and vegetables.

During cooling, heat of respiration decrease as temperature decreases. An average heat of respiration may be calculated between two temperatures T_1 and T_2 knowing the time t for the temperature to change between T_1 and T_2 assuming that the temperature change during this period is linear.

$$q = \frac{a(e)^{bT_1}}{b(T_1 - T_2)}\left[1-(e)^{-b(T_1-T_2)}\right]$$

Total amount of heat generated during time period $t = q \times t$

Note **:** Motors inside a refrigerated room generate heat at the rate of 1025.5 W/hp. Workers inside a room generate approximately 293W per person.

Mechanical Refrigeration:

Refrigerators and freezers use refrigeration cycle to draw heat away from the compartments to keep foods cool. The cycle has four major components: evaporator, compressor, condenser, and an expansion valve. The representation of a refrigeration system is shown in Fig. 9.1.

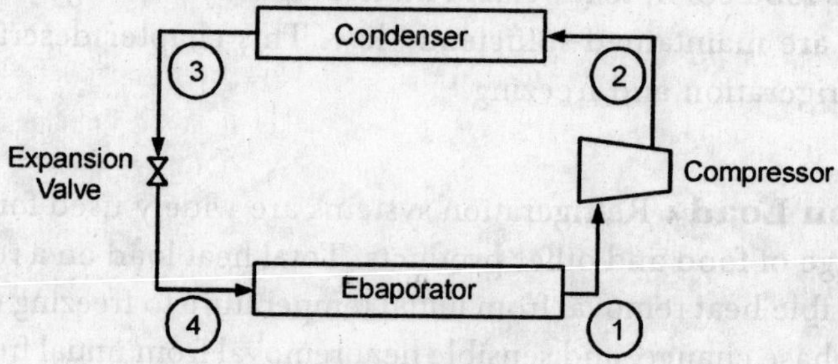

FIG. 9.1. The diagram of a refrigeration system

The refrigeration capacity (qe) of a mechanical refrigeration cycle is the rate at which heat is extracted from the surroundings at the step of evaporation. Referring Fig. 9.2, following equations may be written for different operations of refrigeration cycle:

The equation of energy balance for the evaporator is given as:

$$q_e = \dot{m}(h_1 - h_4)$$

where $\dot{m}$ = rate of circulation of the refrigerant, kg/s

h_1, h_4 = specific enthalpy of the refrigerant at point 1 and 4, J/kg

In the SI system, refrigeration capacity is expressed in watt.

The rate at which heat is rejected to the surroundings, q_c is obtained from the energy balance for the condenser:

$$q_c = \dot{m}(h_3 - h_2)$$

where h_2, h_3 = specific enthalpy of the refrigerant at point 2 and 3, J/kg

The theoretical mechanical power W (watt) supplied to the compressor is:

$$W = \dot{m}(h_2 - h_1)$$

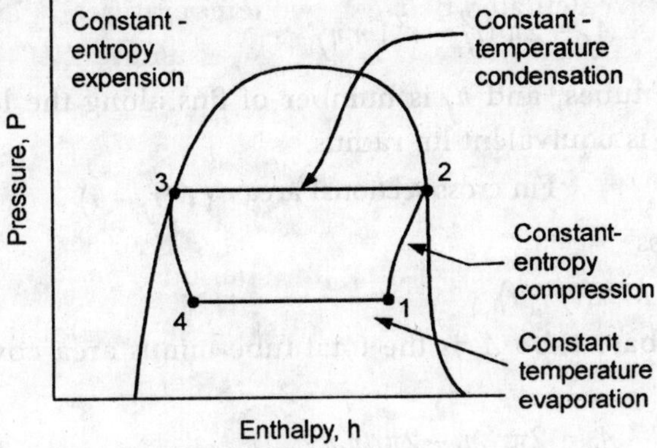

FIG. 9.2 Pressure-enthalpy diagram

Coefficient of Performance (*COP*):

The efficiency of a refrigeration system is expressed as its coefficient of performance (*COP*, dimensionless), defined as:

$$COP = \frac{\text{refrigeration effect}}{\text{work input}} = \frac{q_e}{W} = \frac{h_1 - h_4}{h_2 - h_1}$$

Refrigeration Capacity:

The useful output of a refrigeration system is its refrigeration capacity. The rate at which energy is removed from the cold space of the refrigeration system is the measure of system capacity. The unit used for refrigeration is known as ton of refrigeration. A ton of refrigeration may be defined as the quantity of heat required to be removed from one ton of water at 0 °C in 24 hours to form one ton of ice.

1 ton of refrigeration = 3.52 kW =50 kcal/min=3000 kcal/h

Coefficient of Performance of Reverse Carnot Cycle:

$$(COP)_{\text{refrigeration}} = \frac{\text{heat removed}}{\text{work done}} = \frac{T_1}{T_2 - T_1}$$

where T_1 and T_2 are refrigerated temperature and atmospheric temperature.

Condenser and Evaporator:

The heat transfer surface area of the tubes that comprise the evaporator or condenser coil is increased by the use of fins. Finned heat exchange units are sized in terms of an effective heat transfer surface area (A_{eff}) which is the sum of the area of the bare tube A_t and the effective area of the fin, which is the product of the fin surface area A_f and the fin efficiency η.

$$A_{eff} = A_t + \eta A_f$$

The fin efficiency, η, decreases as the base area of the fin decreases and as the height of the fin increases.

The equivalen fin surface area, A_f, is calculated as follows:

$$A_f = 2\pi\,(r_f^2 - r^2)\, n_t n_f$$

where n_t is number of tubes, and n_f is number of fins along the length of each tube, r is radius of tubes and r_f is equivalent fin radius.

$$\text{Fin cross-sectional area} = t\,(r_f - r)$$

where t = fin thickness

height of fin = $h = (r_f - r)$

The area of the bare tube A_t is the total tube minus area covered by the fins and is given by:

$$A_t = 2\pi r l_t n_t - 2\pi r t n_t n_f$$

where l_t = length

Freezing of Foods:

The storage life of foods is extended by freezing the product. Freezing foods involves the removal of energy from the food. The energy removed to freeze foods is the sensible cooling required to lower the temperature to the freezing point but the primary energy removed is the latent energy for phase change. Freezing time for foods and other products can be predicted by Plank's equation:

$$t_f = \frac{\rho\lambda}{T_f - T_c}\left[\frac{Pa}{h} + \frac{Ra^2}{k}\right]$$

where T_f = freezing time, s

T_f = freezing temperature, °C

T_c = temperature of cooling medium, °C

a = thickness for an infinite slab, diameter for infinite cylinder and sphere

λ = latent heat of fusion per unit volume = ρL_f

k = thermal conductivity of frozen solid

L_f = latent heat of fusion

ρ = density of unfrozen material

The value of P and R are different for different geometries and given as:

Shape	*P*	*R*
Sphere	1/6	1/24
Cylinder	¼	1/16
Slab	½	1/8

When a food material is frozen from both surfaces then,

a = half thickness

The λ refers to the latent heat of freezing of the food and not of pure water. If the mass fraction of water in the food is w and the latent heat of freezing of pure water is λ_0, then λ can be calculated as $\lambda = w\,\lambda_0$.

For an ideal surface contact, h is infinite and Pa/h becomes zero.

For packaged food product, the thermal resistance of a packaging should be taken into account when determining an appropriate value for the heat transfer coefficient in plank's equation. The packaging has the effect of reducing the over all heat transfer coefficient which is given by:

$$\frac{1}{U} = \frac{1}{h} + \frac{x}{k}$$

where x and k are thickness and thermal conductivity of packaging material respectively.

Calculation of Thickness of Ice Layer of Ice Cream in Scraped Surface Heat Exchanger:

Based on heat balance, thickness of ice layer of ice immediately before scrapping a scraped surface heat exchanger may be calculated as:

$$AU\Delta\theta \times t = A \times \delta \times \rho_{ice} \times \lambda_s$$

Or,

$$\delta = \frac{U\Delta\theta \times t}{\rho_{ice}\lambda_s}$$

where Δq = temperature difference

A = heat transfer area

t = time interval between two scrapping operations

$$t = \frac{1}{n \times N}$$

where n is number of blades and N is speed of scrapper shaft.

λ_s = latent heat of solidification of ice

ρ_{ice} = density of ice

Chapter 10

Psychrometrics

Psychrometrics is the study of the physical and thermal properties of air and water vapor mixtures. An understanding of the physical and thermal properties of moist air is the foundation for design and analysis of industrial drying, heating, cooling, storage systems, humidifying and dehumidifying processes.

Properties of Moist Air:

The mixture of dry air and water vapor is called moist air. Dry air consists of 21% oxygen and 79% nitrogen by volume and 23% oxygen and 77% nitrogen by mass. If p_a and p_v are the partial pressure of dry air and water vapor respectively, then by Dalton's law of partial pressure,

$$P = p_v + p_a$$

where P = total pressure (usually atmospheric)

The water vapour pressure (p_v) is the partial pressure by water vapour molecules present in the moist air. When air is fully saturated with water vapour, its vapour pressure is called *saturated vapour pressure* and is designated by p_s. The vapour pressure at saturation is given in steam table for different dry bulb temperatures. Air is said to be dry when it contains no moisture at all.

Unsaturated air (ambient air) = dry air + superheated vapour (water vapour)

Saturated air = dry air + saturated water vapour

The partial pressure of the dry air (p_a) is the difference between atmospheric pressure and the partial pressure of the water vapor also called *vapor pressure*.

$$p_a = P - p_v$$

From ideal gas law on a mole basis, we have:

$$PV = nRT = \frac{m}{M} RT$$

Or, $$PM = \frac{m}{V}RT = \rho RT$$

Or, $$\rho = \frac{PM}{RT}$$

This equation can be used to calculate the density of air.

Mass of air can be calculated using equation:

$$m = \frac{PVM}{RT}$$

where V = volume, m^3

P = pressure, N/m^2

M = molecular weight per kg mole (29 for air)

R = gas constant, Nm/kg mole K

T = absolute temperature, K

n = number of moles

Relative Humidity (*RH*):

RH of an air-water vapour mixture is the ratio of the partial pressure of water vapour in the mixture to the partial pressure of water vapour in saturated air at same dry bulb temperature and pressure. It is often expressed as percentage.

$$RH = \frac{\text{mass of water vapour}}{\text{mass of water vapour at saturation}} = \frac{m_v}{m_s} = \frac{p_v}{p_s} \times 100$$

where p_v = partial pressure of water vapour

p_s = partial pressure of water vapour at saturation

The relative humidity is also defined as the ratio of mole fraction of water vapour (x_v) in a given moist air sample to the mole fraction in an air sample saturated at the same temperature and pressure (x_s).

Thus, $$RH = \frac{x_v}{x_s} \times 100$$

The relative humidity is 100% when the air is saturated with water vapor and 0% when no water vapor is present in the air at all.

Dry bulb Temperature:

It is the temperature recorded by thermometer with a dry bulb and denoted by *T*.

Dew Point Temperature:

The dew point temperature (T_{dp}) is the temperature at which condensation occurs when the air is cooled at constant humidity ratio and constant atmospheric pressure. It may also be defines as the temperature at which a given mixture of air and water vapour would be saturated is called *dew point temperature*. The dew point is also that temperature where the vapor pressure of water equals the partial pressure of water in the air.

$$T_{dp} = T_s \text{ at } p_s = p_v$$

where T_{dp} = dew point temperature; T_s = saturation temperature

At saturation (100% relative humidity), the dry bulb temperature (T), wet-bulb temperature (Tw), and dew point temperature (T_{dp}) are equal. At any other conditions, these temperatures are not equal and follow the order:

$$T > T_w > T_{dp}$$

The difference between dry bulb temperature and wet bulb temperature is called wet bulb depression.

$$\text{wet bulb depression} = T - T_w$$

Humidity:

Humidity of an air water vapour mixture is defined as ratio of mass of water vapour in the mixture to the mass of dry air in the mixture (kg water vapor per kg dry air). It is also known as *specific humidity* or *humidity ratio* or *absolute humidity*.

For an air water vapour mixture, humidity is given by:

$$H = \frac{m_v}{m_a}$$

In term of partial pressure:

$$H = \frac{p_v}{p_a} \cdot \frac{M_v}{M_a} = \frac{p_v}{P - p_v} \cdot \frac{M_v}{M_a} = \frac{p_v}{P - p_v} \cdot \frac{18}{29}$$

where M_v and M_a are molecular weight of water vapour and air respectively.

At all humidities other than 0 or 100 %, the percentage humidity is less than RH.

$$H = 0.622\frac{p_v}{P - p_v} = 0.622\frac{p_v}{p_a} = 0.622\frac{p_s \times RH}{p_a \times 100} \qquad \left(\text{as } pa = P - p_v \text{ and } RH = \frac{p_v}{p_s} \times 100\right)$$

$$\text{Or,} \quad RH = \frac{Hp_a}{0.62\, p_s} \times 100$$

where p_v = partial pressure of water vapour

p_a = partial pressure of dry air

P = total pressure

p_s = partial pressure of water vapour at saturation

P_v can be obtained from steam table at a given dew point temperature.

P_s can be obtained from steam table at a given dry bulb temperature.

The partial pressure of water vapour can be estimated by:

$$p_v = \frac{1.61PH}{1 + 1.61H} = \frac{PH}{0.622 + H}$$

The partial pressure of water vapour (p_v) corresponds to dew point temperature.

Example : If dew point temperature=15 °C, then p_v from steam table = 1707.5 N/m^2

Partial pressure of water vapour (*kPa*) can also be estimated from following empirical equation (Carrier equation):

$$p_v = p_s - \frac{(P - p_s)(T - T_w)}{1500 - 1.44T_w}$$

where p_s = saturation pressure at wet bulb temperature, *kPa*

P = total pressure, *kPa*

T = dry bulb temperature (°C)

T_w = wet bulb temperature (°C)

p_v = actual partial pressure of water vapour at dew point temperature, *kPa*

Saturated Humidity:

The saturation humidity (H_s) is the maximum quantity of water vapor that air can contain at a given temperature, without phase separation.

$$H_s = 0.62\frac{p_s}{P - p_s}$$

where p_s = partial pressure of water vapour at saturation

Percentage Humidity (Degree of Saturation):

It is defined as 100 times the actual humidity H of the air divided by the H_s and expressed as:

$$H_p = \frac{H}{H_s} \times 100$$

The degree of saturation varies from 0 to 1.

Relationship between Percentage Saturation and *RH*:

$$\% \text{ saturation} = \frac{H}{H_s} \times 100 = RH\left(\frac{P - p_s}{P - p_v}\right) \times 100$$

Humid Heat of Air-water Vapor Mixture:

Humid heat of an air water vapour mixture is the amount of heat in kJ required to raise the temperature of 1 kg of dry air plus water vapor present by 1 °C or 1 K.

Humid heat of air water vapour mixture is given by:

$$C_s = C_{pa} + C_{pv}H = 1.005 + 1.88H \text{ , kJ/kg dry air K}$$

where C_{pa} = specific heat of dry air = 1.005 kJ/kg K

C_{pv} = specific heat of water vapor = 1.88 kJ/kg of water vapour

H = humidity ratio, kg water vapour/kg dry air

Enthalpy of Air-water Vapor Mixture:

It is a measure of the energy content of the air and depends upon both the temperature and the moisture content of the air. If T_0 is the datum temperature taken for both components, the total enthalpy is the sensible heat of the air-water vapour mixture plus the latent heat λ_o in J/kg or kJ/kg water vapour of the water vapour at T_0.

The total enthalpy (h) of 1kg of dry air plus its water vapor is given by:

$$h = C_s(T - T_o) + H\lambda_o = (1.005 + 1.88H)(T - T_o) + H\lambda_o$$

where λ_o = latent heat kJ/kg water vapour of water vapour at T_0 = 2501 kJ/kg

T = dry bulb temperature, °C

H = humidity ratio

At base temperature T_0 of 0 °C, the equation becomes:

$$h = (1.005 + 1.88H)T + 2501H = 1.005T + H(2501 + 1.88T)$$

This equation provides a good approximation for the enthalpy of moist air over a wide range of temperatures.

Humid Volume of Air-water Vapor Mixture:

Humid volume (vH) of an air water vapor mixture is the total volume in m^3 of 1 kg of dry air plus the water vapour it contains at 101.325 *kPa* absolute pressure and temperature. At standard temperature and pressure (*STP*), 101.325 kPa and 273 K, 1 kmol of gas will occupy volume of 22.4 m3. Applying the ideal gas equation, we may write:

$$v_H = \frac{22.4}{273}\left(\frac{1}{29} + \frac{H}{18}\right)T \text{ , m}^3\text{/kg of dry air}$$

Or,

$$v_H = (0.00283 + 0.00456H)T$$

where T = dry bulb temperature, K

Mass flow rate of air may be computed by the following relation:

$$\dot{m}_a = \frac{q_a}{\nu_H}$$

where $\dot{m}_a$ = mass flow rate of air, kg/s

q_a = volumetric flow rate of air, m^3/s

nH = humid volume, m^3/kg dry air

Wet Bulb Temperature:

Wet bulb temperature is the temperature indicated by a thermometer covered by a wick saturated with liquid water and in contact with moving air.

The equation of wet bulb line is given as:

$$\frac{H - H_w}{T - T_w} = \frac{h / M_a k_y}{\lambda_w} = \frac{-C_s}{\lambda_w} = \frac{-950}{\lambda_w}$$

where M_a = molecular weight of air

k_y = mass transfer coefficient

T = dry bulb temperature

T_w = wet bulb temperature

h = heat transfer coefficient

λ_w = latent heat of vaporization at wet bulb temperature (T_w)

C_s = 950 J/kg K

The humidity at wet bulb temperature can be calculated by:

$$H_w = 0.62\frac{p_w}{P - p_w}$$

The value of p_w may be taken from steam table at a given wet bulb temperature.

For air water vapour:

$$\frac{h}{M_a k_y} = \text{psychrometric ratio} \approx Cs$$

For air water vapour mixture, the value of this ratio is 0.961.

Adiabatic Saturation Temperature:

The adiabatic saturation temperature is the steady state temperature attained when a large amount of water is contacted with the gas. The equation of adiabatic saturation line is given as:

$$\frac{H - H_s}{T - T_s} = \frac{-C_s}{\lambda_s} = \frac{-950}{\lambda_s}$$

where λ_s = latent heat of vaporization at adiabatic saturation temperature (T_s)

Lewis number Le is given by:

$$Le = \frac{h}{kC_p}$$

where h = surface heat transfer coefficient at the wet-bulb temperature, W/m^2 K

C_p = specific heat of moist air, J/kg K

k = air-film coefficient of mass transfer, kg/m^2 s

For air water vapour mixture, $Le = 1$

Thus, the wet-bulb temperature is normally considered the same as the adiabatic saturation, or thermodynamic wet-bulb temperature

Mixing Process for Two Streams of Air:

Consider two air stream with mass flow rates of m_{a1} and m_{a2}, temperature T_1 and T_2 humidity ratios H_1 and H_2. The mixture has a mass flow rate of m_{a3}, a temperature of T_3 and humidity ratio of H_3.

Writing a total mass balance, a moisture balance, and an enthalpy balance for the air streams (Fig. 10.1) we have:

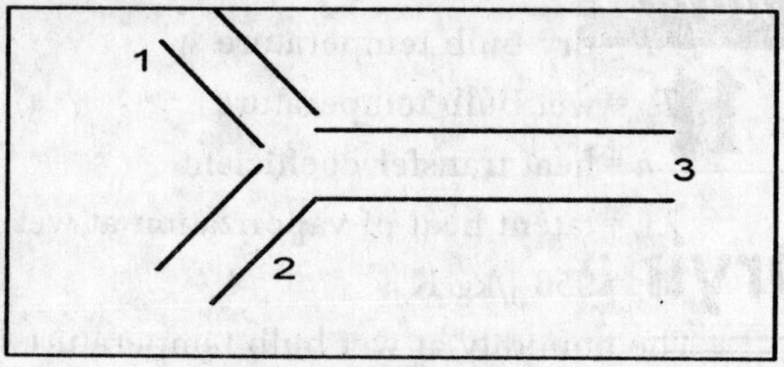

FIG. 10.1. Mixing of two air streams

Total mass balance:

$$m_{a1} + m_{a2} = m_{a3}$$

Enthalpy balance:

$$m_{a1}h_1 + m_{a2}h_2 = m_{a3}h_3$$

Mass balance for water vapour

$$m_{a1}H_1 + m_{a2}H_2 = m_{a3}H_3$$

Solving these equations we have:

$$\frac{m_{a1}}{m_{a2}} = \frac{h_2 - h_3}{h_3 - h_1} = \frac{H_2 - H_3}{H_3 - H_1}$$

Since $h = C_s T + H\lambda_0$

Where T is dry bulb temperature.

$$\therefore \quad m_{a3}h_3 = m_{a1}h_1 + m_{a2}h_2$$

Or, $m_{a3}\left(C_s T_3 + H_3\lambda_0\right) = m_{a1}\left(C_s T_1 + H_1\lambda_0\right) + m_{a2}\left(C_s T_2 + H_2\lambda_0\right)$

$$\left(C_s T_3 + H_3\lambda_0\right) = \frac{m_{a1}}{m_{a3}}\left(C_s T_1 + H_1\lambda_0\right) + \frac{m_{a2}}{m_{a3}}\left(C_s T_2 + H_2\lambda_0\right)$$

Or,
$$T_3 = \left(\frac{m_{a1}T_1 + m_{a2}T_2}{m_{a3}}\right)\frac{C_s}{C_s} + \left(\frac{m_{a1}H_1 + m_{a2}H_2}{m_{a3}}\right)\frac{\lambda_0}{C_s} - \frac{H_3\lambda_0}{C_s}$$

$$T_3 = \left(\frac{m_{a1}T_1 + m_{a2}T_2}{m_{a3}}\right) + (H_3 - H_3)\frac{\lambda_0}{C_s} \qquad \left(\text{As } H_3 = \left(\frac{m_{a1}H_1 + m_{a2}H_2}{m_{a3}}\right)\right)$$

$$\therefore T_3 = \left(\frac{m_{a1}T_1 + m_{a2}T_2}{m_{a3}}\right)$$

The partial water vapour pressure of mixed air may be determined by:

$$p_v = \frac{PH_3}{0.622 + H_3}$$

where P = total pressure

Chapter 11

Drying

Drying is defined as the application of heat under controlled conditions to remove the majority of the water normally present in a food by evaporation. The main purpose of drying is to extend the shelf life of foods by a reduction in water activity. Drying helps in reducing weight, transportation and distribution costs. This chapter describes basic concept of water activity, drying periods and drying methods with their governing equations.

Water Activity:

Water plays an important role in the stability of fresh, frozen and dried foods. It acts as a solvent for chemical, microbiological and enzymatic reactions. Water activity refers to free water available in food materials which takes part in biochemical reaction. Water activity (a_w) is defined as the ratio of the water vapor pressure of the food to the vapor pressure of pure water at the same temperature.

$$a_w = \frac{\text{vapour pressure of water present in food}}{\text{vapour pressure of pure water at same temperature}} = \frac{p}{p_0}$$

Water activity may also be defines as the equilibrium relative humidity (ERH) in which a food would neither gain nor lose moisture.

$$a_w = \frac{\%ERH}{100}$$

The values of water activity of pure water/free water at any temperature above its freezing point is 1. The value of water activity for any foods lies in the range of 0 – 1.

Water activity of solution at specific temperature below freezing can be defined as the vapour pressure of ice divided by the vapour pressure of super cooled water at the same temperature and expressed as:

$$a_w = \frac{\text{vapour pressure of solid water (ice)}}{\text{vapour pressure of supercooled liquid water}}$$

Prediction of Water Activity of High Moisture Foods:

Water Activity for ideal solution : Raoult's law is the basic equation for determination of water activity of ideal solutions. According to Raoult's law, water activity is equal to the mole fraction of water in the solution and can be expressed as:

$$a_w = n_w = \frac{\text{moles of water}}{\text{moles of water + moles of solute}} = \frac{W_w / M_w}{\frac{W_w}{M_w} + \frac{W_s}{M_s}} = \frac{W_w / 18}{\frac{W_w}{18} + \frac{W_s}{M_s}}$$

where, W_w = weight of water

W_s = weight of solute

M_w = molecular weight of water

M_s = molecular weight of solute

n_w = mole fraction of water

The water activity of high moisture foods (with a_w of 0.9 or higher) can be calculated quite accurately by this method. Raoult's law explains adequately the dependence of water activity on water and solute content in foods. Solutes with low molecular weights also provide larger reduction of vapor pressure per unit weight of solute than those with high molecular weights.

Raoult's law is not applicable for macromolecular solute due to the very low molecular weight ratio of water and solute. When ionizing salts are present in the solution, then Raoult's law may be expressed as:

$$a_w = n_w = \frac{W_w / M_w}{\frac{W_w}{M_w} + \varphi \frac{W_s}{M_s}}$$

where ϕ = degree of ionization

For NaCl, degree of ionization = 2

Water Activity for Non-ideal Solution:

In general, water activity for non ideal solution is given by:

$$a_w = \gamma n_w = \gamma (1 - n_s)$$

where γ is activity coefficient which corrects the deviation from non ideality and n_w and n_s is the mole fraction of water and solute.

For a given mass of added solute, n_s is greater for smaller molecules.

Norish Equation:

Norish equation is used for predicting water activity for sugar solution.

$$\log \frac{a_w}{x_w} = -k (1 - x_w)^2$$

Or, $$a_w = x_w 10^{-k(1-x_w)^2}$$

where x_w = mole fraction of water

k = constant depends on solute

The k value of few solutes is given in following table:

Solute	*k value*
Sucrose	2.7
Glucose	0.7
Fructose	0.7
Invert sugars	0.7
Sorbitol	0.85

Ross Equation:

Ross equation is used for most accurate water activity prediction for complex solutions where influence of insoluble solid on water activity is minimal.

$$a_w = (a_{w1})(a_{w2}).......$$

where a_{w1}, a_{w2},.... are water activities of the individual components based on total water in the system. The water activity of a mixture involving several components can be determined from the product of the water activity of each component separately if all the water present in the mixture is mixed with individual components.

Water Activity for Porous Solid Food Materials:

Kelvin-Thompson equation can be used for predicting water activity as follows:

$$a_w = e^{-\frac{M_w \Delta p}{\rho_w RT}}$$

where, Δp = suction pressure = $\frac{2\sigma}{r}$, Pa

r = radius of capillary or pore, m

σ = surface tension of water, N/m

M_w = molecular weight of water

ρ_w = density of water, kg/m^3

T = absolute temperature, K

The water activity can be expressed in term of osmotic pressure. The osmotic pressure of a solution is related to water activity by the following relationship:

$$aw = e^{\frac{M_w P_o}{\rho_w RT}}$$

where R = 8.314 × 103 m^3Pa/kgmol K

ρ_w = density of water, kg/m^3

T = absolute temperature, K

M_w = molecular weight of water

P_o = osmotic pressure, Pa

The osmotic pressure increases with decrease in water activity. As the water activity approaches 1, the osmotic pressure approaches zero.

Effect of Temperature on Water Activity:

Clausius-Clapeyron equation is used to predict the temperature dependence of water activity. The Clausius-Clapeyron equation can be written as:

$$\ln\frac{a_{w1}}{a_{w2}} = \frac{\Delta H}{R}\left[\frac{1}{T_1} - \frac{1}{T_2}\right]$$

where, $\Delta H = q - lw$ = net isosteric heat of sorption or excess heat of sorption, J/kg

q = isosteric heat of sorption, J/kg

λ_w = heat of vaporization of pure water, J/kg

T = absolute temperature, K

R = gas constant, J/kg K

a_{w1} = water activity at temperature T_1, K

a_{w2} = water activity at temperature T_2, K

Effect of Pressure on Water Activity:

At constant moisture content, the variation of water activity with pressure is given by:

$$\ln\frac{a_{w1}}{a_{w_2}} = \frac{M_w}{\rho_w RT}(P_1 - P_2)$$

where, R = gas constant, $m^3 Pa$/kgmole K

P_1, P_2 = total pressures, *Pa*

M_w = molecular weight of water

T = absolute temperature, K

a_{w1} and a_{w2} = water activities at total pressures P_1 and P_2, *Pa*

Moisture Content:

Moisture content can be expressed on wet weight basis (*wb*) and dry weight basis (*db*). Moisture content (*wb*) is most often used in food composition tables whereas moisture content (*db*) is more often encountered with sorption isotherms and drying curves. The wet-basis moisture content expresses the ratio of weight of water to the total weight of the substance. The percentage moisture content on wet weight basis (m) may be expressed as:

$$m = \frac{\text{weight of water}}{\text{weight of sample}} \times 100 = \frac{W_w}{W} \times 100$$

Since, $W = W_w + W_d$

Hence, $$m = \frac{W_w}{W_w + W_d} \times 100$$

Or, $$W_w = \frac{m \times (W_w + W_d)}{100}$$

where, W_w = weight of water

W_d = weight of dry matter (bone dry matter)

The dry-basis moisture content (M) expresses the ratio of the moisture mass present in the material to the mass of the dry matter and may be expressed as:

$$M = \frac{\text{weight of water}}{\text{weight of dry matter}} \times 100 = \frac{W_w}{W_d} \times 100$$

Relationship Between Moisture Content on Wet Basis (*m*) & Dry Basis (*M*):

The relationships between wet and dry moisture content on a percentage basis can be derived as:

$$m = \frac{W_w}{W_w + W_d} \times 100 = \frac{(W_w / W_d) \times 100}{(W_w / W_d + W_d / W_d) \times 100}$$

$$= \frac{M}{(W_w / W_d \times 100 + W_d / W_d \times 100)} \times 100 = \frac{M}{M + 100} \times 100$$

Hence, $$m = \frac{M}{M + 100} \times 100$$

Similarly the moisture content on dry basis can be expressed in term of moisture content on wet basis:

$$M = \frac{m}{100 - m} \times 100$$

where, m = % moisture content wet basis (wb)

M = % moisture content dry basis (db)

The relationships between wet and dry moisture content on a decimal basis can be expressed as:

$$M = \frac{m}{1 - m} \text{ and } m = \frac{M}{1 + M}$$

where m = decimal moisture content wet basis (wb)

M = decimal moisture content dry basis (db)

The amount of water removed from a food material may be calculated by:

$$W_w = W_d (M_0 - M_e)$$

where W_d = dry matter

M_o, & M_e = dry basis moisture content in decimal

The rate of moisture removal from the grain or wet material is:

$$\frac{dw}{dt} = m_a (H_2 - H_1)$$

where H_2 and H_1 are humidity and m_a = mass flow rate of dry air

The weight of grain after drying may be found using:

$$W_2 = W_1 - W_1\left(\frac{m_1 - m_2}{100 - m_2}\right)$$

where W_2 = dried grain

W_1 = weight of undried grain

m_1 = moisture content of undried grain, % wb

m_2 = moisture content of dried grain, % wb

This equation can be expressed in another form as follows:

$$\text{final weight} = \text{initial weight}\left(\frac{100 - m_1}{100 - m_2}\right)$$

Water transport during drying may be calculated by:

$$\dot{m}_w = \frac{q}{\nu}\left(H_f - H_i\right)$$

where q = air flow rate

ν = humid specific volume of air

H_f = increased humidity of air

H_i = initial humidity of air

Amount of Heat and Air Required During Drying:

The amount of heat required in drying food materials = sensible heat for increasing temperature from T_1 to T_2 + amount of moisture removed *x* latent heat of evaporation

Or, $$q = mC_p (T_2 - T_1) + m_w \times \lambda_v$$

where m and C_p are mass and specific heat of material, and m_w is the amount of moisture removed from material.

The amount of heat needed per kg of water removed = $\frac{q}{m_w}$

The mass flow rate of air may be estimated by:

$$q = m_a \times C_p \times (t_2 - t_1)$$

where m_a = mass of air flow rate, kg/s C_p = specific heat and t_1 and t_2 are ambient and heated air temperature.

The volumetric air flow rate may be calculated by:

$$\text{volumetric air flow rate} = \text{mass flow rate} \times \text{specific volume of air}$$

The rate of air supply (kg/s) during grain drying can be directly estimated by:

$$G' = \frac{W_d\left[C_{pg}\left(t_{g2} - t_{g1}\right) + M_1 C_{p_w}\left(t_{g2} - t_{g1}\right) + \left(M_1 - M_2\right)\lambda\right]}{C_{pa}\left(t_2 - t_1\right)\theta}$$

The volumetric flow rate of air is given by;

$$G = \upsilon \times G'$$

where G = volumetric air flow rate, m^3/s

ν = humid volume, m^3/kg

θ = time, s

M_1 & M_2 = moisture content (db), decimal

M_d = bone dry grain

C_{pg} = specific heat of grain

C_{pw} = specific heat of water

C_{pa} = specific heat of air

t_1, t_2 = ambient and heated air temperature

t_{g1}, t_{g2} = initial and final temperature of grain.

Moisture Sorption Isotherm:

The relationship between total moisture content and the corresponding a_w of a food over a range of values at a constant temperature yields a moisture sorption isotherm (MSI) when graphically expressed. Sorption isotherms are typically sigmoid in nature. Various models are available to study sorption isotherms.

***BET* Equation:**

The *BET* isotherm equation is the most widely used model and gives a good fit to data for a variety of foods over the range $0.05 < a_w < 0.45$. It provides an estimate of the monolayer value of moisture adsorbed on the surface.

The *BET* equation can be expressed in the form:

$$\frac{a_w}{(1 - a_w)M} = \frac{1}{M_o C} + \frac{C-1}{M_o C} a_w$$

where M_0 is the monolayer moisture content (db) and M = % m.c (db)

Estimation of the *BET* constants (M_o and C) is generally based on a linearization of the above equation.

$$\frac{a_w}{(1 - a_w)M} = \phi = \frac{1}{M_o C} + \frac{C-1}{M_o C} a_w$$

If the group ϕ is plotted against a_w, a straight line is obtained and M_0 and C are calculated from the intercept and the slope.

GAB Equation:

This equation gives a better fit than the *BET* over a wider range of moisture contents. Guggenheim-Anderson-de Boer (*GAB*) model to predict sorption isotherms is shown below:

$$\frac{M}{M_o} = \frac{CKa_w}{(1 - Ka_w)(1 - Ka_w + CKa_w)}$$

where C and K are constants, both related to the temperature and heat of adsorption. The range of applicability of the *GAB* equation is wider than that of the *BET* model. When K is unity, the equation becomes the *BET* equation.

Henderson Equation:

One of the most widely used equations for biological materials is the Henderson equation:

$$1 - RH = e^{-CTMe^{n}}$$

where c, n = constants based on the material

RH = relative humidity in decimal

T = absolute temperature, K

M_e = dry-basis equilibrium moisture content expressed as a percent

Oswin Model:

$$M = C\left[\frac{a_w}{1 - a_w}\right]^n$$

where C and n are constants.

Smith Model:

Smith developed an empirical model to describe the final curved portion of water sorption isotherm of high molecular weight biopolymers. This model can be written as:

$$M = C_1 + C_2 \ln(1 - a_w)$$

where C_1 and C_2 are constants.

Simultaneous Heat and Mass Transfer in Drying:

Drying is a process of both heat and mass transfer. In drying, moisture is removed by evaporation. The mass transfer equation can be written for a material undergoing dehydration in the form:

$$\dot{m}_w = Ak_g(H_s - H)$$

where $\dot{m}_w$ is the rate of mass of water vapor transferred from the surface to the moving air and A is the surface area of food exposed, H is the humidity of the drying air, k_g is the mass transfer coefficient, kg moles/m^2 · s.

Rate of heating needed to vaporize water at the rate mw will be:

$$q = \dot{m}_w \lambda$$

where λ is latent heat of vaporization at the interface temperature.

Heat transfer needed for vaporization will be:

$$q = Ak_g(H_s - H)\lambda$$

At equilibrium, the heat for vaporizing the mass transferred will be equal the rate of heat transfer.

The rate of heat transfer is:

$$q = hA(T - T_s)$$

where T_s is temperature at interface.

Equation heat and mass transfer equation may be written as:

$$Ak_g(H_s - H)\lambda = hA(T - T_s)$$

$$H = H_s + \frac{hT_s}{k_g\lambda} - \frac{hT}{k_g\lambda}$$

This equation is the equation of a wet bulb line. This line will go through the point T_s and H_s, the wet bulb temperature and the saturation humidity at the wet bulb temperature, respectively.

Drying Rate Periods:

The convection drying process is divided into two drying periods: constant rate drying period and falling rate drying period.

Constant Rate Drying Period:

During constant rate drying period, the rate of evaporation of water from the surface is equal to the rate of moisture migration from interior of product to its surface. The constant drying period continues till critical moisture content is reached. The constant rate drying period is for very short period.

Falling Rate Drying Period:

Falling rate period starts after constant rate period. The moisture content of product from where constant rate drying ceases and falling rate drying starts is called critical moisture content. Most of the agricultural products are dried in falling rate drying period.

Estimations for Total Drying Time:

Estimates of both the constant-rate and the falling-rate periods are needed to estimate the total drying time for a given drying operation.

Calculation of Drying Rate:

The rate of drying depends on the properties of the drier (the dry bulb temp., R.H.), the velocity of the air, surface heat transfer coefficient, the properties of the food (the moisture content, surface area to volume ratio, surface temperature and rate of moisture loss).

To determine the time required to achieve the desired reduction in product moisture content, the rate of moisture removal from the product must be predicted. The equation for moisture removal rate for constant-rate drying period is:

$$R_c = \frac{dw}{dt} = \frac{w_o - w_c}{t_c}$$

Or, time for constant rate period is:

$$t_c = \frac{w_o - w_c}{R_c}$$

where w_0 is the initial moisture content (kg water / kg dry solids) w_c is the critical moisture content (kg water / kg dry solids), R_c is moisture removal rate during constant rate drying (kg/s) and t_c is time for constant rate drying.

The time for falling rate drying is given by:

$$t_f = \frac{w_c}{R_c}\ln\left(\frac{w_c}{w}\right)$$

Hence total drying time becomes:

$$t = t_c + t_f = \frac{w_o - w_c}{R_c} + \frac{w_c}{R_c}\ln\left(\frac{w_c}{w}\right)$$

This indicates that the time for complete drying from some initial moisture content w_o to a desired final moisture content w depends on knowledge of the critical moisture content w_c, the time for constant rate drying t_c, and the rate for constant rate drying R_c.

Other approach of Prediction of Drying Time Under Constant Rate Period:

For constant rate drying period, the moisture removal rate can be described by:

$$\dot{m}_c = \frac{w_o - w_c}{t_c}$$

where $\dot{m}_c$ = moisture removal rate, kg/s

w_c = critical moisture content, kg water/kg dry solids

w_0 = initial moisture content, kg water/kg dry solids

t_c = drying time for constant rate drying, s

During constant rate drying period, heat is transferred from hot air to the product surface while water vapour is transferred from product surface to the heated air. The rate of heat transfer is expressed as:

$$q = hA(T_a - T_w)$$

where q = rate of heat transfer, W

A = area available for heat transfer, m^2

T_a = hot air temperature, °C

T_w = wet-bulb temperature (product surface temperature), °C

The heat transfer coefficient (h) is related to the mass flux of air using the following equations:

$$h = 14.3G^{0.8} \quad \text{(When air flows parallel to the drying surface)}$$

and

$$h = 24.2G^{0.37} \quad \text{(When air flows perpendicular to the drying surface)}$$

$$G = \rho v$$

where h = heat transfer coefficient between air flowing through a bed of solids and solids, W/m^2 K

G = mass flux of air, kg/m^{2}s

The amount of water vapour transfer during constant rate drying is given by the following mass transfer equation:

$$\dot{m}_c = \frac{K_m A M_w P}{0.622RT}(H_s - H_a)$$

where K_m = convective mass transfer coefficient, m/s

A = product surface area, m^2

M_w = molecular weight of water

P = atmospheric pressure, *Pa*

R = gas constant

T = absolute temperature, $[(Ta + Tp)/2] + 273$, K

T_a = hot air temperature, °C

T_p = product surface temperature, °C

H_a = humidity ratio of air (kg water vapour/kg dry air)

H_s = humidity ratio at product surface (kg water vapour/kg dry air)

Heat required for phase change of water at product surface temperature is:

$$q = \dot{m}_c \lambda_v$$

where λv = latent heat of vaporization of water at wet bulb temperature of heated air, J/kg

Combining $q = \dot{m}_c \lambda_v$ and $q = hA(T_a - T_w)$, the following equation for rate water vapour transfer is obtained:

$$\dot{m}_c = \frac{w_o - w_c}{t_c} = \frac{hA(T_a - T_w)}{\lambda_v}$$

Or,

$$t_c = \frac{\lambda_v (w_0 - w_c)}{hA(T_a - T_w)}$$

This is the required equation for the prediction of the duration of the constant rate period of drying based on heat transfer. This equation can be used for estimation of constant rate drying time.

Similarly the equation for the prediction of time for constant rate period of drying based on mass transfer can be given as:

$$t_c = \frac{0.622RT(w_0 - w_c)}{K_m A M_w P(H_s - H_a)}$$

This expression indicates that the constant rate drying time is inversely proportional to difference between humidity ratio at product surface and of heated air.

The constant drying rate may also be computed the following equations:

$$R_c = \frac{q}{A\lambda_w} = \frac{h}{\lambda_w}(T - T_w)$$

and $$R_c = \frac{w}{At_c}(x_1 - x_2) \qquad \text{(When } x_1 > x_2\text{)}$$

where R_c = constant drying rate, kg water/s. m^2

T = hot air temperature, °C

T_w = wet bulb temperature, °C

A = exposed area, m^2

q = rate of heat transfer, W

Total evaporation rate = $R_c \times A$, kg water/s

w = mass of dry solid, kg

x_1 = initial moisture content (db, fraction)

x_2 = final moisture content (db, fraction)

Falling Rate Peri od:

The equation for drying time (t_f) in falling rate period for materials with an infinite plate geometry in which moisture movement is controlled by diffusion is:

$$t_f = \frac{4d_c^2}{D\pi^2}\ln\left[\frac{8}{\pi^2}\left(\frac{w_c - w_e}{w - w_e}\right)\right]$$

where w is the average moisture content at time t (db), w_e is the equilibrium moisture content (db), m_c is the moisture content at the start of the falling rate period (db), D is the mass diffusivity (m^2/s) and d_c is characteristic dimension, half thickness of slab, m.

For spherical product, the equation for drying time (t_f) in falling rate period is given by:

$$t_f = \frac{d_c^2}{D\pi^2}\ln\left[\frac{6}{\pi^2}\left(\frac{w_c - w_e}{w - w_e}\right)\right]$$

where d_c is characteristic dimension, radius of sphere, m.

Equation for time of drying of material when liquid diffusion of moisture controls drying is:

$$t = \frac{4x^2}{\pi^2 D_L}\ln\frac{8X_1}{\pi_2 X}$$

where D_L is liquid diffusion coefficient in m^2/s or diffusivity of moisture through solid

x = half thickness of slab when drying occurs from both surfaces.

x = total thickness when drying occurs from top surface

X_1 = initial free moisture content = $X_{t1} - X_e$

$X = X_t - X_e$

X = average free moisture content at time t

X_e = equilibrium moisture content (EMC)

X_{t1} = initial moisture content at start of drying when $t = 0$

X_t = average total moisture content at time t

When air used in drying is dry, the EMC is zero.

Drying Rate Constant:

Drying rate constant can be obtained from thin layer drying equation. In thin layer drying, materials are fully exposed to heated air. The thickness of material normally taken is up to 15 cm.

Thin layer drying models:

Following are the thin layer drying models:

Exponential model:

$$\frac{M - M_e}{M_o - M_e} = e^{-kt}$$

Or,
$$t = \frac{1}{k}\ln\frac{M - M_e}{M_o - M_e}$$

The moisture ratio (MR) is given by:

$$MR = \frac{M - M_e}{M_o - M_e}$$

where k = drying constant, per sec

t = time, sec

The drying constant k may be related as:

$$k = \alpha v^n Ps$$

where v = velocity, m/min

P_s = pressure, kg/cm^2

α, n = constant

For two different drying times, the above equation may be expressed as:

$$\frac{M_1 - M_e}{M_o - M_e} = e^{-kt_1}$$

and
$$\frac{M_2 - M_e}{M_o - M_e} = e^{-kt_2}$$

Generalized Exponential model:

$$\frac{M - Me}{Mo - Me} = Ae^{-kt}$$

Page's model:

$$\frac{M - Me}{Mo - Me} = e^{-ktn}$$

Where n is constant of model.

Logarithmic model:

$$\frac{M - M_e}{M_o - M_e} = A + B\log(t)$$

where A and B are constant of model.

All moisture content is on dry basis.

Half Response Time:

It is defined as the time necessary to obtain a moisture content ratio of one half in a drying process. Similarly one-fourth response time is defined as the time necessary to obtain a moisture content ratio of one-fourth in a drying process.

We have $$\frac{M - Me}{Mo - Me} = e^{-kt}$$

By definition of one half response time, we may write:

$$\frac{M - M_e}{M_o - M_e} = \frac{1}{2} \quad \text{and} \quad t = t_{1/2}$$

Hence $$\frac{1}{2} = e^{-kt_{1/2}}$$

Or, $$\ln\frac{1}{2} = -kt_{1/2}\ln e$$

$$\Rightarrow \quad \ln 2 = kt_{1/2}$$

$$\therefore \quad t_{1/2} = \frac{\ln 2}{k}$$

Similarly by definition of one-fourth response time, we may write:

$$t_{1/4} = \frac{\ln 4}{k} \qquad \left(\text{as } \frac{M - M_e}{M_o - M_e} = \frac{1}{4}\right)$$

Knowing value of k, $t_{1/2}$ and $t_{1/4}$ may be computed.

Deep Bed Drying:

In deep bed drying, materials are not fully exposed to hot air. The thickness of material is more than 15 cm. Deep bed drying system has been analyzed by Hukill. The Hukill analysis is suitable for correlating the drying period, product moisture and product depth factors for the solutions of the drying problems.

In deep bed drying, the amount of grain in each depth is calculated by using the following heat balance:

$$\frac{dQ}{d\theta} \times Cp \times \Delta t = \Delta M \frac{dw}{d\theta} h_{fg}$$

where $\frac{dQ}{d\theta}$ = air flow rate, kg/s

C_p = specific heat of air, kcal/kg °C

Δt = maximum temperature drop of drying air, °C

$\Delta M = Mo - Me$, %db

$\frac{dw}{d\theta}$ = moisture removal from the grain volume under consideration, kg/s

h_{fg} = latent heat of evaporation, kcal/kg

$$\text{Amount of grain in each depth factor } (w) = \frac{dw}{d\theta} \times \theta_{1/2}$$

where $\theta_{1/2}$ = one half response time

$$\text{Number of depth factor} = \frac{\text{dry weight of paddy}}{\text{amount of moisture removed}}$$

$$\text{thickness of each depth factor} = \frac{\text{depth of grain to be dried}}{\text{number of depth factors}}$$

$$\text{time unit} = \frac{\text{total drying time}}{\text{half response time}}$$

$$MR = \frac{M - M_e}{M_o - M_e}$$

Moisture ratio is taken from graph based on time unit and depth factor and thus moisture content of grains can be determined.

The velocity of drying front in deep bed drying is given by:

$$v = m_a \left(\frac{\rho_a}{\rho_m}\right)\left(\frac{H_f - H_i}{M_f - M_i}\right)$$

where Hi = initial humidity

H_f = final humidity

M_i and M_f = initial and final moisture content (db) in fraction

ρ_a = density of air

ρ_m = density of material

m_a = mass flow rate of dry air

Time of Advance of Drying Front:

The time period taken by the drying front to reach the top of the bin is called *maximum drying rate period.*

Time taken by drying front to reach the top of the bed can be calculated by:

$$\theta_1 = \frac{W_d(M_1 - M_x)}{AG(H_s - H_1)\times 100}$$

where M_1 = initial moisture content of grain (% db)

M_x = average moisture content of grain (% db) at the end of drying front advance at the top

θ_1 = time of advance, s

A = cross sectional area of dryer through which air passes, m^2

G = mass velocity of dry air, kg/m^2s

H_s = humidity of saturated air leaving dryer, kg/kg

H_1 = humidity of air entering into dryer, kg/kg

W_d = weight of bone dry grain in the bin, kg

The time of drying for decreasing rate period can be expressed by the following equation:

$$\theta_2 = \frac{1}{k}\ln\frac{(M_x - M_e)}{(M - Me)}$$

where θ_2 = time of drying during decreasing rate period, s

M_e = EMC (db)

K = drying constant, 1/s

M = average m.c (db) at the end of decreasing rate period

M_x = average initial m.c (db) at the beginning of decreasing rate period

The total drying time for grains in the bin is the sum of the time required for the maximum drying rate and decreasing rate period.

$$\text{Total drying time} = \theta = \theta_1 + \theta_2$$

Dryer Performance:

The performance of any dryer depends on the design of overall drying system, maintenance and methods of operation. Following parameters are used to evaluate a dryer performance:

Heat Utilization Factor (*HUF*):

The utilization factor of a drying system is the ratio of drop in temperature of drying air by drying process and the increase in the temperature of ambient air by heating and is given by:

$$HUF = \frac{\text{heat utilized}}{\text{heat supplied}} = \frac{\text{drop in dry bulb temperature of drying air}}{\text{increase in dry bulb temperature of ambient air}} = \frac{t_2 - t_3}{t_2 - t_1}$$

where HUF = heat utilization factor

t_1 = dry bulb temperature of ambient air, °C

t_2 = dry bulb temperature of heated air, °C

t_3 = dry bulb temperature of exhaust air, °C

It may be more than one under certain drying condition. The heat utilization is usually less than 100%but can exceed 100%.

Coefficient of performance (*COP*): *COP* of a grain dryer is expressed mathematically by following relation:

$$COP = \frac{t_3 - t_1}{t_2 - t_1}$$

where t_1 = dry bulb temperature of ambient air, °C

t_2 = dry bulb temperature of heated air, °C

t_3 = dry bulb temperature of exhaust air, °C

Relationship Between *HUF* and *COP*:

$$HUF = 1 - COP$$

The overall thermal efficiency of a drying system may be expressed as:

$$\text{overall thermal efficiency,\%} = \frac{\text{energy used for evaporation}}{\text{heat energy supplied}} \times 100$$

Drying Methods:

Following drying methods are commonly used in food processing industry:

Spray Drying : Spray drying is used for drying of liquid foods. One of the most common liquids typically dried is milk. Spray drying involves the atomization of liquid foods into a spray, and contact between spray and drying medium resulting in moisture evaporation. The drying of the spray continues until the desired moisture content in the dried particles is achieved, and the product is recovered from the air. Drying of liquid food product is carried out in a spray dryer. The dried material is separated from air in a cyclone separator.

Energy requirement for atomization of milk: When a drop of liquid is sprayed into a number of droplets, its surface area increases.

Energy required = work done = increase in surface area x surface tension

The energy required to atomize a milk drop into a milk droplet is given by:

$$E = \Delta SA \times \sigma = \sigma \times \pi D^2 \left(N^{1/3} - 1\right)$$

where s = surface tension, N/m

ΔSA = change in surface area, m^2

D = diameter of drop (bigger), m

Surface area of drop of diameter $D = \pi D^2$

When a drop of diameter D is atomized into a droplet of diameter d, then the number of droplet N may be calculated by the equation:

$$N = \frac{\text{volume of drop}}{\text{volume of droplet}} = \frac{\frac{\pi}{6}D^3}{\frac{\pi}{6}d^3} = \frac{D^3}{d^3} = \left(\frac{D}{d}\right)^3$$

Or,
$$\frac{D}{d} = (N)^{1/3}$$

Or,
$$d = \frac{D}{N^{1/3}}$$

Total surface area of droplet of diameter $d = \pi d^2 \times N$

Putting value d we have:

$$\text{Total surface area} = \pi \times \frac{D^2}{N^{\frac{2}{3}}} \times N = \pi D^2 N^{1/3}$$

Hence, change in surface area $= \pi D^2 N^{1/3} - \pi D^2 = \pi D^2 (N^{1/3} - 1)$

The total energy required to atomize the given volume of milk

$$= \sigma \times \pi D^2 (N^{1/3} - 1) \times n$$

where n is number of drops of milk.

The number of drops of milk n may be calculated by:

$$n = \frac{\text{volume of milk}}{\text{volume of one drop}} = \frac{V_m}{\frac{\pi}{6}D^3}$$

This equation of energy requirement during atomization can be employed for any liquid food.

The energy required in spraying can be expressed in term of a spherical drop of R mm radius and N droplet of equal size of radius r mm for a given surface tension of liquid as follows:

$$\text{Energy required} = \text{increase in surface area } x \text{ surface tension}$$

$$\text{Radius of drop} = R \text{ mm} = R \, x \, 10^{-3} \text{ m}$$

$$\text{Surface area of drop} = 4\pi R^2 = 4\pi R^2 \, x \, 10^{-6} \text{ m}^2$$

$$\text{Volume of original drop} = \frac{4}{3}\pi R^3 = \frac{4}{3}\pi R^3 \times 10^{-9} \text{ m}^3$$

$$\text{Volume of one droplet} = \frac{4}{3}\pi r^3 = \frac{4}{3}\pi r^3 \times 10^{-9}\ \text{m}^3$$

Now, $$\frac{4}{3}\pi r^3 \times 10^{-9} \times N = \text{volume of original drop} = \frac{4}{3}\pi R^3 \times 10^{-9}$$

i.e. $$r = \frac{R}{(N)^{1/3}}$$

$$\text{Surface area of each droplet} = 4\pi r^2 \ x\ 10^{-6}\ \text{m}^2$$

$$\text{Surface area of all droplet} = N \ x\ 4\pi r^2 \ x\ 10^{-6}\ \text{m}^2$$

$$\text{Increase in surface area} = N \ x\ 4\pi r^2 \ x\ 10^{-6}\ \text{m}^2 - 4\pi R^2 \ x\ 10^{-6}\ \text{m}^2$$

Hence,

Energy required = increase in surface area *x* surface tension

$$= (N \ x\ 4\pi r^2 \ x\ 10^{-6}\ \text{m}^2 - 4\pi R^2 \ x\ 10^{-6}\ \text{m}^2) \times \text{surface tension (N/m), J}$$

Drying Time for Droplets:

Drying of droplets takes place both in constant rate and falling rate periods.

Constant Rate Period:

The drying time during the constant rate period is given by the following expression:

$$t_c = \frac{\lambda \rho_w \left(D_0^2 - D_c^2\right)}{8k_a (T_a - T_w)}$$

where Ta = dry bulb temperature ; T_w = wet bulb temperature (surface temperature)

k_a = thermal conductivity of air; D_0 = initial droplet diameter,

D_c = diameter at the end of the constant rate period

Falling Rate Period:

Drying time during falling rate period is:

$$t_f = \frac{\lambda \rho_d D_c^2}{6k_a (T_a - T_w)}(w_c - w_f)$$

where D_c = constant diameter

ρ_d = density of dry particle

λ = latent heat of vaporization

Other Drying Time Calculation Formula:

Time required to evaporate a drop of water of initial diameter *d* to final diameter zero is:

$$t = \frac{\lambda \rho d_0^{\,2}}{8k_a (T_a - T_w)}$$

where T_a = dry bulb temperature of air ; T_w = wet bulb temperature,

k_a = thermal conductivity of air; d_0 = initial droplet diameter

ρ = liquid density, λ = latent heat of vaporization

The drying time required for a droplet to reach from diameter d_1 to d_2 is given by:

$$t = \frac{\lambda\left(\rho_1 d_1^2 - \rho_2 d_2^2\right)}{8k_a\left(T_a - T_w\right)}$$

where d_2 diameter is the droplet diameter at the end of constant rate period, ρ_1 and ρ_2 are densities of product at the stage 1 and 2 respectively.

Amount of Heat and Air Required During Drying:

The amount of heat required in drying liquid food = heat used in heating liquid food (sensible heat) + heat used in evaporating water (latent heat)

$$q = \dot{m}C_p\left(T_2 - T_1\right) + \dot{m}_w\lambda_v$$

where T_1, T_2 = initial and evaporation temperature of product

$\dot{m}$ = mass flow rate of liquid food

$\dot{m}_w$ = mass flow rate of water removed

λ_v = latent heat of evaporation at evaporation temperature

This heat must be equal to heat supplied by hot air and is given by:

$$q = \dot{m}_a C_p\left(t_2 - t_1\right)$$

where t_1, t_2 = drying air temperature and exit air temperature of air

$\dot{m}_a$ = mass flow rate of air

Equating heat supplied by air and heat used in drying liquid food, amount of air required during drying can be computed.

The amount of heat required in heating air is:

$$q = \dot{m}_a C_p\left(T_f - T_i\right)$$

where T_f and T_i are final and initial air temperature.

This heat must be equal to heat provided by steam during condensation. Hence,

$$q = \dot{m}_s\lambda$$

where λ = latent heat of steam

$\dot{m}_s$ = mass flow rate of steam

Thermal efficiency of spray dryer is given by:

$$\eta_t = \frac{\left(T_1 - T_2\right)}{\left(T_1 - T_a\right)} \times 100$$

where T_a = ambient air temperature

T_1 = temperature to which air is heated

T_2 = temperature of air leaving the dryer

When radiation loss is included, then the equation becomes:

$$\eta_t = \frac{\left(1-\frac{R}{100}\right)(T_1-T_2)}{(T_1-T_a)}$$

where R = radiation loss (%)

Cyclones:

Cyclones are one of the main methods used to separate gas-solid systems. The solids move radially to the walls, slide down the walls, and are collected at the bottom.

Terminal velocity (v_t) of the smallest particle that can be removed from the cyclone may be given by:

$$v_t = \frac{0.2A_i D_o g}{\pi z D v_o}$$

where v_o = air inlet velocity, D_o = outlet chamber diameter, A_i = inlet cross sectional area, D = diameter of main cyclone chamber, z = height of cyclone

Terminal velocity can also be found using Stoke's Law:

$$v_t = \frac{D^2(\rho_p-\rho)g}{18\mu}$$

By combining these two equations we can find the diameter of the smallest particle that can be removed using the cyclone:

$$\frac{D^2(\rho_p-\rho)g}{18\mu} = \frac{0.2A_i D_o g}{\pi z D v_o}$$

Hence, $$D_p = \sqrt{\frac{3.6A_i.D_o.\mu}{\pi.z.D.v_o\rho_p}}$$

where μ = viscosity of the air

Drum Drying:

Drum drying is used for drying liquid foods such as milk. Liquid food is applied as a thin film to the surface of a heated drum, and the dried solids are then scraped off with a knife.

The equation for estimating evaporation rate due to conduction heat transfer from drum to foodstuff is:

$$\dot{m}\lambda = UA(T_s - T_p)$$

$$q = UA(Ts - Tp)$$

where U = overall heat-transfer coefficient

λ = latent heat of vaporization at boiling point

$\dot{m}$ = rate of vapour formation

A = area of drying surface on the drum

T_s = temperature of roller surface(steam temperature)

T_p = product temperature

The effective drying area on the drum is given by:

$$A = \frac{3}{4} \times \text{total surface area} = \frac{3}{4} \times (\pi DL)$$

where D = diameter, m ; L = length, m

When effective area is known, total area of drum can be calculated as:

$$\text{total surface area} = \frac{4}{3} \times \text{effective area}$$

The value of U can be estimated by:

$$\frac{1}{U} = \frac{1}{h_1} + \frac{x}{k} + \frac{1}{h_2}$$

where h_1 and h_2 are the heat film coefficients (W/m^2 K) for the hot fluid and the cold fluid respectively, x is drum wall thickness (m) and k is the thermal conductivity of the wall (W/mK). The overall heat transfer coefficient (U) provides a measure of the efficiency of the heat transfer process.

Total volume of material on drum can be calculated by:

$$V = \frac{3}{4} \times (\pi DL) \times t \text{, m}^3$$

where t = thickness of film spread on drum, m

Total mass of material on drum can be calculated by:

$$m = V \times \rho = \frac{3}{4}(\pi DL) \times t \times \rho$$

where ρ = density of food material

Rate of moisture evaporation $\dot{m}_w = q/\lambda$

Writing mass balance equation for solid, we have:

$$m_f x_f = m_p x_p$$

where m_f = mass of feed

m_p = mass of concentrated food

x_f and x_p = fraction of solid in feed and concentrated product

Mass of moisture evaporated can be calculated as:

$$m_w = m - m_p$$

Residence time (t) is calculated as:

$$t = \frac{\text{mass of water evaporated}}{\text{rate of moisture evaporation}} = \frac{m_w}{\dot{m}_w},\ \text{s}$$

Time required (T) for one complete revolution is given as:

$$T = \frac{4}{3} \times t,\ \text{s/revolution}$$

Hence, speed of drum (N) may be computed as:

$$N = \frac{1}{T},\ \text{rps}$$

Freeze Drying:

Freeze-drying also known as lyophilization is a drying process typically used to preserve a perishable material or make the material more convenient for transport. In freeze drying, heat transfer occurs by conduction from the heated shelves, by convection from the air inside the drying chamber to the exposed surfaces and by radiation. Freeze-drying works by freezing the material and then reducing the surrounding pressure and providing enough heat to allow the frozen water in the material to sublime directly from the solid phase to the vapour phase.

Equation for freeze drying time is given by:

$$t = \frac{x^2 \rho_f \lambda_s \left(m_i - m_f\right)}{8 k_d \left(T_s - T_i\right)}$$

where t = drying time, s

k_d = thermal conductivity of the dry layer, W/m.K

T_s, T_i = temperature at the slab surface and at the sublimation front, respectively, K.

ρ_f = density of the frozen food, kg/m^3

m_i, m_f = initial and final water content, respectively, kg/kg.

λ_S = latent heat of sublimation (J/kg)

x = slab thickness, m

Latent heat of sublimation, which can be taken as 2838 kJ kg^{-1}.

Fluidized bed drying:

The air velocity at which fluidization occurs is called *minimum fluidization velocity* and is calculated for spherical particles using the formula:

$$v = \frac{(\rho_s - \rho)}{\mu} \frac{d^2 \varepsilon^3}{180(1-\varepsilon)}$$

where v = velocity in m/s

d = diameter of particle, m

ε = voidage of bed

ρ_s = density of solid, kg/m^3

ρ = density of air, kg/m^3

μ = viscosity of air, Ns/m^2

The velocity at which entrainment of particle in air occurs is called entrainment velocity and is calculated by:

$$v_e = \sqrt{\frac{4d(\rho_s - \rho)}{3C_d\rho}} \qquad \text{where } C_d = \text{drag coefficient}$$

Recirculation Ratio for Recirculatory Dryer:

In recirculatory dryer, a part of exhaust air is fed to inlet side of blower. Fresh air and diverted exhaust air are mixed and then heated. Thus wastage of energy is minimized as the energy required foe heating mixed air is less than heating fresh air. The recirculation ratio (R_R) is defined as the ratio of mass of the exhaust air to the total mass of fresh and exhaust air. It can also be defined as:

$$R_R = \frac{\text{mixed air temperature-ambient air temperature}}{\text{exhaust air temperature-ambient air temperature}}$$

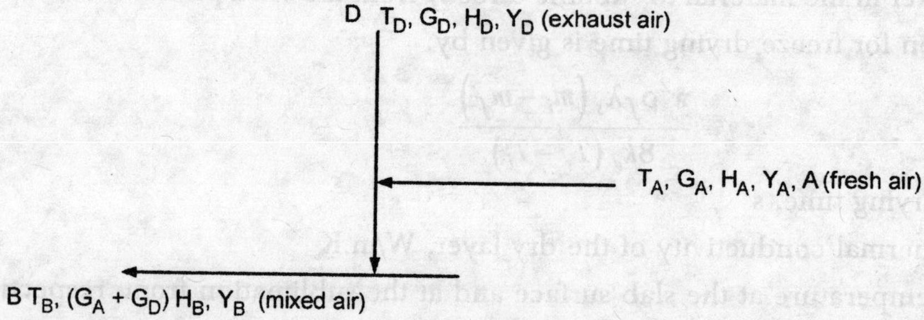

FIG. 11.1 Recirculation of exhaust air

Let Y = humidity

G = mass flow rate

T = temperature

H = enthalpy

A, B and D are for fresh, mixed and exhaust air.

Referring Fig. 11.1 we may write the enthalpy balance as follows:

$$G_D H_D + G_A H_A = (G_A + G_D) H_B$$

$$G_D(H_D - H_B) = G_A(H_B - H_A)$$

$$\frac{H_D - H_B}{H_B - H_A} = \frac{G_A}{G_D}$$

Adding 1 on both sides we have:

$$\frac{G_D + G_A}{G_D} = \frac{H_D - H_A}{H_B - H_A}$$

or,

$$\frac{G_D}{G_D + G_A} = \frac{H_B - H_A}{H_D - H_A} \approx \frac{T_B - T_A}{T_D - T_A}$$

Hence, $\text{Recirculation ratio} = \dfrac{G_D}{G_D + G_A}$

Now from moisture balance we have:

$$G_D Y_D + G_A Y_A = (G_A + G_D) Y_B$$

Hence, $\text{Recirculation ratio} = \dfrac{G_D}{G_D + G_A} = \dfrac{Y_B - Y_A}{Y_D - Y_A}$

The percent shrinkage of dried product can be calculated by:

$$\%\ \text{shrinkage} = \frac{\text{original volume-dry volume}}{\text{original volume}} \times 100$$

The Rehydration ratio may be calculated as:

$$RR = \frac{W_r}{W_d}$$

where W_r = weight of rehydrated sample

W_d = weight of dehydrated sample

Estimation of Heat Requirement for Parboiling:

Parboiling is carried out to improve the milling quality of paddy. It is a hydrothermal treatment followed by drying. It consists of soaking, steaming and drying.

Soaking Operation:

The total water required for the soaking operation is:

$$W = W_d \left(m - m_o\right) + W_p$$

where W = weight of water, kg

W_d = weight of paddy, kg

m = final moisture content (% wb)

m_o = initial moisture content (% wb)

W_p = weight of water required to fill the pore spaces, kg

$$W_p = \text{porosity} \times \frac{\text{weight of paddy}}{\text{density of paddy}} \times \text{density of water}$$

where porosity is in fraction.

•The ratio of the volume of voids between grains to the total volume occupied by the bulk grain is called the void ratio or porosity.

The amount of heat required to raise the temperature of water from T_1 to T_2 is:

$$Q_{so} = WC_p (T_2 - T_1)$$

where W = total amount of water

C_p = specific heat of water

Steaming Operation:

The heat gained by paddy during steaming operation is:

$$Q_{st} = W_p C_p T + W_x C_{pw} T$$

where W_p = weight of dry paddy

C_p = specific heat of paddy

T = temperature difference between steamed and soaked paddy = $T_{st} - T_{so}$

T_{st} = paddy temperature just after steaming

T_{so} = paddy temperature just after soaking

W_x = weight of water in soaked paddy

C_{pw} = specific heat of water

Drying Operation:

Heat required to raise air temperature from T_1 to T_2 is:

$$Q_a = q\rho C_p (T_2 - T_1)$$

where Q_a = heat required to raise air temperature

q = air flow rate

ρ = density of air

C_p = specific heat of air

Hence total heat required for parboiling = $Q_{so} + Q_{st} + Q_a$

Chapter

12

Evaporation

Evaporation is an important unit operation employed to remove water from dilute liquid food to obtain concentrated liquid products. Removal of water from liquid food increases microbiological stability and shelf life, and reduces transportation and storage costs. Applications of evaporation include concentration of milk, fruit and vegetable juices, and syrup solutions. This chapter presents the governing equations of single effect, double effect and triple effect evaporators.

Material and Heat Balance for Single Effect Evaporator:

Mass Balance:

The overall mass balance is:

$$\dot{m}_f = \dot{m}_p + \dot{m}_v$$

where $\dot{m}_f$, $\dot{m}_p$ and $\dot{m}_v$ are the mass flow rate of feed (kg/s), product (kg/s) and vapour (kg/s) respectively.

Material balance for the solids is written as follows:

$$\dot{m}_f x_f = \dot{m}_p x_p + \dot{m}_v x_v$$

where x_f, x_p and x_v are mass fraction of solute or non-soluble solids in feed, product and vapour respectively. Since there is no solute in vapour stream hence $x_v = 0$ and then the equation become:

$$\dot{m}_f x_f = \dot{m}_p x_p$$

and $$\dot{m}_v = \dot{m}_f \left(1 - \frac{x_f}{x_p}\right)$$

Heat Balance:

Heat supplied by steam = Sensible heat + Latent heat of vaporization

$$\dot{m}_s \lambda_s = \dot{m}_f C_{pf} \left(T_b - T_f\right) + \dot{m}_v \lambda_v$$

where $\dot{m}_v = \dot{m}_f - \dot{m}_p$

$T_b = T_b$ = boiling point of liquid

T_f = feed temperature

C_{pf} = specific heat of feed

λ_s = latent heat of condensing steam

λ_v = latent heat of vaporization of water

The left hand side of the equation must be equal to the rate at which heat is transferred from the steam to the feed.

i.e. $$q = \dot{m}_s \lambda_s = UA(T_s - T_b)$$

Or, $$\dot{m}_s = \frac{UA(T_s - T_b)}{\lambda_s}$$

where T_b = boiling point of liquid, K

T_s = temperature of steam, K

A = heat transfer area, m^2

q = rate of heat transfer, W

U = over all heat transfer coefficient, W/m^2K

$\dot{m}_s$ = steam flow rate, kg/s

This equation can be used to estimate steam flow rate.

The heat needed to be transferred from steam to the product for accomplishing the specified extent of evaporation is given by the following equation:

$$q = \dot{m}_s H_s - \dot{m}_c H_c = \dot{m}_s \lambda_s$$

where H_s = enthalpy of steam

H_c = enthalpy of condensate

$\dot{m}_s$ = steam flow rate, kg/s

$\dot{m}_c$ = condensate flow rate, kg/s

The heat transfer area of single effect evaporator may be calculated by:

$$A = \frac{m_s \lambda_s}{U(T_s - T_b)} = \frac{q}{U(T_s - T_b)}$$

Overall Heat Transfer Coefficient (U):

The overall resistance to heat transfer is the sum of three resistances in series, namely, that of the condensing steam film, that of the solid wall and that of the boiling liquid.

$$\frac{1}{U} = \frac{1}{h_c} + \frac{x}{k} + \frac{1}{h_b}$$

where h_c and h_b are heat transfer coefficients of condensing steam and boiling liquid films respectively.

x = thickness of the solid wall, m

k = thermal conductivity of the solid, (W/m.K)

The heat transfer area $A = n\pi dL$

Where n is number of tubes, L is length and d is diameter of tubes.

Evaporator Efficiency:

A common measure of the efficiency of an evaporator is the mass of vapour generated per unit mass of steam admitted into the evaporator. This quantity is known as steam economy.

$$\text{steam economyd} = \frac{\text{amount of water evaporated}}{\text{amount of steam used}} = \frac{m_v}{m_s}$$

Heat Balance for Double Effect Evaporators:

Heat balance for double effects evaporator may be made as follows:

Effect 1:

$$q_1 = \dot{m}_s\lambda_s = \dot{m}_f C_p\left(T_{b1} - T_f\right) + \dot{m}_{v1}\lambda_1 = U_1 A_1 \Delta T_1$$

where $\Delta T_1 = T_s - T_{b1}$

Effect 2:

$$q_2 = \dot{m}_{v1}\lambda_1 = \left(\dot{m}_f - \dot{m}_{v1}\right)C_p\left(T_{b1} - T_{b2}\right) + \dot{m}_{v2}\lambda_2 = U_2 A_2 \Delta T_2$$

where $\Delta T_2 = T_{b1} - T_{b2}$

$\dot{m}_f$ = liquid flow rate of feed

$\dot{m}_s$ = flow rate of steam fed to the first effect

$\dot{m}_{v1}$ = flow rate of vapor produced in first effect

$\dot{m}_{v2}$ = flow rate of vapor produced in second effect

λ_1, λ_2 are latent heat values at temperature

T_{b1}, T_{b2} which can be obtained from steam tables.

$\dot{m}_v$ = flow rate of vapour produced

C_p = specific heat capacity of the liquid (assumed to be constant)

T_s = temperature of steam

T_{b1} = evaporating temperature in first effect

T_{b2} = evaporating temperature in second effect

U_1 = overall heat transfer coefficient in first effect

U_2 = overall heat transfer coefficient in second effect

A_1 = heat transfer area in first effect

A_2 = heat transfer area in second effect

Latent heat of steam at temperature T can be obtained by the equation:

Latent heat of steam = enthalpy of steam-enthalpy of condensate

i.e. $$\lambda_T = 2501 + 1.88T - 4.18T$$

Total capacity of second effect evaporators can be obtained by adding the value of q for each effect which is given by:

$$q = q_1 + q_2 = U_1 A_1 \Delta T_1 + U_2 A_2 \Delta T_2 = \dot{m}_s \lambda_s$$

If U and A are same for both effects then

$$q = UA(\Delta T_1 + \Delta T_2) = UA\Delta T$$

Where, $$\Delta T = \Delta T_1 + \Delta T_2 = T_s - T_{b2}$$

The total ΔT in double effect evaporators would be the difference between the steam temperature and the vapor temperature in the last effect.

The heat transfer area for each effect can be estimated by the following equations:

$$A_1 = \frac{\dot{m}_s \lambda_s}{U_1 \Delta T_1}$$

$$A_2 = \frac{\dot{m}_{v1} \lambda_1}{U_2 \Delta T_2}$$

The steam economy can be calculated as:

$$\text{steam economy} = \frac{\text{amount of water evaporated}}{\text{amount of steam used}} = \frac{\dot{m}_{v1} + \dot{m}_{v2}}{\dot{m}_s}$$

Mass and Heat Balance for Triple Effect Evaporators:

Mass balance:

$$\dot{m}_f = \dot{m}_{v1} + \dot{m}_{v2} + \dot{m}_{v3} + \dot{m}_p$$

where $\dot{m}_f$ = liquid flow rate of feed

$\dot{m}_p$ = flow rate of product

$\dot{m}_{v1}$ = flow rate of vapor produced in first effect

$\dot{m}_{v2}$ = flow rate of vapor produced in second effect

$\dot{m}_{v3}$ = flow rate of vapor produced in third effect

Solid balance:

$$x_f \dot{m}_f = x_p \dot{m}_p$$

where x_f is solid fraction in feed and x_p is solid fraction in product in third effect.

Heat balance : Considering three effect evaporators in which the temperatures and pressures are T_1, T_2, T_3, and P_1, P_2, P_3, respectively, in each unit and if the liquor has no boiling point rise, then the heat transmitted per unit time across each effect may be expressed as:

Effect 1:

$$q_1 = \dot{m}_s\lambda_s = \dot{m}_f C_p\left(T_{b1} - T_f\right) + \dot{m}_{v1}\lambda_1 = U_1 A_1 \Delta T_1$$

where $\Delta T_1 = T_s - T_{b1}$

Effect 2:

$$q_2 = \dot{m}_{v1}\lambda_1 = \left(\dot{m}_f - \dot{m}_{v1}\right)C_p\left(T_{b1} - T_{b2}\right) + \dot{m}_{v2}\lambda_2 = U_2 A_2 \Delta T_2$$

where $\Delta T_2 = T_{b1} - T_{b2}$

Effect 3:

$$q_3 = \dot{m}_{v2}\lambda_2 = \left(\dot{m}_f - \dot{m}_{v1} - \dot{m}_{v2}\right)C_p\left(T_{b2} - T_{b3}\right) + \dot{m}_{v3}\lambda_3 = U_3 A_3 \Delta T_3$$

where $\Delta T_3 = T_{b2} - T_{b3}$

where T_s = temperature of steam

$\dot{m}_f$ = liquid flow rate of feed

$\dot{m}_v$ = flow rate of vapour produced

C_p = specific heat capacity of the liquid (assumed to be constant)

$\dot{m}_s$ = flow rate of steam fed to the first effect

T_{b1} = evaporating temperature in first effect

T_{b2} = evaporating temperature in second effect

T_{b3} = evaporating temperature in third effect

U_1 = overall heat transfer coefficient in first effect

U_2 = overall heat transfer coefficient in second effect

U_3 = overall heat transfer coefficient in third effect

A_1 = heat transfer area in first effect

A_2 = heat transfer area in second effect

A_3 = heat transfer area in third effect

λ_1, λ_2 and λ_3 are latent heat values at temperature T_{b1}, T_{b2}, T_{b3} which can be obtained from steam tables.

The heat transfer area for each effect can be estimated by the following equations:

$$A_1 = \frac{\dot{m}_s\lambda_s}{U_1\Delta T_1}$$

$$A_2 = \frac{\dot{m}_{v1}\lambda_1}{U_2\Delta T_2}$$

$$A_3 = \frac{\dot{m}_{v2}\lambda_2}{U_3\Delta T_3}$$

Equating the mass flow rate of vapour produced in each effect and neglecting the sensible heat changes, if $\dot{m}_{v1}$, $\dot{m}_{v2}$ $\dot{m}_{v3}$ are the respective mass flow rate of vapour produced in effects 1, 2 and 3, and $\dot{m}_s$ mass flow rate of steam fed to first effect then we may write:

$$\dot{m}_{v1}\lambda_1 \quad \dot{m}_{v2}\lambda_2 = \dot{m}_{v3}\lambda_3 = \dot{m}_s\lambda_s$$

The sum of the mass flow rate of vapour produced in each effect must be equal to the total mass flow rate of water evaporated in all three effects.

i.e. $$\dot{m}_{v1} + \dot{m}_{v2} + \dot{m}_{v3} = \dot{m}_{vt}$$

where $\dot{m}_{vt}$ = total mass flow rate of water evaporated

The steam economy can be calculated as:

$$\text{steam economy} = \frac{\text{amount of water evaporated}}{\text{amount of steam used}} = \frac{\dot{m}_{v1} + \dot{m}_{v2} + \dot{m}_{v3}}{\dot{m}_s}$$

The amount of energy required in evaporation of water at different temperature in a three effect evaporator is:

$$Q = m_{v1}\lambda_{T1} + m_{v2}\lambda_{T2} + m_{v3}\lambda_{T3}$$

where m_{v1}, m_{v2} and m_{v3} are amount of vapour produced in first, second and third effect evaporator respectively and λ_{T1}, λ_{T2} and λ_{T3} are latent heat of evaporation at temperature T_1, T_2 and T_3 respectively.

Total Capacity of a Three Effect Evaporators:

Total capacity of a three effect evaporators can be obtained by adding the value of q for each effect which is given by:

$$q = q_1 + q_2 + q_3 = U_1A_1\Delta T_1 + U_2A_2\Delta T_2 + U_3A_3\Delta T_3$$

If U and A are same for all effects then

$$q = UA\left(\Delta T_1 + \Delta T_2 + \Delta T_3\right) = UA\Delta T$$

where, $\Delta T = \Delta T_1 + \Delta T_2 + \Delta T_3 = T_s - T_{b3}$

The total ΔT in triple effect evaporators would be the difference between the steam temperature and the vapor temperature in the last effect. A boiling point rise would decrease the available ΔT.

$$\Delta T = T_s - T_v - \Delta T_{b1} - \Delta T_{b2} - \Delta T_{b3}$$

where ΔT = overall temperature drop for heat transfer, T_s = steam temperature, T_v = vapor temperature in the last effect, ΔT_{b1}, ΔT_{b2}, ΔT_{b3} = boiling point rise in effects 1, 2 and 3.

The boiling point rise can be expressed as follows:

$$\Delta T_b = 0.51 \text{ m}$$

where ΔT_b in °C is the increase in the boiling point of a solution with molality *m*, above the boiling point of pure water at the given absolute pressure.

$$m = \frac{x_s / M_s}{x_w / 1000}$$

where x_s is mass fraction of solute, x_w is mass fraction of water, M_s is molecular weight of solute.

Example: Molality(*m*) for a 30% solution of hexose sugar can be calculated as:

$$m = \frac{x_s / M_s}{x_w / 1000} = \frac{0.3/180}{0.7/1000} = 2.38$$

= as the molecular weight of a hexose sugar is 180.

Hence $\Delta T_b = 0.51\text{m} = 0.51(2.38) = 1.21\ ^\circ\text{C}$

Temperature Drops in Triple Effect Evaporators:

Since $\Delta T_1 \propto \frac{1}{U_1}$ (as $q_1 = U_1 A_1 \Delta T_1$)

and over all temperature drop = (in case of no boiling point rise)

Hence temperature drop in first effect, second effect and third effect can be predicted by using following equations:

$$\Delta T_1 = \frac{\frac{1}{U_1}}{\left(\frac{1}{U_1} + \frac{1}{U_2} + \frac{1}{U_3}\right)} \Delta T$$

$$\Delta T_2 = \frac{\frac{1}{U_2}}{\left(\frac{1}{U_1} + \frac{1}{U_2} + \frac{1}{U_3}\right)} \Delta T$$

$$\Delta T_3 = \frac{\frac{1}{U_3}}{\left(\frac{1}{U_1} + \frac{1}{U_2} + \frac{1}{U_3}\right)} \Delta T$$

The overall heat transfer coefficient for triple effect evaporators can be calculated as follows:

$$\frac{1}{U}=\frac{1}{U_1}+\frac{1}{U_2}+\frac{1}{U_3}$$

Water Consumption for Direct Contact Condensers:

The water consumption can be estimated by a heat balances for a direct contact condenser. For direct contact condensers, the amount of cooling water required per unit amount of vapor condensed can be determined by:

$$\dot{m}_v H_s + \dot{m}_w C_p (T_1 - 273) = (\dot{m}_v + \dot{m}_w) C_p (T_2 - 273)$$

where $\dot{m}_v$ = vapour flow rate to the condenser, kg/s at temperature T_s

$\dot{m}_w$ = cooling water flow rate, kg/s at an entry temperature of T_1 and a leaving temperature of T_2

H_s = enthalpy of vapor at Ts

The amount of water vapor with the noncondensible gases leaving the condenser can be evaluated by:

$$w_v = \frac{18 \times p_c}{29(p_v - p_c)}$$

where w_v is kg water vapor/kg air, p_c is vapor pressure of water at temperature of condensate-cooling water mixture, and p_v is absolute pressure inside the evaporator.

Falling Film Evaporator:

Mass flow rate of vapour produced in single tube falling film evaporator is given by:

$$\dot{m}_v = \frac{\pi d L U \Delta T}{\lambda}$$

The velocity of vapour in the tube is given by:

$$v_v = \frac{Q}{A} = \frac{4\dot{m}_v \vartheta}{\pi d^2}$$

where $\dot{m}_v$ = mass flow rate of vapour, kg/s

Solving these two equations we get:

$$v_v = \frac{4\pi d L U \Delta T \vartheta}{\lambda \pi d^2} = \frac{4 L U \Delta T \vartheta}{\lambda d}$$

where d = diameter of tube

L = length of tube

U = overall heat transfer coefficient

λ = heat of evaporation

ϑ = specific volume of vapour, m^3/kg

ΔT = temperature difference between steam and boiling liquid

This is the desired velocity of vapour in a falling film evaporator.

The average velocity of film is given by:

$$\overline{v} = \frac{\rho g \delta^2}{3\mu} \qquad \text{where } \delta = \text{film thickness}$$

Film width = πd

$$A = \pi d \delta$$

$$\overline{v} = \frac{Q}{A} = \frac{\dot{m}}{\rho \pi d \delta}$$

Comparing these two equations we get:

$$\therefore \quad \frac{\dot{m}}{\rho \pi d \delta} = \frac{\rho g \delta^2}{3\mu} = \frac{g \delta^2}{3\nu} \qquad \left(\text{as } \nu = \frac{\mu}{\rho}\right)$$

Or;
$$\delta = \sqrt[3]{\frac{3\dot{m}\upsilon}{\pi d g \rho}}$$

where ν = kinematic viscosity

The film thickness can be estimated by this equation.

Chapter 13

Physical Separation Processes

Physical separation processes are commonly used in food industry to separate food component or desirable component from undesirable ones. This chapter presents the physical separation process such as filtration, centrifugation and membrane separation.

Filtration:

Filtration is an operation by which solid particles are separated from a liquid or gas by forcing the mixture through a porous medium that retains the particles. The resulting liquor is termed as filtrate and the separated solids are termed as filter cake. Filtration is used to clarify liquids by the removal of small amounts of solid particles (*e.g.* wine, beer, oils and syrups). The rate of filtration is expressed as follows:

Rate of filtration = driving force/resistance to flow

Rate of Filtration:

The rate of filtration defined as the volume of filtrate obtained per unit time, characterizes the capacity of a filter. The basic law of fluid flow through porous media is known as the Darcy law which is expressed as:

$$Q = \frac{dV}{dt} = \frac{A\Delta p}{\mu R}$$

where V = filtrate volume, m^3

Q = filtrate flow rate, m^3/s

A = filter area (normal to the direction of flow), m^2

ΔP = pressure drop across the porous bed, Pa

R = resistance of the bed to flow, m^{-1}

μ = viscosity of the fluid, Pa.s

Filtrate Flow through Filter Cake:

The total pressure drop across the filter is the sum of the pressure drop across the filter medium (filter cloth and precoat), "P_m, and cake, "P_c.

i.e. $$\Delta P = \Delta P_m + \Delta P_c$$

The medium resistance R_m is:

$$R_m = \frac{\Delta P_m}{\mu v}$$

And the specific cake resistance is:

$$\alpha = \frac{\Delta P_c}{\mu v\,(m / A)}$$

where v is velocity of filtrate, A is filter area, μ is filtrate viscosity and m is mass of filter cake.

The SI nit of R_m and α are m^{-1} and m/kg respectively.

Now we may write:

$$\Delta P = \Delta P_m + \Delta P_c = \alpha \mu v \frac{m}{A} + R_m \mu v$$

Let V = volume of filtrate and

c = concentration of cake solids in the suspension to be filtered then m = V.c

Filtrate velocity $\quad v = \dfrac{1}{A}\dfrac{dV}{dt}$

Hence, $\quad \Delta P = \dfrac{\mu\,(dV / dt)}{A}\left[\dfrac{\alpha V c}{A} + R_m\right]$

Or, $\quad \dfrac{dt}{dV} = \dfrac{\mu}{A \cdot \Delta P}\left[\dfrac{\alpha V c}{A} + R_m\right]$

This equation is known as *Sperry equation* which is the most widely used model for filtrate flow through filter cakes.

In the case of cake filtration, the total resistance R is the sum of two resistances in series, namely, the resistance of the filter medium R_f and that of the cake R_c and given by:

$$R = R_f + R_c$$

In batch filtration, cake thickness L increases with increasing filtrate volume. If the volume of cake deposited per unit volume of filtrate obtained is v, then we may write:

$$L = \frac{vV}{A}$$

Specific cake resistance may also be expressed in another form as given by:

$$\alpha = \frac{k(1-\varepsilon)S_o^2}{\rho_p \varepsilon^3}$$

where k = constant

ε = porosity of cake

S_o = specific surface area of particle per m^3 volume of solid particle

ρ_p = density of solid particle in cake

Volume of filtrate (V) is related to amount of accumulated dry cake (W) by the equation:

$$W = C_s V$$

$$C_s = \frac{\rho C_x}{1 - mC_x}$$

where V = volume of filtrate, m^3

C_x = mass fraction of solid in slurry

m = mass ratio of wet cake to dry cake

ρ = density of filtrate, kg/m^3

C_s = kg of solids/m^3 of filtrate

Constant-pressure Filtration:

Usually filtration is carried out under conditions of constant pressure. Filtration equation for constant pressure filtration is:

$$t = \frac{K_p V^2}{2} + BV$$

where V = volume of filtrate collected in time t

$$K_p = \frac{\mu \alpha C_s}{\Delta P A^2}$$

$$B = \frac{\mu R_m}{A \Delta p}$$

where R_m is resistance of filter medium to filtrate flow in m^{-1}.

This equation shows that a plot of t/V against V will be linear, and the values of α and R_m can be determined from the slope and intercept.

Continuous Filtration:

A rotary vacuum drum filter is an example of continuous filtration in which pressure drop is held constant during filtration. In continuous vacuum filters, the filtrate is sucked through a moving porous filter medium. The solids remaining on the filter medium are removed, usually by scraping-off with a blade. In continuous filtration, the resistance of filter medium is normally negligible compared to cake resistance.

For rotary vacuum drum filter:

$$\text{Flow rate} = \frac{V}{At_c} = \left[\frac{2f\Delta P}{\mu \alpha t_c C_s}\right]^{0.5}$$

where t_c = total filter cycle time

f = fraction of submergence of drum surface in slurry

C_s = kg of solids/m^3 of filtrate

The filter time t is less than total cycle time t_c and related as:

$$t = ft_c$$

To calculate flow rate of filtrate following relation can be used:

$$\frac{V}{t_c} = \frac{C_x}{C_s} \times \dot{m}_s$$

where $\dot{m}_s$ = mass flow rate of slurry, kg/s

C_s = kg of solid/m^3 of filtrate

C_x = mass fraction of solid in slurry

Centrifugal Filtration:

In centrifugal filtration, centrifugal force is employed to speed up the filtration. The equation of centrifugal filtration is given by:

$$q = \frac{\rho\omega^2 \left(r_2^2 - r_1^2\right)}{2\mu\left(\frac{m_c \alpha}{A^2} + \frac{R_m}{A}\right)}$$

where q = filtrate flow rate, m^3/s

ρ_1 = inner radius of liquid surface

ρ_2 = inside radius of basket

$m_c = C_s \cdot V$, mass of cake deposited on filter

A = flow area, m^2

Settling and Sedimentation:

In settling and sedimentation particles are separated from the fluid by gravitational forces acting on the particles. Application of settling and sedimentation include settling of solid food particle from a liquid food, settling of a slurry from a soybean leaching process etc.

Theory of Particle Movement Through a Fluid:

Laminar fluid flow around immersed particles :

Fluid flow around individual particles is of interest in many applications, such as settling of particles in a suspension, centrifugation, fluidization, pneumatic transport etc. A particle falling freely in a fluid experiences three forces: gravitational force, (F_g acting downward), force of friction or resistance (drag force) (F_d acting upward), and the force due to buoyancy (F_b acting upward. Referring Fig.1) and making a force balance we have:

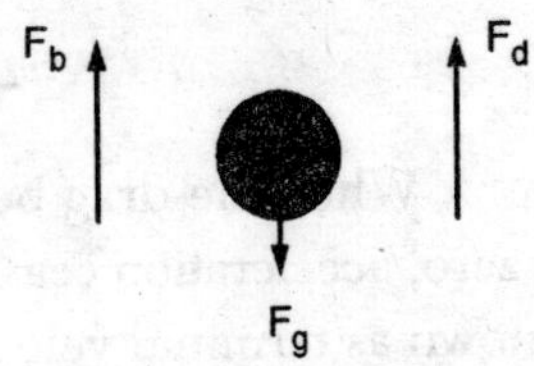

FIG. 13.1 Forces acting on a particle falling through fluid

$$\text{Net force } (F_{\text{Net}}) = \text{Gravitatonal force } (F_g) - \text{Buoyancy force } (F_b) - \text{Drag force } (F_d)$$

The force of buoyancy (F_b) is equal to the weight of the liquid displaced and is given by:

$$F_b = \text{volume of fluid displaced} \times \text{density of fluid} \times g$$
$$= \text{volume of particle} \times \text{density of fluid} \times g = V_p \rho g$$

Since $$V_p = \frac{m_p}{\rho_p}$$

where m_p is mass of particle and V_p is volume of particle.

Hence, $$F_b = \frac{\rho m_p g}{\rho_p}$$

$$\text{gravitation force} = F_g = m_p g$$

$$\text{Drag force} = F_D = \frac{C_d \rho v^2 A_p}{2}$$

For a spherical particle:

$$m_p = \frac{\pi D_p^3 \rho_p}{6}$$

$$A_p = \frac{\pi D_p^2}{4}$$

where D_p = diameter of the particle, m
ρ_p = density of the particle, kg/m^3
ρ = density of the liquid, kg/m^3
C_D = drag coefficient
v = velocity of the particle, m/s
A_p = projected area of the particle on a plane normal to the direction of flow

Resultant force (net force) must be equal to force due to acceleration ($m\ dv/dt$).

Hence, $$m_p \frac{dv}{dt} = F_g - F_b - F_d$$

$$m_p \frac{dv}{dt} = m_p g - \frac{\rho m_p g}{\rho_p} - \frac{C_d v^2 \rho A_p}{2}$$

When the drag becomes equal to the gravity force, the net force acting on the particle is zero, acceleration ceases and the particle continues to move downwards at a constant velocity, known as terminal velocity or settling velocity (v_t), calculated by setting the net force to zero.

$$\frac{dv}{dt} = 0, \ v = v_t$$

Solving above equation, we may write:

$$v_t = \sqrt{\frac{4(\rho_p - \rho) g D_p}{3 C_d \rho}}$$

For spherical particles, the drag coefficient for laminar flow region is given by:

$$C_d = \frac{24}{Re} = \frac{24}{\rho v D_p / \mu}$$

Hence, $$v_t = \frac{g D_p^2 (\rho_p - \rho_f)}{18\mu}$$

This is the fundamental equation for movement of particles in fluids. This is Stoke's law and gives the terminal velocity for a single smooth, rigid sphere falling in a homogeneous fluid as a function of the size and density of particle and density and viscosity of fluid.

The sedimentation/flotation velocity of the particle or droplets can be determined by this equation.

For a particle moving in a centrifugal field, g may be replaced by $a_c = \omega^2 r$

Hence $$v_t = \frac{\omega^2 r D_p^2 (\rho_p - \rho_f)}{18\mu}$$

where r = radial distance from centre of rotation

This equation can be used for determination of sedimentation velocity of fat globule in a centrifugal force field.

From this equation, we may write:

$$vt \infty \omega^2 D_p^2$$

Or $$\frac{vt_1}{vt_2} = \frac{\omega_1^2 \, Dp_1^2}{\omega_2^2 \, Dp_2^2}$$

This equation can be used for calculation of terminal velocity in two different given conditions.

Reynolds number for free fall of particle:

$$Re = \frac{\rho_f v_p D_p}{\mu_f}$$

where ρ_f and μ_f are for fluid density and viscosity, v_p is velocity of particle and D_p is diameter of particle.

In free settling of particle, settling of particles in not impeded by each other while in hindered settling, settling of particles is impeded by other particles. The drag coefficient in hindered settling is greater than in free settling.

Turbulent Fluid Flow Around Immersed Particles:

For Reynolds number between 2 and 500 the following empirical equation is often used:

$$C_D = \frac{18.5}{Re^{0.6}}$$

At higher Re, the drag coefficient becomes nearly constant (independent of Re). A good approximation for this range is $C_D = 0.44$.

Settling Tank:

The maximum permissible feed rate of a settling tank for the separation of the particles of diameter d_p is:

$$Q_{max} = \frac{A d_p^2 (\rho_p - \rho) g}{18\mu}$$

where d_p = particle diameter, m

ρ, ρ_p = density of the liquid and the particle, respectively, kg/m^3

μ = viscosity of the liquid, Pa.s

g = acceleration due to gravity, m/s^2

A = cross-sectional area and Q = the volumetric flow rate of the suspension.

This equation can be used to calculate the minimum size of particles that can be totally retained in a settling tank of cross-sectional area A, fed at a volumetric rate of Q.

Differential Settling:

The separation of solid particles into several size fractions based on the settling velocities in a medium is called differential settling or classification. The density of the medium is less than that of either of the two substances to be separated. In differential settling both light and heavy materials settle through the medium.

The terminal velocity of component A (high density material) and component B(low density material) can be written as:

$$v_{tA} = \sqrt{\frac{4(\rho_A - \rho) g D_{pA}}{3 C_{dA} \rho}}$$

$$v_{tB} = \sqrt{\frac{4(\rho_B - \rho) g D_{pB}}{3 C_{dB} \rho}}$$

For particles of equal settling velocity, $v_{tA} = v_{tB}$ we may write:

$$\frac{D_{pA}}{D_{pB}} = \frac{\rho_{pB} - \rho}{\rho_{pA} - \rho} \cdot \frac{C_{dA}}{C_{dB}}$$

For particles that are essentially sphere at very Reynolds number in turbulent Newton's law region, C_d is constant and $C_{DA} = C_{DB}$, then

$$\frac{D_{pA}}{D_{pB}} = \frac{\rho_{pB} - \rho}{\rho_{pA} - \rho}$$

For laminar Stoke's law settling:

$$C_{dA} = \frac{24\mu}{D_{pA} v_{tA} \rho}$$

$$C_{DB} = \frac{24\mu}{D_{pB} v_{tB} \rho}$$

For Stoke's law settling, $v_{tA} = v_{tB}$

Hence, $$\frac{D_{pA}}{D_{pB}} = \left(\frac{\rho_{pB} - \rho}{\rho_{pA} - \rho}\right)^{0.5}$$

For particle settling in turbulent Newton's law region:

$$\frac{v_{tA}}{v_{tB}} = \left(\frac{\rho_{pA} - \rho}{\rho_{pB} - \rho}\right)^{0.5}$$

Centrifugal Separation:

The particles that do not settle easily in gravity settlers can be separated from fluids by centrifugal force. Centrifugal separation is achieved many separation systems where a rotational movement is imparted to the mixture.

Settling in Tubular Bowl Centrifuge:

The flow rate of the machine for total clarification is given by:

$$q = V \times \frac{\omega^2 d_p^{\,2} (\rho_p - \rho)}{18\mu \ln \frac{r_2}{r1}} = \frac{\pi b \left(r_2^{\,2} - r_1^{\,2}\right) \omega^2 d_p^{\,2} (\rho_p - \rho)}{18\mu \ln \frac{r_2}{r1}}$$

where V = bowl volume ; ρ_p = particle density

ρ = liquid density ; μ = liquid viscosity

b = height of bowl

The particles having diameters smaller than that calculated by this equation do not reach the wall of bowl and moves with exit liquid. The critical diameter is defined as the diameter of a particle that reaches ½ the distance between r_1 and r_2.

The critical particle diameter of the largest particles in the exit stream may be estimated by the expression:

$$q_c = \frac{\omega^2 d_{pc}^{\,2} (\rho_p - \rho) V}{18\mu \ln\left(\frac{2r_2}{r_1 + r_2}\right)}$$

where d_{pc} = critical particle diameter

V = volume of bowl

$$V = \pi b\left(r_2^2 - r_1^2\right)$$

where b = effective length/height of the tubular bowl

At this flow rate q_c, particles with a diameter greater than D_{pc} will predominately settle to the wall and most smaller particle will remains in the liquid.

Residence time t is the ratio of volume of liquid V in the bowl and feed volumetric flow rate and is given by:

$$t = \frac{18\mu}{\omega^2 \left(\rho_p - \rho\right) d_p^2} \ln \frac{r_2}{r_1}$$

Separation of Liquid in a Centrifuge:

Liquid-liquid separation in which the liquids are immiscible but finely dispersed as an emulsion are common operations in the food industry. It is particularly common in the dairy industry in which milk is separated into skim milk and cream. The location of liquid-liquid interface position is very important in the centrifuge design. A boundary region between the liquids at a given centrifuge speed forms at a radius r_n where the hydrostatic pressure of the two layers is equal. This is termed the neutral zone and is important in equipment design to determine the position of feed and discharge pipes. Equation for interface position in the centrifuge is:

$$r_n^2 = \frac{\rho_H r_H^2 - \rho_L r_L^2}{\rho_H - \rho_L}$$

where ρ_H = density of heavy liquid

ρ_L = density of light liquid

r_H = radius to surface of heavy liquid

r_n = radius to liquid-liquid interface

r_L = radius to surface of light liquid layer

This relationship is used to place the feed inlet and product outlets in the centrifuge to get maximum separation.

The pressure on the wall of the centrifuge is given by:

$$P = \frac{\rho\omega^2}{2}\left(r_2^2 - r_1^2\right)$$

Disc-bowl Centrifugal Cream Separator:

It is used for cream separation from milk. The flow rate of milk through disc in a centrifugal separator is given by:

$$q = \frac{(2\pi)^3}{3} z \tan\alpha\left(r_o^3 - r_i^3\right)\frac{n^2 d^2 \Delta\rho}{18\mu} \times c$$

where c = correction factor, 0.5-0.7

q = flow rate of milk, m^3/s

z = number of disc

α = disc angle of inclination

d = limiting diameter of fat globules, m

n = rotation of disc, revolution per second

μ = viscosity, kg/ms

Δ_ρ = density difference between the medium and fat globules

r_o = outer radius at which particles must be separated out

r_i = inner radius at which light particle enters the space between the discs

The energy required to start up a centrifugal separator is given by:

$$E = \pi^3 \rho_B n^2 \left(r_o^4 - r_i^4\right) L$$

where E = energy, J

ρ_B = density of bowl, kg/m^3

n = rotation of disc, rps

L = length where mass is concentrated, m

r_0, r_i = outer and inner radius of disc respectively, m

Power required to accelerate a centrifuge is given by:

$$P = \frac{1}{2} m \left(2\pi n R_i\right)^2$$

where P = power, J/s or W (as $J = kgm^2/s^2$)

m = mass flow rate, kg/s

R_i = inner radius of bowl, m

n = rotation of disc, rps

The tensile stress exerted by liquid and material of bowl is given by:

$$\sigma = \omega^2 \left[\frac{PR_i^{\,3}}{2t} + \rho_B R_m^{\,2}\right]$$

where ω = angular velocity, rad/s

P = pressure exerted by liquid, Pa

Ri = inner radius of bowl, m

t = thickness of bowl wall, m

ρ_B = density of the bowl, kg/m^3

R_m = mean radius of bowl, m

Efficiency of Centrifugal Separator:

$$\text{Efficiency of centrifugal separator} = \frac{\text{Centrifugal force}}{\text{Gravity force}} = \frac{m\omega^2 r}{mg} = \frac{\omega^2 r}{g}$$

Membrane separation : It is used for separating constituents of foods on a molecular basis where the foods are in solution and where a solution is separated from one less concentrated by a semi permeable membrane.

The general equation of permeate flux is:

Permeate Flux = permeate volume/membrane area × time

Osmotic Pressure of Solution:

The term osmosis refers to the spontaneous transfer of water from a more dilute into a more concentrated solution through a membrane. In order to stop osmotic transfer of water into a solution, a certain pressure, called osmotic pressure, must be exerted against the direction of the transfer.

The osmotic pressure of a dilute non-ionized solution can be obtained by Van't Hoff's equation:

$$\pi = \frac{CRT}{M}$$

where C = solute concentration, kg/m^3

T = absolute temperature, K

R = gas constant, m^3 atm/kg mol K

M = molecular weight of solute

The osmotic pressure for ionized solutes, this becomes:

$$\pi = \frac{iCRT}{M}$$

where i is the degree of ionization.

For NaCl, $i = 2$ and for $CaCl_2$, $i = 3$

Rate of Flow through Membranes:

The net driving force for reverse osmosis is the difference between the applied differential pressure ΔP, and the differential osmotic pressure, $\Delta\Pi$, which resists the flow in the desired "reverse" direction. The equation used is:

$$\frac{dm}{dt} = KA(\Delta P - \Delta\pi)$$

where dm/dt is the rate of mass transfer (Kg/s), K is the mass transfer coefficient (Kg/m^2sPa), A the area through which the transfer is taking place (m^2), ΔP is the net applied pressure (Pa) and ΔP is the net osmotic pressure across the membrane (Pa). ΔP is the difference in the applied pressure on the solutions at each side of the membrane and $\Delta\Pi$ is the difference in the osmotic pressures of the two solutions.

Flux Equation for Reverse Osmosis:

The reverse osmosis is widely used for concentration and clarification of fruit juices and desalination of salty water. The reverse osmosis is mainly concerned with solutions containing smaller molecules such as sugars and salts.

The filtration rate flux by *RO* is directly proportional to the difference between applied hydrostatic pressure and osmotic pressure of the feed solution. It can be expressed by the following relation:

$$Nw = \frac{(\Delta p - \Delta\pi)}{R_c + R_m}$$

where N_w is the filtration rate, R_c is resistance of the cake which accumulates on the upstream surface of membrane, R_m is the resistance of membrane and $\Delta\pi$ and Δp are the differences in the hydrostatic and osmotic pressure between feed solution and filtrate.

Flux Equation for Ultrafiltration:

Ultrafiltration is commonly used in dairy industry for separation of protein from milk apart from other uses. Flux equation for diffusion of solvent through membrane is:

$$N_w = A_w(\Delta p - \Delta\pi)$$

where N_w = water flux, kg/s m^2

$A_w = P_w/L_m$

Pw = solvent membrane permeability, kg slvent/s.m.atm

L_m = membrane thickness

A_w = solvent permeability constant, kg solvent/s.m^2 atm

$\Delta p = P_1 - P_2$

P_1 = pressure exerted on feed, atm

P_2 = pressure on product solution, atm

$\Delta\pi = \pi_1 - \pi_2$=osmotic pressure of feed solution-osmotic pressure of product solution

Temperature Dependence of Membrane Permeation Rates:

Temperature affects liquid permeation rates through membranes in proportion to the change in viscosity of the fluid with temperature. If the solvent is water, and permeate flux at one temperature is given, the permeation rate at any other temperature can be calculated by:

$$\frac{J_{T1}}{J_{T2}} = \frac{\mu_{T2}}{\mu_{T1}}$$

where J_{T1} and J_{T2} are fluxes and π_{T1} and π_{T2} are viscosities at T_1 and T_2 respectively.

Membrane Performance:

The equation for rate of flow of ware through a membrane is given by:

$$\dot{m}_w = \frac{K_w A(\Delta P - \Delta\pi)}{t}$$

where $\dot{m}_w$ is rate of water flow rate (kg/s), A is area (m^2), ΔP is the net applied pressure (*Pa*) and $\Delta\Pi$ is the net osmotic pressure across the membrane (*Pa*), K_w is the coefficient of water permeability through the membrane (Kg/m^{2}Pa).

Concentration factor and rejection are two important processing parameters for all pressure activated processes. The concentration factor (f) is defined as follows:

$$f = \frac{V_f}{V_c}$$

where V_f is the feed volume and V_c is the final concentrate volume.

The rejection factor (R) of solute through a membrane is defined expressed by:

$$R = \frac{C_f - C_p}{C_f} = 1 - \frac{C_p}{C_f}$$

where C_f is the solute concentration of component in the feed and C_p is the solute concentration in the permeate.

Rejection factor normally lies between 0 to 1 or 0 to 100%.

When $C_p = 0$, $R = 1$, all the component is retained in the feed.

When $C_p = C_f$, $R = 0$, the component is freely permeating.

Chapter
14

Food Packaging, Handling and Storage

Packaging, handling and storage are an integral part of any food processing industry. Raw and processed products are packed to increase their shelf life. The permeability of packaging material plays an important role in selection of right film. The raw materials and processed packed materials need to be moved from one point to another point in food industry for storage or distribution. In this chapter permeability of packaging film, food handling equipment and storage structures are presented.

Permeability of Packaging Film:

Gases and vapors can permeate through packaging films by macroscopic or microscopic pores and pinholes by a molecular mechanism, known as diffusion. The diffusion law applies for the case of gas transport in one direction (from the atmosphere into a package) which is expressed as:

$$N_A = -D_{AB}\frac{dC}{dz}$$

where N_A is the flux of gas (mol/sm^2), D_{AB} is diffusion coefficient (m^2/s), C is concentration of gas (mol/m^3), z is distance (m)

If D_{AB} is a constant and steady state condition exists for a solid slab, then

$$N_A = \frac{D_{AB}\left(C_{A1} - C_{A2}\right)}{z_2 - z_1}$$

where C_{A1} and C_{A2} are concentration at point 1 and 2 respectively.

Applying Henry's Law, concentration (C) may be related to the partial pressure p as follows:

$$C_A = \frac{Sp_A}{22.414}, \text{ kg mol A/m}^3 \text{ solid}$$

where S = solubility of the solute (gas) in a solid (mol/[m^3 atm]) and p_A is partial pressure of gas (atm).

Hence,
$$N_A = \frac{D_{AB}S\left(p_{A1} - p_{A2}\right)}{22.414\left(z_2 - z_1\right)} = \frac{P_M\left(p_{A1} - p_{A2}\right)}{22.414\left(z_2 - z\right)}$$

(as $C_{A1} = Sp_{A1}/22.414$, $C_{A2} = Sp_{A2}/22.414$)

where p_{A1} and p_{A2} are the partial pressure of a gaseous component at each side of the film respectively and P_M is permeability ($P_M = D_{AB}S$), $m^3(STP)/m^2s$ (atm)/m.

Permeability:

The permeability is defined as m^3 of solute gas at *STP* (0°C temperature and 1 atm pressure) diffusing per second per m^2 cross sectional area through a solid 1 m thick under a pressure difference of 1 atmospheric pressure.

Diffusion through a multi layered packaging material having thickness $z_1, z_2, \ldots$ and permeability $P_{M1}, P_{M2} \ldots$ is given by:

$$N_A = \frac{p_{A1} - p_{A2}}{22.414\left[\frac{z_1}{P_{M_1}} + \frac{z_2}{P_{M_2}} + \ldots\ldots\ldots\right]}$$

where N_A = diffusion flux, $kmol/sm^2$

$p_{A1} - p_{A2}$ = overall partial pressure difference

This equation can be used in case of diffusion through multilayer packaging films.

The amount of moisture transferred to a packet of given size can be estimated by:

Amount of moisture added = N_A × surface area × time

The effect of temperature on permeability coefficient can be predicted by:

$$B = B_o e^{\left(\frac{-E_a}{RT}\right)}$$

where E_a is the activation energy for permeability (J/mol) and B_o is a constant.

Gas Transmission Rate (G.T.R.):

Gas permeation is an important consideration in packaging foods with plastics, since food packaging plastics are permeable to moisture, oxygen, carbon dioxide, nitrogen, and other gases. Proper design of a packaging system is essential to enhance the keeping quality of foods. Gas permeability based on Fick's first law of diffusion is described with the following equation:

$$GTR = P\left(p_1 - p_2\right)$$

Or,
$$GTR = \frac{Q}{At}$$

where, *GTR* = gas transmission rate

Q = quantity of gas transmitted (mass, volume or concentration)

A = film area exposed

t = time

P = permeance

$p_1 - p_2$ = partial pressure difference of the gas across the film

For transmittance of water vapor, *GTR* is referred to as *WVTR* (Water Vapor Transmission Rate), and permeance is referred to as *WVP* (Water Vapor Permeance). Hence, from above equation:

$$WVTR = WVP\,(p_1 - p_2)$$

$$WVTR = WVP\,(RH_1 - RH_2)\,p_s \qquad \left(\text{as } RH = \frac{p}{p_s}\right)$$

Hence, $$Q = WVP\,(RH_1 - RH_2)\,p_s\,At$$

where p = partial pressure of water vapor

p_s = saturated water vapor pressure

Permeability may also be expressed as:

$$P_M = WVP\,.\,z$$

where z = film thickness

The permeability of a film to water vapour is usually expressed as g/m^2 day (i.e. per 24 h) and is also known as the water vapour transfer rate (*WVTR*).

Permeability of Multilayer Material in Series and Parallel:

Total permeability of the packaging material in series is given by:

$$P_{MT} = \frac{\Delta z_1 + \Delta z_2 + \Delta z_3}{\dfrac{\Delta z_1}{P_{M1}} + \dfrac{\Delta z_2}{P_{M2}} + \dfrac{\Delta z_3}{P_{M3}}}$$

where Δz_1, Δz_2, Δz_3 are the thickness of packaging material or film and P_{M1}, P_{M2} and P_{M3} are their respective permeability.

This equation can be used to calculate the permeability constant for any multilayer material.

The total permeability of the packaging material for arrangement in parallel is given by:

$$P_{MT} = \frac{P_{M1}A_1 + P_{M2}A_2 + P_{M3}A_3}{A_1 + A_2 + A_3}$$

where A_1, A_2 and A_3 are area of respective film and P_{M1}, P_{M2} and P_{M3} are their respective permeability.

Decontamination of Packaging Film by Radiation:

The packaging film is decontaminated by applying appropriate dose of radiation. The absorbed dose (D) is the amount of energy absorbed (E) per unit mass (m) of the matter during the time that it is exposed to the radiation:

$$D = \frac{E}{m}$$

In the International System, the absorbed dose is measured in Gray (*Gy*), which is one joule of energy absorbed per kilogram of mass of the matter. Sometimes rad ("radiation absorbed dose") is also used.

$$1\ Gy = 1\ \text{J/kg}$$

$$1\ Gy = 100\ \text{rad}$$

Shelf Life Estimation:

The equation used for calculation of shelf life of packaged dry foods is:

$$\ln\frac{M_e - M_i}{M_e - M_c} = \left(\frac{P}{X}\right)\times\left(\frac{AP_o t_s}{W_s b}\right)$$

where M_e = equilibrium moisture content of the food, M_i = initial moisture content the food, M_c = critical moisture content of the food, P/X = permeability of packaging material(g water day^{-1} m^2 (mm Hg)$^{-1}$, A = area of package (m^2), Ws = weight of dry solids in the food, P_0 = vapour pressure of pure water at the storage temperature (*Torr*), b = slope of the moisture sorption isotherm (*g* water/g solids per unit a_w) and t_s = time to the end of the shelf life (days)

Material Handling:

Materials handling is defined as the organized movement of a specific material from one place to another, at the right time and in the right quantity. It may involve lifting, moving horizontally or vertically. It is an important factor in the smooth operation of any food processing plant and can greatly affect the quality of the product and the cost and profitability of the operation. The two important material handling equipments (bucket elevator and screw conveyor) are described here:

Bucket elevator : A bucket elevator consists of buckets attached to a chain or belt that revolves around two pulleys one at the top and other at the bottom. The bucket elevator is a very efficient device for the vertical conveyance of bulk grains. Bucket elevators are used to handle particulate, free-flowing substances such as sugar, beans, and cereals. The buckets are loaded at the bottom of the system and tipped out at the top.

In elevating of grains the discharge from bucket elevators is a combination of centrifugal and gravitational discharge. The mass of grain is subjected to two forces at the point the bucket starts to turn around the pulley. These forces are the gravity forces W and the centrifugal force F_c.

The magnitude of the centrifugal force which orient outward is given by:

$$F_c = \frac{mv^2}{r}$$

where m is mass of the grain, v is velocity of grain, and r is the effective radius.

In order to produce centrifugal discharge, F_c and W must be equal at a point near the top of the travel.

Hence $$W = F_c = \frac{mv^2}{r} = mg$$

$$v^2 = gr \text{ or } v = \sqrt{gr}$$

where g is the acceleration due to gravity

Since $$v = 2\pi rN$$

where N is the speed of rotation.

Hence, $$N = \frac{\sqrt{g}}{2\pi\sqrt{r}}$$

This equation shows the relationship between the effective head-wheel radius and its revolutions per second for the most satisfactory discharge conditions.

Theoretical capacity : Theoretical capacity of bucket elevator (kg/s) is given by:

C = capacity of one bucket (m^3) × number of bucket lifted per second × density of material

$$\text{Volume of one bucket} = \frac{r^2\theta l}{2}$$

where r = radius of curvature, m
l = length of bucket, m
θ = angle subtended by segment in radians

Horse power : Theoretical horse power of bucket elevator can be calculated using the following equation:

$$HP = \frac{KCL}{75}$$

where L = lift of elevator, m
C = Capacity, kg/s
K = factor, 1.2 to 1.5 (1.2 for elevators loaded on the bottom side and 1.5 for elevators loaded on the upside)

Screw conveyor : Screw conveyors are used for the handling of a wide variety of materials horizontally, at an inclination and even vertically. Screw conveyors are used to handle finely divided powders (*e.g.* : milk powder, flour, etc.), granular materials of all types (*e.g.* : barley, corn, rice, rye, wheat, cottonseed, soy beans, etc) and viscous food materials such as sugar beet pulp.

Theoretical capacity : Theoretical capacity of screw conveyor (kg/s) is given by:

$$C = \frac{\pi}{4}(D^2 - d^2)\,pN\rho$$

where D = screw diameter, m
p = pitch (distance from the centre of one thread to the centre of the next thread), m
N = revolution per second

d = shaft diameter, m

r = density of material, kg/m^3

Horse power : The horse power for screw conveyor for horizontal operation may be estimated by:

$$HP = \frac{KCL}{75}$$

where C = capacity, kg/s

L = conveyor length, m

K = material factor, 0.4 for paddy

Storage structures : Silos and bins are commonly used as storage structures for storing food grains. Silos and bins are classified into two groups depending upon the relative dimensions of the container: shallow bin and deep bin.

Shallow bin : A bin whose relative dimension are such that the plane of rupture meets the grain surface before it strikes the opposite side is called shallow bin.

A structure (bin) may be considered as shallow if : $h < L \tan\left(\frac{90 + \phi}{2}\right)$

where ϕ the angle of repose of material, h is depth and L is length of storage structure.

A grain bin is also referred to as a shallow bin when depth of grain is less or equal to equivalent diameter. The equivalent diameter is 4 times the hydraulic radius of bin which is defined as:

$$R = \frac{A}{P} = \frac{D}{4}$$

where R = hydraulic radius

A = area of cross section of bin

P = perimeter of bin

D = diameter of bin

So for shallow bin, $h \le 4R$ where h = depth of grain

Angle of repose : The angle between the horizontal and inclination of heap formed during free fall of granular material is called angle of repose. It is an indicator of the product's ability to flow. The angle of repose depends on size, shape, moisture content and orientation of particles.

The tangent of angle of internal friction of material is called coefficient of friction between two layers of particles.

For homogeneous mass, angle of repose = angle of internal friction

In practice, angle of repose is smaller than angle of internal friction.

To determine lateral pressure in shallow bin, Rankine's theory and Airy's theory are commonly used.

Rankine's theory: This theory is widely used in shallow bin design. The intensity of lateral pressure on the sides of shallow bin is determined by Rankine's theory. According to it, the lateral pressure inside a shallow bin is given by:

$$P_l = whK = wh\left(\frac{1-\sin\theta}{1+\sin\theta}\right)$$

where h = depth of grain

θ = angle of internal friction of grain

w = specific weight of grain

K = Rankine's coefficient

$$K = \frac{\text{lateral pressure}}{\text{vertical pressure}} = \frac{P_l}{P_v} = \frac{1-\sin\theta}{1+\sin\theta}$$

When angle of internal friction of grain = natural angle of repose, then we may write:

$$P_l = whK = wh\left(\frac{1-\sin\phi}{1+\sin\phi}\right)$$

where ϕ the angle of repose of material.

Airy theory for shallow bin: According to Airy's theory, the lateral pressure exerted by grains in a shallow bin is given by:

$$P_l = wh\left[\frac{1}{\sqrt{\mu(\mu+\mu')}+\sqrt{1+\mu^2}}\right]^2$$

where h = depth of grain

w = specific weight of grain or grain bulk density

μ = coefficient of friction of grain on grain

= tan θ_i, θ_i is the angle of internal friction

μ' = tan θ_w, θ_w is the angle of wall friction

Maximum dynamic pressure = 4 × maximum lateral pressure

Maximum lateral pressure expected = 5 × maximum lateral pressure

$$\%\text{ load transferred to vertical wall of bin} = \frac{L_t - L_v}{L_t}$$

where L_t = total load of grain

L_v = vertical load

Total load of grain = density of grain ×volume of bin

$$\text{Volume of bin} = \frac{\pi D^2 H}{4}$$

where D is diameter and H is height of bin.

$$P_v = \frac{P_l}{K}$$

$$\text{Vertical load} = P_v \frac{\pi D^2}{4}$$

Deep bin : A bin in which plane of rupture meets the opposite side before it emerges from grain is called deep bin.

A structure (bin) may be considered as deep if:

$$h > L \tan\left(\frac{90 + \phi}{2}\right)$$

where ϕ the angle of repose of material, h is is depth and L is length of storage structure.

A grain bin is also referred to as a deep bin when depth of grain is greater than equivalent diameter.

i.e. $h > 4R$ where h = depth of grain

In deep bin, a part of load is resisted by friction between the materials stored and side walls of the bin/silo. This results in reduction of lateral pressure. To determine the lateral pressure in deep bin, Jensen's theory and Airy's theory are commonly used.

Jensen theory for deep bin : Jensen considered the friction between grain and bin wall and proposed the following formula for predicting lateral pressure inside a silo:

$$P_l = \frac{wR}{\mu}\left[1 - e^{-\frac{\mu K h}{R}}\right]$$

where P_l = lateral pressure

w = grain bulk density

R = hydraulic radius of the bin

K = ratio of lateral to vertical pressure (Rankine Coefficient)

μ = coefficient of friction of grain on the bin wall = $\tan \theta_w$

θ = angle of friction between grain and bin wall

h = dept of grain

$$k = \frac{\text{lateral pressure}}{\text{vertical pressure}} = \frac{p_l}{p_v} = \frac{1 - \sin\theta_w}{1 - \sin\theta_w}$$

Or, $P_l = KP_v$

Other important parameters used in design of bins are given below:

Height of upper cone of stored grains in a silo : The height of upper cone of stored grains in a silo is given by:

$$z = r \tan\theta$$

where r = radius of cylindrical bin

θ = minimum angle of internal friction

Characteristic abscissa in the silo is given by the following expression:

$$A = \frac{R}{\mu K}$$

where μ = coefficient of friction of grain on wall = tan θ_w

R = hydraulic radius

The maximum lateral pressure of a bin may be given by the following expression:

$$P_{max} = \frac{w_{max} R}{\mu}$$

where w_{max} = maximum bulk density

μ = coefficient of minimum friction of grain on wall = tan θ_w

Height of grain storage (h) = total height-z

The lateral pressure at various depth of silo may be calculated by:

$$P_h = P_{max}\left[1-\left(1+\frac{h}{A}\right)^{-2}\right]$$

The total load on the bottom of a silo can be estimated by:

$$L = w_{max} s\left[h\left(1+\frac{h}{A}\right)^{-1}+\frac{z}{3}\right]$$

where s = cross sectional area of silo, m^2

w_{max} = maximum bulk density, kg/m^3

L = load, kg

A = characteristic abscissa

For a cylindrical silo, $s = \frac{\pi D^2}{4}$ where d = diameter

For a square silo, $s = a^2$ where a = length of side of silo

GREEK A

Greek Le
Alpha
Beta
Gamma
Delta
Epsilon
Zeta
Eta
Theta
Iota
Kappa
Lambda
Mu
Nu
Xi
Omicron
Pi
Rho
Sigma
Tau
Upsilon
Phi
Chi
Psi
Omega

APPENDIX-A

GREEK ALPHABETS:

Greek Letters	*Lower case*	*Upper case*
Alpha	α	Α
Beta	β	Β
Gamma	γ	Γ
Delta	δ	Δ
Epsilon	ε	Ε
Zeta	ζ	Ζ
Eta	η	Η
Theta	θ	Θ
Iota	ι	Ι
Kappa	κ	Κ
Lambda	λ	Λ
Mu	μ	Μ
Nu	ν	Ν
Xi	ξ	Ξ
Omicron	ο	Ο
Pi	π	Π
Rho	ρ	Ρ
Sigma	σ	Σ
Tau	τ	Τ
Upsilon	υ	Υ
Phi	φ	Φ
Chi	χ	Χ
Psi	ψ	Ψ
Omega	ω	Ω

NUMERALS :

Roman Numeral	*Arabic Numeral*
I	1
IV	4
V	5
IX	9
X	10
XV	15
XIX	19
XX	20
XL	40
L	50
LX	60
XC	90
C	100
CI	101
CL	150
CC	200
CD	400
D	500
DC	600
CM	900
M	1000

APPENDIX-B

UNITS AND DIMENSIONS

1. SYSTEMS OF UNITS

There are four standardized systems of units which are given below:

(i) CGS (Metric)

(ii) FPS (British)

(iii) MKS System

(iv) SI system

System of Units	*Length*	*Mass*	*Time*
CGS	Centimeter	Gram	Second
FPS	Foot	Pound	Second
MKS	Meter	Kilogram	Second
SI	Meter	Kilogram	Second

Fundamental and Derived Units:

Fundamental Unit **:** The unit of a physical quantity which is independent of any other quantity is called a fundamental unit. The SI unit of fundamental quantities is shown in the table below:

Quantity	*SI Unit*	*Symbol*
Length	Meter	m
Mass	Kilogram	kg
Time	Second	s
Electric current	Ampere	A
Temperature	Kelvin	K
Amount of substance	Mole	mol
Luminous intensity	Candela	cd

Supplementary SI Units:

Quantity	*SI Unit*	*Symbol*
Plane angle	Radian	Rad
Solid angle	Steradian	Sr

Derived Unit **:** The unit of physical quantity which can be expressed in term of fundamental unit is called derived unit. Following are the derived units:

Quantity	*SI Unit*
Area	m^2
Volume	m^3
Specific volume	m^3/kg
Velocity, speed	m/s
Linear acceleration	m/s^2
Density	kg/m^3
Surface tension	N/m, kg/s^2
Enthalpy	J/kg
Dynamic viscosity	Pa. s, $N.s/m^2$, kg/m s
Frequency	Hz or cycle/s, s-1
Mass flux	kg/s m^2
Heat flux	J/s m^2 or W/m^2
Permeability of plastic film	m^3 (STP)/(s.m^2 Pa)/m
Mass diffusivity	m^2/s
Thermal diffusivity	m^2/s
Mass transfer co-efficient	m/s, kg/s m^2Pa
Rate constant	s^{-1}
Rittinger's constant	m^4/ kg
Kick's constant	m^3/ kg
Rate of heat transfer	J/s, W
Mass velocity	kg/m^2s
Thermal resistance	°C / W
Specific surface area	m^2/kg
Activation energy	J/mol
Concentration flux	mole/m^2s
Fouling factor	m^2K/W
Humid heat	J /kg K

Quantity	***SI Unit***
Latent heat of vaporization	J/kg
Stefan-Boltzmann constant	W/ m^2 K4
Thermal storage capacity	J/m^3 K
Momentum flux	kg/m s^2
Bond work index	J/kg
Modulus of elasticity	N/m^2
Universal gas constant	Pam^3/mol K or J/ mol K
Specific cake resistance	m/kg
Filter medium resistance	m^{-1}
Angular velocity	rad/s
Angular acceleration	rad/s^2
Momentum	kgm/s
Angular momentum	kgm^2/s
Cœfficient of linear expansion	K^{-1}
Concentration (of amount of substance)	mol/m^3
Force	N, kgm/s^2
Pressure, stress	Pa, N/m^2, kg/m.s^2
Work, energy, heat	J, N m, kg m^2/s^2
Power, radiant flux	W, J/s, Nm/s, kg m^2/s^3
Mass flow rate	kg/s
Volumetric flow	m^3/s
Kinematic viscosity	m^2/s
Torque	Nm
Entropy	J/K
Heat capacity	J/K
Heat flux density	W/m^2
Energy density	J/m^3
Specific energy	J/kg
Specific entropy	J/kg K
Specific heat capacity	J/kg K
Latent heat	J/kg
Electric charge density	C/m^3

Quantity	*SI Unit*
Molar energy	J/mol
Entropy	J/mol K
Molar entropy	J/K
Molar heat capacity	J/mol K
Surface charge density	C/m^2
Thermal conductivity	W /m K
Coefficient of heat transfer	W/m^2K
Absorbed dose	Gy (Gray), J/kg or m^2s^{-2}
Diffusion cœfficient	m^2/s
Electric potential	V (Volt)
Electric resistance	Ω (ohm)
Electric charge	C (Coulomb), A.s
Electric current density	A/m^2
Electric dipole moment	Cm
Electric field strength	V /m
Capacitance	F (Farad)
Magnetic flux	Wb (Weber), V·s
Conductance	S (Siemens)
Magnetic flux density	T(Tesla), Wb/m^2
Magnetic field strength	A/m (ampere per meter)
Magnetic dipole moment	Wbm
Moment of force	Nm
Radiant intensity	W/Sr
Vacuum	torr
Respiration rate	s^{-1}
Decimal reduction time	s
Death rate constant or velocity constant	s^{-1}
Absolute roughness	m
Inductance	Henry (H), Wb/A
Illuminance	lux
Luminous flux	lumen

2. DIMENSIONS

Dimensions of the primary quantities are:

Quantity	*Dimension*
Length	L
Mass	M
Time	T
Temperature	θ

Dimensions of derived quantities can be expressed in terms of the fundamental dimensions which are given below:

Physical quantity	*Dimensions*
Surface tension	ML^0T^{-2}
Viscosity	$ML^{-1}T^{-1}$
Thermal resistance	$M^{-1}L^{-2}T^3$ K
Planck's constant	$ML^2\,T^{-1}$
Momentum flux	$ML^{-1}T^{-2}$
Kinematic viscosity	L^2T^{-1}
Diffusivity	L^2T^{-1}
Rittinger's constant	$L^4\,M^{-1}$
Kick's constant	$L^3\,M^{-1}$
Enthalpy	$L^2\,T^{-2}$
Momentum	MLT^{-1}
Pressure or stress	$ML^{-1}\,T^{-2}$
Energy, work, heat	$ML^2\,T^{-2}$
Power	$ML^2\,T^{-3}$
Specific heat	$L^2T^{-2}\,\theta^{-1}$
Thermal conductivity	$MLT^{-3}\,\theta^{-1}$
Heat transfer coefficient	$MT^{-2}\,\theta^{-1}$
Mass transfer coefficient	ML^0T^{-1}
Acceleration	LT^{-2}
Impulse	MLT^{-1}
Angular momentum	ML^2T^{-1}
Force	MLT^{-2}

Physical quantity	*Dimensions*
Kick's constant	$L^3 M^{-1}$
Rittinger's constant	$L^4 M^{-1}$
Latent heat	$L^2 T^{-2}$
Speed, velocity	LT^{-1}
Torque	ML^2T^{-2}
Frequency	T^{-1}
Young modulus of elasticity	$ML^{-1}T^{-2}$
Potential Energy	ML^2T^{-2}
Mass flow rate	MT^{-1}
Pressure, Shear stress	$ML^{-1} T^{-2}$
Volume	L^3
Angular velocity	T^{-1}
Area	L^2
Density	ML^{-3}
Potential Energy	ML^2T^{-2}
Mass flow rate	MT^{-1}
Pressure, Shear stress	$ML^{-1}T^{-2}$
Volume	L^3
Angular velocity	T^{-1}
Area	L^2
Density	ML^{-3}
Potential Energy	ML^2T^{-2}
Mass flow rate	MT^{-1}
Pressure, Shear stress	$ML^{-1}T^{-2}$
Volume	L^3
Angular velocity	T^{-1}
Area	L^2
Density	ML^{-3}
Frequency	T^{-1}
Young modulus of elasticity	$ML^{-1}T^{-2}$
Potential Energy	ML^2T^{-2}
Mass flow rate	MT^{-1}
Pressure, Shear stress	$ML^{-1}T^{-2}$

Physical quantity	*Dimensions*
Volume	L^3
Angular velocity	T^{-1}
Area	L^2
Density	ML^{-3}
Heat transfer rate	ML^2T^{-3}
Overall heat transfer coefficient	$MT^{-3}\theta^{-1}$
Surface energy	MT^{-2}
Velocity gradient, Angular velocity	T^{-1}
Angular acceleration	T^{-2}

3. FUNDAMENTAL CONSTANTS

Name	*Symbol*	*Numerical Value*
Avogadro's number	N	6.023×10^{26} /(kg mol)
Boltzmann's constant	k	1.380×10^{-23} J/k
Stefan-Boltzmann constant	σ	5.67×10^{-8} W/(m^2K^4)
Electron volt	eV	1.602×10^{-19} J
Electron charge	e	1.602×10^{-19} C
Faraday constant	F	9.65×10^7 C/(kg mol)
Planck's constant	h	6.626×10^{-34} J s
Standard gravitational acceleration	g	9.80665 m/s^2
Universal constant of gravitation	G	6.67×10^{-11} N m^2/kg^2
Speed of light in air	c	3.00×10^8 m/ s
Electron charge	e	-1.60×10^{-19} C
Ton	1 ton	1.00×10^3 kg

4. UNIVERSAL GAS CONSTANT (R)

Value of R	*Units*
1.9872	g cal/g mol K
82.057	cm^3 atm/g mol K
8314.34	J/kg mol K
8.314	kJ/kg mol K
82.057×10^{-3}	m^3 atm/kg mol K
8314.34	kg m^2/s^2 kg mol K
8314.34	m^3 Pa/kg mol K

5. VALUES OF SOME USEFUL NUMBERS

$$\pi = 3.14$$

$$e = 2.7182818$$

$$\sqrt{2} = 1.4142136$$

$$\sqrt{3} = 1.7320508$$

$$\ln 2 = 0.693$$

$$\ln 10 = 2.303$$

6. SI PREFIXES

SI Prefixes	*Symbol*	*Exponent Value*
Tera	T	1012
Giga	G	109
Mega	M	106
Kilo	K	103
Hecto	H	102
Deca	da	101
Deci	d	10-1
Centi	c	10-2
Milli	m	10-3
Micro	μ	10-6
Nano	n	10-9
Pico	p	10-12

APPENDIX-C

CONVERSION FACTORS

Mass:

1 kg = 1000g = 2.2 lb

1 g = 10^{-3} kg

1 lb = 0.454 kg = 453.593 g

1 ton (metric) = 1000 kg

Length:

1 m = 10 decametre (dm) =100 cm = 1000 mm = 10^6μm = 3.28 ft = 39.37 in = 1.0936 yd

1 in. = 2.54 cm = 25.40 mm = 0.0254 m = 0.0833 ft = 0.02778 yd

1 yd = 3 ft = 0.9144 m

1 cm = 0.3937 in = 10^{-2} m

1 ft = 12 in = 0.3048 m

1Å (angstrom) = 10^{-10} m

1 μm = 10^{-6} m = 10^{-4} cm = 10^{-3} mm

1 decametre (dm) = 10 m

1 hectometre (hm) = 100 m

1 km = 1000 m = 0.6214 mile

5280 ft = 1 mile

1760 yd = 1 mile

1 mile = 1.61 km

Area:

1 m^2 = 10.8 ft^2 =10000 cm^2 = 1000000 mm^2

1 in.^{2} = 6.45 cm^2 = 645 mm^2

1 cm^2 = 0.1550 in^2

1 ft^2 = 144 in2 = 0.0929 m^2

1 sq hectometre (1 hm^2) = 10000 m^2 = 1 hectare (ha)

1 sq km (1 km^2) = 1 000 000 m^2

1 yd^2 = 9 ft^2

1 acre = 0.405 ha= 43560 ft^2

1 sq mile = 2.59 km^2

1 ha = 0.01 km^2 = 10000 m^2 = 2.471 acre

Volume:

1 m^3 = 106 cm^3 = 103 L (liter) = 264.17 gal (US) = 35.3 ft^3

1 ft^3 = 1728 in.^{3} = 0.02832 m^3 = 28.32 L

1 gal (US) = 3.7854 L = 3785.4 cm^3 = 0.003785 m^3 = 0.13368 ft^3

1 dm^3 = 1 litre

1 litre = = 0.001 m^3 = 1000 cm^3 = 61 in.^{3} = 10^{-3} m^3 = 0.2642 gal. (U.S.) = 0.0353 ft^3

1 mL = 1 cm^3

1 yd^3 = 27 ft^3 = 0.7646 m^3

1 in.^{3} = 16.4 cm^3 = 0.0164 litre

1 cm^3 = 0.06102 in^3

Temperature:

°F = 1.8 (°C) + 32

°C = (°F – 32)/1.8

°R = °F + 460

K = °C + 273

ΔT K = ΔT ΔC = 1.8 ΔT °F

Δ °C = Δ°K

Speed/Velocity:

1 km/h = 0.278 m/s

1 m/s = 3.28 ft/s = 3.60 km/h

1 ft/s = 0.3048 m/s

Standard Acceleration Of Gravity

g=9.80 m/s2=980 cm/s2=32.174 ft/s2

Density:

1 g/cm^3 = 1000 kg/m^3 = 62.428 lb/ft^3 = 0.0361 lb/in^3

1 lb/ft^3 = 16.0185 kg/m^3

1 g/ml=1000 kg/m^3

Volumetric Flow Rate:

1 ft^3/s = 449 gal/min = 0.02832 m^3/s

1 ft^3/min = 0.0004719 m^3/s = 0.4719 L/s

1 m^3/s = 35.31 ft^3/s = 1000 L/s

Force:

1 lbf = 4.448 N

1 N = 1 kg m/s^2 = 105 dyne = 105 g cm/s^2 = 0.225 lbf

1 dyne = 1 g cm/s^2 = 10^{-5} kg. m/s^2 = 10^{-5} N

1 kgf = 9.807 N = 2.205 lbf

Pressure and Stress:

At sea level atmospheric pressure equals 101.3 kPa or 14.7 psi.

1 bar = 105 Pa =1.033 kgf/cm^2 = 14.5038 lbf/in^2 = 0.987 atm = 10.2 m H^2O = 33.48 ft H^2O

1 Pa = 1 N/m^2 = 10 $dyne/cm^2$ = 9.8692 $\times 10^{-6}$ atm = 7.5 $\times$ 10^{-3} torr

1 lbf/in^2 = 6894.8 Pa = 6.804 $\times$ 10^{-2} atm = 6.895 kPa = 2.309 ft H^2O = 2.0360 in. Hg

1 $dyne/cm^2$ = 0.10 Pa = 10^{-6} bar = 0.987 $\times$ 10^{-6} atm

1 atm = 1.01325 $\times$ 105 N/m^2 = 101.325 kPa = 14.696 psi = 1.01325 bar = 760 torr = 760 mm Hg

1 psi = 1 $lbf/in.^2$ = 6.895 kPa = 2.03 in. mercury = 51.7 mm mercury

1 bar = 105 N/m^2 = 14.5 psi = 100 kPa = 0.1 MPa

1 kPa = 0.294 in. mercury = 7.5 mm mercury = 4.02 in. water = 10^2 mm water

1 kPa = 4.02 in. water = 102 mm water

1 torr = 1 mmHg=133.32 Pa

Heat, Energy, Work, Power and Torque:

1btu (British Thermal Unit) = 252.16 cal=1.05506 kJ

1 hp = 550 ft-lbf/s = 746 W = 0.746 kW = 0.7068 BTU/s

1 W = 1 J/s = 0.23901 cal/s = 3.414 Btu/h =14.340 cal/min

1 Btu/h = 0.2931 W = 0.2931 J/s

1 N m = 1 J = 100 N cm =1 kg m^2 s-2 = 107 dyne cm = 0.7376 ft lbf = 0.23901 cal

1 dyne cm = 10^{-7} N m = 10^{-5} N cm

1 erg = 1 dyne cm = 1 $\times$ 10^{-7} J

1 BTU = 1055 J = 1.055kJ = 252.16 cal

1 cal = 4.184 J

1 kcal = 4.18 $\times$ 103 J

1 kW = 0.948 Btu/s

1 BTU/h = 0.293W

1 J/s = 1 W = 0.23901 cal/s

1 kW = 1.341 HP = 860 kcal/h

1 HP = 75 kgm/s

1 J = 107 ergs = 1 Nm = 1kg-m^2/s^2 == 10^7 g. cm^2/s^2

1 kWh = 3600 kJ = 3.6 MJ = 3413 Btu

1 ton refrigeration = 3.519 kW

1 hp.h = 0.7457 kW.h = 2544.5 btu

1 kcal/g mol = 4.1840 × 103 kJ/kg mol

Specific Heat, Latent Heat, Thermal Conductivity and Heat Transfer Coefficient:

1 Btu/lb °F = 4.187 k J/kg K

1 BTU/lb = 2.326 × 103 J/kg

1 Btu /h ft °F = 1.730 W/m K

1 Btu/ ft^2 h °F = 5.678 W/m^2 K

1 Btu/ft h °F = 1.731 J/ms °C

Heat Flux and Heat Flow:

1 btu/h.ft^2 = 3.1546 w/m^2

1 btu/h = 0.29307 W

1 cal/h = 1.1622 × 10^{-3} W

Dynamic (Absolute) Viscosity and Kinematic Viscosity:

1 P (Poise) = 1 dyne s/cm^2 = 0.1 Pa s = 100 cP = 100 mPa s = 1 g/cm s = 0.1 Ns/m^2

1 Pa s = 1000 cP = 10 P = 1 kg/m s = 1 N s/m^2 = 0.67197 lb/ft s

1 cP = 1 mPa s = 0.001 Pa s = 0.01 P = 10^{-3} Pa.s=10^{-3} kg/m.s = 10^{-3} N.s/m^2

1 centistoke (cSt) =10^{-2} cm^2/s = 0.000001 m^2/s = 1 mm^2/s = 5.58001 in^2 /hr = 0.00155 in^2 /s

1 St = 100 cSt = 0.0001 m^2/ s

1 m^2 /s = 10^{-5} cSt = 10.76 ft^2/ s

1 St (Stoke) = 1 cm^2/s=10-4 m^2/s

1 cm^2/s=3.875 ft^2/h

1 m^2/s = 3.875 × 104 ft^2/h = 10000 stokes

1 cm^2/s = 10^{-4} m^2/s

1 m^2/h = 10.764 ft^2/h

Mass Flux and Molar Flux:

1 g/s.cm^2 = 7.3734 × 10^3 lbm/h.ft^2

1 g mol/s.cm^2 = 7.3734 × 10^3 lb mol/h. ft^2 = 10 kg mol/s.m^2 = 1 × 10^4 g mol/s.m^2

1lb mol/h. ft^2 = 1.3562 × 10^{-3} kg mol/s.m^2

BIBLIOGRAPHY

1. Ahmed T. (1997). Dairy Plant Engineering and Management (4th Ed.), Kitab Mahal, New Delhi
2. Araullo, E. V.; Padua, D. B graham, Michael (1985). Rice Post Harvest Technology, Oxford & IBH Publishing co. Pvt. Ltd., New Delhi
3. Alfa Laval/Tetra Pak (1995). Dairy Processing Handbook, Tetra Pak Processing Systems, S-221 86, Lund, Sweden
4. Bala, B. K. (1997). Drying and Storage of Cerẹals Grains, Oxford & IBH Publishing co. Pvt. Ltd., New Delhi
5. Barbosa-C´anovas, Gustavo V.; Ortega-Rivas, Enrique; Juliano, Pablo and Yan, Hong (2005). Food Powders: Physical Properties, Processing, and Functionality, Kluwer Academic/ Plenum Publishers, New York
6. Berk, Zeki (2009). Food Process Engineering and Technology, Elsevier Inc., USA
7. Batty, J. Clair and Folkman, Steven L. (1983). Food engineering fundamentals, John Wiley and Sons, Inc., USA
8. Brennan, J. G., J. R. Butters, N. D. Cowell, and A. E. V. Lilly. (1990). Food Engineering Operations (3rd edition) Elsevier, London, UK.
9. Brennan, James G. (2006). Food Processing Handbook, WILEY-VCH Verlag GmbH amd Co. KGaA, Weinheim, Germany
10. Brooker, D. B., Bakker Arkema, F. W. and Hall, C. W. (1974). Drying Cereal Grains. The AVI Publishers
11. Burton, H. (1988). Ultra-High-Temperature Processing of Milk and Milk Products, Elsevier Science Publishing Co., Inc. New York, USA
12. Chakraverty, A. (1995). Post-harvest Technology of Cereals, Pulses and Oilseeds, Oxford & IBH Publishing co. Pvt. Ltd., New Delhi
13. Datta, A. K. (2001). Transport Phenomena in Food Process Engineering, Himalaya Publishing House, Mumbai
14. Earle, R. L. (1985). Unit Operations in Food Processing, Pregman Press
15. Fellows, P. J. ((2000). Food Processing Technology, Woodhead Publishing, Cambridge, UK

16. Geankoplis, J. Christie (1997). Transport Process and Unit Operations (3rd edition), Prantice-Hall of India, New Delhi

17. Greenkorn, R. A. and Kessler, D. P. (1972). Transfer Operations, McGraw Hill, New Delhi

18. Focust, Alan S; Wenzel, A. Leonard; Clump, W. Curtis, Maus, Louis and Andesrsen, L. Bryce (1980). Principles of Unit Operation (2nd edition), John Wiley and Sons, New York, USA

19. Heldman, D. R and Hartel, R. W. (1997). Principles of Food Processing, Chapman and Hall, New York, USA

20. Henderson S. and Perry, S.M. (1976). Agricultural Process Engineering (5th sdition), AVI Publishers.

21. Holman, Jack P. (1986). Heat Transfer. McGraw-Hill, New York, USA

22. Karel, Marcus and Lund, Darvl B. (2003). Physical Principles Preservation of Food (2nd edition), Marcel Dekker, Inc., U.S.A.

23. Lewis, M. J. (1990) Physical Properties of Foods and Food Processing Systems. Woodhead Publishing, Cambridge, UK

24. Lewis, M. J. and Heppell, N. J. (2000). Continuous Thermal Processing of Foods: pasteurization and UHT sterilization, Aspen, Gaithersburg, UK

25. Loncin M. and Merson R. L. (1979). Food Engineering–Principles and Selected Applications, Academic Press, UK

26. Maroulis, Zacharias B. and Saravacos, George D. (2003). Food Process Design, Marcel Dekker, Inc , New York, U S A

27. McCabe, W. L. and Smith, J. C. (1999). Unit Operations of Chemical Engineering, McGraw Hill, USA

28. Mohsenin, N. N. (1980). Physical Properties of Plant and Animal Materials, Gordon and Breach Science Publishers, New York, USA

29. Nag, P. K. (1985). Engineering thermodynamics, Tata McGraw Hill Publishing Co. Ltd., New Delhi

30. Rahman, M.S. (1995). Food Properties Handbook. CRC Press, New York, USA

31. Rao, M. A., and Rizvi. S. S. H. (1995). Engineering Properties of Foods (2nd edition), Marcel Dekker, New York, USA

32. Roberts, T. C. (2002). Food Plant Engineering Systems, CRC Press, New York, USA.

33. Romeo T. Toledo (2007). Fundamentals of Food Process Engineering (3rd edition), Springer Science Publisher, New York, USA

34. Sahay K. M. and Singh, K. K. (1994). Unit Operation of Agricultural Processing. Vikas Publishing House, New Delhi

35. Sahin, Serpil and Sumnu, Servet G¨ul¨um (2006). Physical Properties of Foods, Springer Science Publisher, New York, USA

36. Sharma, Shri K, Mulvaney, Steven J. and Rizvi, S. S. H. (2000). Food Process Engineering Theory and Laboratory Experiments, John Wiley and Sons, Inc. New York, USA

37. Singh, R. P., and Heldman, D. R. (1993). Introduction to Food Engineering. Academic Press, San Diego, CA.

38. Smith, P. G. (2004). Introduction to Food Process Engineering, McGraw Hill.

39. Treybal R. E. (1981). Mass Transfer Operations. McGraw Hill.

40. Valentan, Kenneth J., Rostein, Enrique and Singh, R. Paul (1997), Handbook of Food Engineering Practice, CRC Press, New York, USA

41. Wilhelm, L.R., Suter, D.A. and Brusewitz, G. H. (2005). Food and Process Engineering Technology, American Society of Agricultural Engineering, USA

Index